THE ARTIFACTS OF UAXACTUN

GUATEMALA

A. V. KIDDER

Publication 576

Carnegie Institution of Washington
Washington, D. C.
1947

THE LORD BALTIMORE PRESS, BALTIMORE, MARYLAND
MERIDEN GRAVURE COMPANY, MERIDEN, CONNECTICUT

Contents

Figures

Introduction

In the normal course of events this paper would have constituted an appendix to the report of A. L. Smith on his excavations at Uaxactun, or that of R. E. Smith on the pottery of that site. Service by their authors in connection with the war effort, however, has so retarded completion of these reports that it seems best to publish on the artifacts without further delay. Until the appearance of the above-mentioned reports, the reader may refer for background material to O. G. and E. B. Ricketson's monograph on the excavations at Uaxactun between 1926 and 1931 (Ricketson and Ricketson, 1937; as it will constantly be quoted, this work will hereafter be referred to as RR) and S. G. Morley's discussion of the site and its inscriptions (Morley, 1938, vol. 1).

Uaxactun, situated in the dense forest of the northern part of the Department of the Peten, was discovered by S. G. Morley in 1916. It was again visited by him in 1920; and when, in 1923, he organized the Carnegie Institution's Maya archaeological program he selected Uaxactun, Chichen Itza, and Tayasal as three cities whose intensive investigation could be expected to throw light on the entire course of pre-Columbian Maya history. Tayasal, on Lake Peten, was chosen because pure Maya culture flourished there until late in the seventeenth century; Chichen Itza, in northern Yucatan, because it was an important center from relatively early times until shortly before the Spanish conquest; Uaxactun because it contained both the earliest and the latest Long Count inscriptions, the dates ranging from 8.14.10.13.15 to 10.3.0.0.0 or, according to the Goodman-Martinez-Thompson correlation of Maya and Christian chronology, from A.D. 328 to 889. This constitutes the longest recorded occupancy of any Maya city now known. Dr. Morley therefore believed that Uaxactun could be counted upon to provide information not only on the beginnings of Maya civilization but also on its development through a period of nearly six centuries. His expectations have been fully realized.

A preliminary survey by Frans Blom in 1924 was followed by excavations under the direction of Oliver G. Ricketson and A. Ledyard Smith, carried on from 1926 to 1937 in the several semi-independent groups of ruined structures which make up the site. Between 1926 and 1931 major attention was devoted to Group E. Work in Group A, begun in 1930, continued through 1937.

In Group E there was discovered Structure E-VII sub, the oldest example of Maya architecture so far recognized. It is a massive stucco-covered pyramid decorated with grotesque masks, preserved in extraordinarily perfect condition beneath a later pyramid (see Proskouriakoff, 1946, pl. 1). Of even greater archaeological importance was the finding, under the Group E plaza, of deposits of village refuse laid down before the rise of Classic Maya culture. The pottery and particularly the little clay figurines from this midden are closely allied stylistically, and presumably were contemporaneous, with Archaic remains of types which had long been known in Mexico and the Guatemala highlands, but of which representatives had not previously come to light in the lowland Maya area. The Group E subplaza materials enabled Mrs. Ricketson (RR, ch. 10) to establish ceramic phases antedating the Classic pottery sequence previously worked out for Peten by Vaillant on the basis of Merwin's finds at the nearby site of Holmul (Merwin and Vaillant, 1932). Mrs. Ricketson's pre-Classic phases were designated Uaxactun I-A and I-B. Her Uaxactun II corresponds to Holmul II–IV, covering the first part of the Classic or Old Empire period of the Maya or, as Thompson has called it, the Initial Series period; her Uaxactun III corresponds to Holmul V, the latter part of the Classic or Initial Series period.

The field seasons of 1930 and 1931 were devoted to the final intensive stratigraphic studies of the subplaza deposits of Group E. During those years work was also inaugurated at Group A, the largest at Uaxactun. There R. E. Smith excavated Structure A-I, whose several superimposed buildings provided valuable data on architectural development and contained burials and caches adding much new information on the later ceramic phases (A. L. Smith, 1932; R. E. Smith, 1937). The principal activity at Group A, however, was the thorough dissection by A. L. Smith and E. M. Shook of Structure A-V, a building which, in its later stages, became a very large example of the multichambered "palace" type, but whose foundations date from pre-Classic times and whose growth involved a long series of demolitions, additions, and alterations of plan. Its excavation, requiring eight field seasons, was an extraordinarily difficult piece of work, certainly the most complex architectural investigation ever undertaken in the New World. The intelligence and resourcefulness of Smith and Shook in solving the manifold practical problems it presented and in recording and interpreting their finds are beyond praise. The results amply justify their efforts, for they were able to work out in great detail the changes in architectural design and building practice that took place during the at least six centuries of Structure A-V's existence (see Proskouriakoff, 1946, pls. 28–35, a set of drawings illustrating its growth).

R. E. Smith, associated with his brother from 1930 onward, devoted himself to study of the pottery. His work was greatly facilitated by the fact that the builders of Uax-

1

actun, unlike those of most other Maya cities that have so far been examined, utilized much household refuse, including great numbers of potsherds, in the rubble fill of substructures and walls. Thus there became available extensive ceramic samples of all periods. Collections of this sort, however, are seldom entirely free from admixtures of earlier material. But recognition of the pieces resulting from such adulteration was accomplished by R. E. Smith by means of check excavations in other buildings and in deposits of rubbish which had not been rehandled. Pit 2 in a well-stratified midden in Group A was particularly valuable in this respect. Furthermore, Structure A-V contained many burials accompanied by offerings of pottery. These could be assigned to successive stages in the development of A-V, and other relatively datable interments were found elsewhere. The mortuary pottery served both to check further on the sherds and to supply fuller data on vessel form and decoration than could be had from fragments. New stratigraphic tests were also made in Group E to gather additional information as to the pre-Classic wares that were very scantily represented at Group A.

On the basis of the above materials, R. E. Smith recognizes (1936a, 1946b, 1940) four sequent ceramic phases at Uaxactun: Mamom, Chicanel, Tzakol, Tepeu. Mamom, in the new style, corresponds to Mrs. Ricketson's I-A, Chicanel to her I-B. Both are pre-Classic. Tzakol, comprising three sequent subphases, corresponds to Mrs. Ricketson's II and is akin to Vaillant's Holmul II–IV (Holmul I seems not to appear at Uaxactun) and Thompson's (1939) San Jose II. It was the first or Early Classic phase. It came into being at about the same time as did the practice of erecting inscribed stelae and the first use of the corbeled vault. The Smiths believe it to have dated from before 8.15.0.0.0 to about 9.8.0.0.0, a stretch of at least 260 years which also, in terms of A. L. Smith's architectural classification, covers Phase I of the vault. Tepeu, the second or Late Classic phase, corresponds to Mrs. Ricketson's III, Holmul V, San Jose III and IV, and to A. L. Smith's Phase II of the vault. Tepeu, like Tzakol, is divisible into three subphases and is believed to have lasted from about 9.8.0.0.0 to the abandonment of Uaxactun. As this took place at some time after 10.3.0.0.0, Tepeu covers a period of perhaps more than 320 years.

The present report deals with the artifacts, other than pottery vessels and clay figurines, found in all excavations except those in Group E that were recorded by the Ricketsons. There are significant differences between the two collections. The artifacts described by Mrs. Ricketson (RR, chs. 6–9) came, for the most part, from the Group E subplaza deposits of the Mamom and Chicanel phases and therefore represent the earliest periods in the life of Uaxactun; whereas the material here considered dates almost exclusively from the Tzakol and Tepeu horizons, for with the exception of limited check excavations by R. E. Smith in Group E, practically all the work of later years was done in Groups A and B, in which next to no Mamom and very few Chicanel remains were found. As a matter of fact, a large proportion of the specimens are from deposits in the latest rooms and above the latest court floors in Structure A-V. Another difference is due to the fact that in Group E there were few and poorly stocked graves, while in Groups A, B, and C a large number were encountered, mostly in Structure A-V. Many, particularly those of the Tzakol phase, contained lavish offerings. The present collection therefore is much the richer in ornaments and other mortuary furniture.

In spite of the great amount of work that was done at Uaxactun, the total "take" of nonceramic utilitarian artifacts was very small. Scarcity of such artifacts has also obtained at all other lowland Maya sites that have been investigated. To some extent this is doubtless the result of the limited attention which has so far been paid to house sites and middens, archaeologists having confined themselves almost exclusively to the excavation of temples and other ceremonial structures in and about which implements for daily use would naturally not have accumulated in quantity. But even such digging as has been done in humbler precincts has been surprisingly unproductive. One can only conclude that the Maya actually used relatively few chipped and ground stone tools and tools of bone, their place presumably having often been taken by implements of the extremely hard woods so abundant in the lowlands. Woods, both hard and soft, had to be worked, however, not only to make small objects but also to procure house materials and beams for ceremonial structures, to say nothing of the enormous amounts which, as Morris has pointed out, were required for burning lime (Morris, Charlot, and Morris, 1931, p. 219). Furthermore, there was the constant cutting of forest growths involved in clearing fields.

For minor operations obsidian surely was much used, and employment of obsidian flake-blades and raw chips, found abundantly in sites even at great distances from the highland sources of supply, probably explains the rarity of small, secondarily chipped implements. Obsidian, however, is too brittle to be effective for chopping. Certain large flint artifacts to be described below may have served as axes, although they seem ill-adapted for such use. All in all, it would appear that much of the heavy work must have been done by charring and scraping; and, in the preparation of corn land, the larger trees, killed and rendered leafless by girdling, might well have been allowed to remain standing, as is the practice even today in Peten and on the south coast of Guatemala.

Whatever the reason, the artifact collection is small. And, from the point of view of technological development, it is unsatisfactory in that the majority of the tomb specimens are of a single phase—Tzakol—and the greater part of the utilitarian objects are from superficial deposits laid down in very late times when Group A, at least, seems to have been abandoned as a ceremonial center and its buildings, evidently already semiruinous, were being used as dwelling places by the remnants of a once flourishing community.

Although, as the final section of this report will make evident, few conclusions either as to local developments or relations with other groups can as yet be drawn, it is certain that when data on more Maya sites and on other Mesoamerican groups become available, the artifacts of Uaxactun will take on greater meaning. For this reason, the exact provenience, the cultural horizon, and the catalogue number of each specimen illustrated have been tabulated. Because of the heavy cost of printing such material, it is not included in the present report, but one copy has been placed in the library of the Peabody Museum of Harvard University and one, which will be sent on request to any student desiring to consult it, in the files of the Institution's Division of Historical Research. The Uaxactun card catalogue, also on file at the Division office, was prepared by Mrs. Ricketson and, in later years, by Mrs. R. E. Smith. It contains notes on and measurements of every specimen, and drawings or photographs of most of them. The photographs in this report were made by my daughter, Mrs. Barbara Aldana; the drawings are by Sr. Antonio Tejeda F., Sr. Victor Lucas, and Miss Tatiana Proskouriakoff. For identification of mammal and reptile bones I am greatly indebted to Dr. Adolph Murie and the late Dr. Glover Allen; for those of birds to Dr. Alexander Wetmore; and for the very few organic remains recovered to Dr. Paul A. Vestal.

1

Objects of Stone

CHIPPED STONE

At Uaxactun, as at most other Maya sites that have been investigated, chipped stone artifacts were relatively rare. Most specimens fall into well-defined categories of one sort or another. Grouping is therefore a fairly simple matter. But how to arrange the resultant classification, in order that it may be useful to those whose major interest is in typology and distribution as well as to those primarily concerned with the light such objects can shed upon the life of the people of Uaxactun, is somewhat of a problem. The system which I employed in presenting material of this kind from Pecos (Kidder, 1932), and which was followed by Mrs. Ricketson for that recovered during the earlier years of the Uaxactun project (RR), was based primarily on the amount of chipping undergone by the objects, and secondarily on their form. This was satisfactory enough for such simple and almost exclusively utilitarian implements as those of Pecos, but it is much less so in the present case, for when applied to the small but much more varied Uaxactun collection, it brings together pieces radically different in material, size, workmanship, and function. The Pecos type of classification is therefore inconvenient for either typological or what might be called paleo-ethnological studies. I have accordingly tried to serve both interests by separating utilitarian implements from ceremonial objects. It is of course not always possible to be certain whether a given specimen was designed for ritual or for practical use. In the case of the so-called eccentric flints and obsidians there is naturally not the doubt that arises when one is concerned with knifelike objects and projectile points, which might well have been employed for either or both purposes. In such cases I have classed as ceremonial those pieces found in substela and other obviously cult caches and those from graves which, because of unusually elaborate form or fine workmanship or because others of the same type most often occur in caches, seem unlikely to have been put to everyday use.

I have next segregated the specimens on the basis of the type of stone employed in their manufacture. At Uaxactun this seems necessary because coarse local flints were used only for certain sorts of tools; finer, perhaps imported, stones for others; and the surely imported obsidian for still others. This diversity of raw material should, it seems to me, be emphasized not only because of differences in the form of the finished product, but also because problems of custom and of trade are involved. Only in the subclassifications within the above major categories are specific function, form, and type of chipping taken into account. In order to reconcile the method with that of Mrs. Ricketson I include in the appropriate places in my descriptions, references (preceded by the letters RR) to objects of each sort illustrated by her.

A word as to nomenclature. I apply the term *chip* to

amorphous pieces of flint or obsidian which, once struck, were not further altered; or were altered by, rather than for, use. Most of these were probably by-products of entirely unpredetermined form, but some were doubtless produced by breaking up larger bodies of stone with the object of obtaining sizable, keen-edged fragments. *Flakes* are elongated, gently curved pieces of flint or obsidian struck from cores. They commonly served as blanks for the manufacture of implements, many of which retain the curvature and considerable areas of the original surfaces of the flake. *Flake-blades,* at Uaxactun only of obsidian, are long, thin, narrow flakes struck from specially prepared cores. Their form was definitely premeditated and they were almost always put to use without modification.

UTILITARIAN IMPLEMENTS

I. Implements of White Flint

Material. Color varies from mouse gray (rare) to nearly pure white; most pieces more or less clouded with pinkish lavender. Some specimens contain small cavities, their interiors crusted with lime; others bear remnants of the coarse-textured white lime crust of the original nodules. Presumably a native stone.

A. Chopping (?) or general utility tools, pointed at one end, rounded at the other, 53.

    1. *Standard form,* 44 (fig. 61,*c-k*. RR, fig. 119,*a*; pl. 54,*b*,1–7). L 12–14 cm., W 6–7 cm., T 3–4 cm. Crudely chipped, edges ragged, retouching uncommon. Bear moderate signs of use, usually on rounded end, whose edge is often somewhat dulled by battering. On one whole specimen (fig. 61,*k*) and one fragment the rounded edge and both faces for 4–6 cm. back from the edge bear a glassy polish like that of Illinois flint "spades." This is evidently the result of use in digging.

    2. *Standard form re-used,* 5 (fig. 61,*a,a',b,b'*). Both ends shortened and blunted by long use, presumably as pecking- or hammerstones.

    3. *Extra-long,* 4. L 17–27 cm., W 6–7 cm., T 2.75–4 cm. Closely resemble standard form, but as there are no specimens intermediate in length, these probably constitute a separate subtype.

    4. *Extra-fine, thin,* 1 (fig. 61,*j*). L 22 cm., W 7 cm., T 2.5 cm. Actually somewhat, and relative to length much, thinner than standard form; contour more even, edges sharper, due to retouching. Specimen apparently never used.

COMMENT. These heavy and for the most part crudely chipped implements occurred in refuse deposits of all phases at Uaxactun, never in caches or graves. They were certainly common in the earliest times, as most of the more than 50 listed by Mrs. Ricketson came from the subplaza (Mamom phase) beds in Group E. A number of the specimens here treated were found in Pit 14, Group A, in refuse of the Tzakol phase. Others occurred in accumulations above the latest floors of Structure A-V. There is no apparent change in form from beginning to end. Tools of exactly the same sort and also those made from the low-grade local flints that occur in the limestone throughout Peten were found by Thompson at San Jose and Benque Viejo in British Honduras (1939, p. 169 and pl. 25,*c*; 1940, p. 25 and pl. 6,*a,c*). Others are from the Rio Hondo and Indian Church, British Honduras (Mus. Amer. Ind.). "Roughly chipped celts" are recorded from Holmul by Merwin and Vaillant (1932, p. 43) and by the Ganns (1939, p. 27) from Nohmul, British Honduras—in both cases with burials. The type, however, does not seem to have been in use in northern Yucatan in the later periods, as they are not mentioned by Morris in his careful study of large stone tools occurring at Chichen Itza (Morris, Charlot, and Morris, 1931, p. 211); nor are any listed in the catalogue of finds from that site. From the chultuns of Labna, however, E. H. Thompson (1897*a*, figs. 5, 8) recovered specimens apparently identical to those of the Peten. The major occupation of Labna was certainly earlier than that of "Mexican" Chichen Itza.

The function of these implements is problematical. Their rounded edges do not seem sharp enough to have served for cutting wood, nor are their pointed ends sufficiently acute to have made efficient picks. They are so thick that mounting, either by insertion in a helve or by wrapping with a slender haft, would hardly have been practicable. The polish seen on a few examples, from Uaxactun and Benque Viejo, is almost certainly due to protracted use in the earth. Battering of the extremities indicates at least occasional employment for the working of stone, but the blunt-ended specimens next to be described probably more often served that purpose. Thus one must suppose them to have been general utility tools. In spite of their seeming ineffectiveness for such work, they may regularly have been used for chopping, for no other implement came to light at Uaxactun that could reasonably be classed as an axe—all but one of the polished celts (p. 38) are much too small and light— and it is obvious that vast amounts of wood had, in some way or other, constantly to be cut. In this connection see Morris' interesting discussion of wood consumption in the burning of architectural lime (Morris, Charlot, and Morris, 1931, p. 219). The longer one thinks of it the more one marvels at what the Maya were able to accomplish without benefit of metal tools in such a densely forested country as Peten.

B. Pecking or pounding tools, blunt-ended, 11.

    1. *Standard form,* 8 (fig. 61,*m-o*). L 9.5–11 cm., W 3–3.75 cm., T 2–3 cm. Ends rounded to square,

one end sometimes tapering to blunt point. Chipping crude. Slight battering at ends, particularly at small ends of pointed specimens.

2. *Standard, extra-long,* 1 (fig. 61,*l*). L 15.5 cm., W 4.7 cm., T 3 cm. One end battered.

3. *Triangular section,* 2. Identical to standard form save that one face is almost flat.

COMMENT. These objects were also found in deposits of all periods. Nothing exactly like them appears in the literature. That they are not merely examples of the foregoing group that have been reduced in size by wear is indicated by their greater slenderness. They do not show heavy use. Such marks as they bear suggest service as pecking tools. There is no polishing of the normally very blunt ends; we therefore believe Mrs. Ricketson to be mistaken in consider-

D. Drill (??) thin, tapering, 1 (fig. 61,*q*). L 18.5 cm., W 3.1 cm., T 2 cm. Oval section. Chip-scars on faces and edges softened by long use, nearly obliterated at pointed end. Wear becomes progressively less pronounced toward unworn butt. The smoothed surfaces are dull, not glossily earth-polished.

E. Drills, small, stubby, 10 (fig. 1). L 2.5–5.5 cm. Produced from thick flakes, of which each specimen retains some of the original surfaces and some a certain amount of the original curvature. Crudely chipped; roughly quadrangular or triangular in section; unretouched save at one end, where they have been brought to what was presumably once a sharp point, but which is now worn (in some cases greatly) to a rounded termination. The

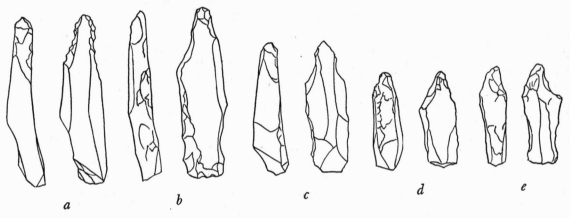

a   b   c   d   e

FIG. 1—FLINT DRILLS

Specimens of this crude type, of which 10 lay together in a Tzakol deposit, were the only drills, either of flint or obsidian, found at Uaxactun. L of *b*, 5 cm.

ing specimens apparently of this type to have been "straight-shafted drills" (RR, pl. 55,*a*,8–14).

C. Rubbing tools, chisel-like, 2. No. 1 (fig. 61,*r*): L 17.5 cm., W 4.8 cm., T 2.5 cm. Triangular section, one side flat, other keeled; one end square, other pointed; edges even, straight, retouched. Square end sharp-edged; flat side for 5 cm. back from square end polished. This cannot have been produced by use in the ground, as other side of end is unaltered. Pointed end unbattered and bears bit of lime crust. No. 2 (fig. 61,*p*): L 17 cm., W 3.1 cm., T 2 cm. Oval section; one end blunt with remnant of lime crust; other, square, sharp-edged, chipped to shallow gouge-form; under side at gouge end wear-smoothed for half length of tool, upper side unworn. Both these implements fit the hand well, and had evidently been long used for some work, perhaps on hides, that has altered the under surface without dulling the chisel edge. No. 1 from a Tepeu deposit; No. 2, early, probably Chicanel.

plane surfaces of the butt offer a good grip and the implements can be rotated effectively between the thumb and first two fingers. Probably so used, rather than hafted.

COMMENT. All were found together in Cut 4, Pit 2, Group A, a Tzakol stratum; none elsewhere at Uaxactun. They were doubtless drills. Carefully formed stone drills, either straight or winged, appear to have been next to unknown in Mesoamerica, at least from the time of the Middle Cultures on. It will be interesting to learn, when preceramic remains are found, whether such implements as drills and well-made scraping tools were commoner then than they seem to have been in later times. The Uaxactun specimens called by Mrs. Ricketson scraper-drills (RR, pl. 55,*b*,6–13) are also crude. The only finely chipped drill I have seen from the Maya area is from Holmul: a straight-shafted specimen of white flint, quadrangular in section, with keen, much-worn point. It is 3.5 cm. long (Peabody Mus. Harvard).

F. Scrapers, flat, 3 (RR, pl. 55,*b*,1–5). No. 1 (fig. 62,*a*): L 8 cm., W 7 cm., T 2.6 cm. Possibly re-used example of Type A-1. Large end chipped to blunt quasi-"snub-nosed" form. No. 2 (fig. 62,*c*): L 6.8 cm., W 6 cm., T 1 cm. Thin chip; one face unworked, slightly convex; entire periphery retouched to sharp edge. No. 3 (fig. 62,*b*): L 6.6 cm., W 4 cm., T 1.9 cm. Crudely chipped, "crusty" piece, one end retouched to sharp edge.

G. Scrapers (?), turtleback, 6 (fig. 62,*d-g*; RR, pl. 55,*b*,3). L 10–11 cm., W 8–10 cm., T 3.5–5 cm. Thick oval to nearly round; made from flakes struck from nodules, some of whose lime crust usually remains (see fig. 62, *d,e,g*). One face retains original inner surface of flake

type was found below the plaza floor in Group E (RR, pl. 55,*b*,3). The turtleback should not be confused with the so-called snub-nosed or humpbacked scraper, an implement not produced in flint, so far as I know, anywhere in Meso-america, but which was made of obsidian by people of the Middle Cultures of the Valley of Mexico (see p. 14).

H. Scraper-drills, 1 (cf. RR, pl. 55,*b*,6–8,10–13). L 8.5 cm., T .2 cm. Broad end chipped on one side only, tapering point chipped to rounded section and shows considerable wear.

COMMENT. This appears to be a two-purpose implement. It is better fashioned than those illustrated by Mrs. Ricketson but, like them, it is of early date, hers having been found

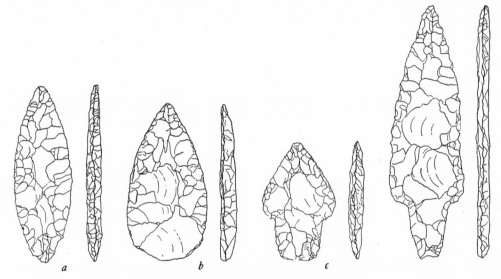

FIG. 2—FLINT POINTS, SYNOPTIC SERIES
Scale ½.

unaltered or very little chipped; other face well chipped to produce evenly rounded edge and symmetrically arched surface. Edges of all slightly worn.

COMMENT. Both the flat specimens and the turtlebacks were doubtless scrapers. Well-formed flint examples such as these are exceedingly rare throughout the Maya country, the various scraping processes employed in woodworking, the preparation of hides, etc. having evidently been carried out with odd chips of flint little or not at all retouched, like those illustrated by Mrs. Ricketson (RR, pl. 55,*b*,1,2,4,5), or with the sharp edges of obsidian chips or flakes. One of the Uaxactun flat scrapers (fig. 62,*a*) was found under the most deeply buried platform of Structure A-V and is there-fore assignable to the Chicanel phase; another (fig. 62,*c*) is from Tepeu refuse above the latest floor of A-V. All the turtlebacks are from late deposits in Structures A-V, -XV, and -XVIII, but that the form was also produced in more ancient times is likely, as a piece which seems to be of this

in the Mamom deposit in Group E and the present speci-men in Pyramid A, a Chicanel building forming the core of Structure A-I (R. E. Smith, 1937). This type of tool seems to have gone out of use in later times.

II. IMPLEMENTS OF FINER, USUALLY DARK, FLINT

Material. Predominantly dark-colored, most specimens brown; a few chocolate-brown and light brown to pinkish brown, two jet-black, one pearly white (fig. 65,*b*,4). The butts of a number of specimens show the white patination of the original nodule's exterior (see fig. 65,*a*,1; *b*,5,6,9,10; *c*,3). This flint works excellently, permitting manufacture of thin, keen-edged implements. That of lighter color is of poorer quality and may be local. I presume the darker stone to have been imported.

A. Projectile points or knives, unstemmed, 27.
  1. *Pointed at both ends,* 13 (figs. 2,*a*; 65,*a*,1–9). L 6–9.3 cm., W averages 1/3 L, T .5–1 cm. In com-

parison to Types A-2 and B-1-a these points are crudely chipped, particularly those of lighter-colored stone (fig. 65,*a*,5–7).

2. *Pointed at one end, rounded at other,* 14 (figs. 2,*b*; 65,*b*,3–11). L 6–10 cm., W of typical specimens varies from 2/5 to 1/2 L, T .5–.7 cm. Excellently fashioned, primary chips thrown far across face, sharp retouched edges. Because of their relatively heavy, little retouched butts it seems certain that these points served as knives, although some of the finest and thinnest might have been lance points. All are seemingly too large and heavy for use on atlatl darts. Two examples (fig. 65,*b*,3,4) are what might be called a reversed form, as their points are less acute and their rounded ends have been retouched to a keen edge. That of white stone (fig. 65,*b*,4) bears a high polish on both faces running back about 1 cm. from the almost square larger end. Its use is unknown, but Gann (1918, p. 89, fig. 33) records from the Rio Hondo, British Honduras, a thin and finely chipped implement, highly polished on one side near the larger end and bearing traces of blue paint. This he thinks may have been a paint grinder. Our second "reversed" specimen (fig. 65,*b*,3) perhaps served as an end-scraper.

COMMENT. Specimens of both the above subtypes were found in the deposits below the plaza floor in Group E, but they do not appear in Mrs. Ricketson's illustrations (RR, pl. 54) in which these forms are represented by examples of the same shapes but of larger size, some belonging to the category of heavy white flint implements already discussed, others to the group of ceremonial flints to be considered hereafter (p. 18). The present material is for the most part from A-V, where it occurred both in buried construction of the Tzakol and Tepeu phases and in late surface refuse, from which came the two finest pieces (fig. 65,*b*, 9,10). As to the chronological and geographical ranges of similar small unstemmed flint implements in Mesoamerica I can supply no useful information, as these unimpressive little objects have seldom received illustration or even notice in the literature. As a matter of fact, it is possible that because of their utility and the ease of their manufacture they were made throughout the region at all times and so will never be helpful for the differentiation of cultures or of periods. But Vaillant, who conscientiously recorded all material, no matter how unspectacular, found during his extensive excavations in Middle Culture sites in the Valley of Mexico, figures no examples of either subtype. There is a very well chipped example, pointed at one end, rounded at the other, in white flint from the Sacred Cenote at Chichen Itza (Peabody Mus. Harvard). Linné (1934, fig. 258) illustrates a single jasper specimen, pointed at both ends, from

Xolalpan, a suburb of Teotihuacan; Strong (1935, fig. 15,*d*) one of felsite from Roatan, Bay Islands, Honduras; W. and D. H. Popenoe (1931, fig. 1) a crude example of gray flint, 12 cm. long, from Lancetilla, Honduras.

What I have said of the possible lack of archaeological value of the above implements does not apply to the much larger "sacrificial" knives, which are also unstemmed. These, as will be pointed out below (p. 18), may prove very useful indicators of trade relations or culture contacts.

B. Projectile points or knives, stemmed, 43.

1. *Tapering stem, short blade,* 8 (figs. 2,*c*; 65,*a*,10–13). L of all but one (fig. 65,*a*,13) 6.1–6.4 cm., W 3.6–4 cm., T averages .7 cm. A very uniform group: broad, thin-edged blade; wide, slightly tapering stem with squarish butt; stem much more roughly chipped than blade.

2. *Tapering stem, long blade,* 33 (figs. 2,*d*; 65,*c*,*d*; RR, pl. 5,*a*,1–3,6,7). L 4–13 cm., both extremes exceptional, typical examples 7–9 cm.; for W variation see illustration; T .5–.8 cm. There is considerable variation in workmanship but most specimens are thin and symmetrically shaped with sharp retouched edges. Stems taper to often rather carelessly finished butts, which sometimes end in a plane surface at right-angles to long axis of implement, evidently a vestige of the striking table of the nodule or core from which flake was detached. Most specimens of brown flint, some retaining white patination on butt (fig. 65,*c*,3; *d*,5).

3. *Expanding stem,* 2 (fig. 65,*b*,1,2). L 6.3, 8.3 cm. (probably originally 9 cm. or more); W 3.6, 2.5 cm.; T .6, 1.2 cm. Stems produced by the chipping out of side notches. No. 1 (fig. 65,*b*,1) of typical brown flint, well chipped. No. 2 (fig. 65,*b*,2) cream-colored flint, crudely chipped, thick; seems to be an example of the slimmer variety of Type II-A-1 (cf. fig. 65,*a*,5–7), notched as an afterthought.

COMMENT. No stemmed flint points were found in the early deposits of Group E (RR, p. 185), and almost all those from other parts of the site came from above the floors of late (Tepeu) rooms and courts; a few, however, were in rooms of the Tzakol phase. All eight of the tapering-stemmed, short-bladed specimens were taken from the most recent surface refuse in Structure A-V. All but the single large short-bladed point seem suitable in size and weight for mounting on atlatl darts; but even the smallest of the long-bladed subtype are probably too thick and heavy for such use. Whether they and the larger ones were knives or spearheads is problematical. It should be noted in this connection that very small stemmed points, usually and probably correctly believed to be arrowheads, were not found at Uaxactun, either in flint or obsidian; nor, as far as I know, have they occurred anywhere in Guatemala, save for a single rather crude one of obsidian recovered by Dutton and Hobbs at Tajumulco in the extreme western part of the republic (1943, fig. 24,*k*). Stone arrowpoints of any sort are, indeed, extremely rare in most parts of Central America, although specimens of obsidian are common in Central Mexico. These, together with a few of flint, are discussed below (p. 12).

As in the case of the unstemmed points, the literature yields scant data as to the distribution of those with stems; but representatives of the Uaxactun type with long blade and rounded shoulders merging without sharp break into a rela-

ing stem should be noted. None was found during the five years' work reported upon by the Ricketsons and but two subsequently (fig. 65,*b*,1; the second, fig. 65,*b*,2, seems to be a makeshift adaptation of an unstemmed piece); nor did they occur at San Jose. In late deposits at Chichen Itza, on the other hand, they greatly outnumbered those with tapering triangular stem. As may be seen in figure 63,*a-e*, the Chichen Itza specimens were produced by chipping two large rounded notches near the base of a point with almost square butt. That this subtype may have been in general use in the Yucatan peninsula is suggested by an example from El Carmen figured by Maler (1912, pl. 5). These should be distinguished from the very fine thin points of

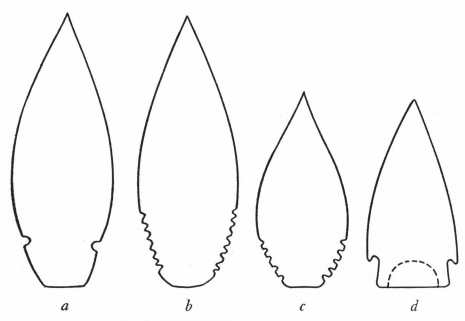

FIG. 3.—FLINT POINTS FROM CHICHEN ITZA

Of beautiful stone and superlatively fine workmanship. Probably heads of ceremonial atlatl darts. *a-c*: Translucent green chalcedony, cache in Temple of the Cones. (Courtesy American Museum of Natural History.) *d*: Pure white flint, Sacred Cenote. Dotted area on butt retains gummy black hafting adhesive. (Courtesy Peabody Museum, Harvard.) Natural size.

tively broad, tapering stem (fig. 65,*c,d*) have been found at Holmul and Copan (Peabody Mus. Harvard) and at San Jose and Baking Pot, British Honduras (Thompson, 1939, pl. 27,*a*,6; Ricketson, 1929, pl. 14,*g*). No example of this sort is in the considerable collection of chipped points from Chichen Itza, the few with tapering stem from that site having short, but usually well-marked, shoulders and a definitely triangular stem (fig. 63,*f*). Several specimens from San Jose approach the latter form but are less well shaped (Thompson, 1939, pl. 25,*a*,5,8–10; *c*,4). Vaillant (1934, fig. 32) illustrates a specimen with almost straight-sided stem and barblike shoulders from a late, perhaps Teotihuacan III, horizon at Gualupita in Morelos.

The great rarity, at Uaxactun, of flint points with expand-

white stone from the Sacred Cenote at Chichen Itza (fig. 3,*d*; see also a specimen from the High Priest's Grave [Thompson and Thompson, 1938, fig. 18,*j*]), which were almost certainly for use on atlatl darts, as they resemble in shape the points on such projectiles shown in the sculptures; and as the gummy black adhesive still remaining on their stems is restricted in area (fig. 3,*d*), rather than spread over the whole stem, as would have been the case had they been mounted in the wider hafts usually employed for stone knives. Four points identical in shape and of superlative workmanship, but made of a beautiful translucent green chalcedony, formed part of a remarkable cache of chipped objects unearthed many years ago at Chichen Itza by Le Plongeon in the hearting of the "Tomb of Coh," now known

2

as the Temple of the Cones, north of the Castillo. With them were numerous equally fine points of white stone; these are unique, as far as I know, in that many of them have a series of very small notches on either side of the base (fig. 3,b,c). There are also two more conventionally notched (fig. 3,a). In addition, there were in the cache a magnificent unstemmed chipped object with expanding base, presumably a knife (Le Plongeon, 1896, pl. LXIII), and a leaf-shaped obsidian blade (specimens in Amer. Mus. Nat. Hist., cat. no. 30-1949). Although the points of white and green stone were presumably atlatl dart heads and to that extent utilitarian, the beauty of their material, the excellence of their chipping, and the fact that they were found in the Sacred Cenote, High Priest's Grave, and Temple of the Cones renders it probable that they were designed for special, very likely ceremonial, use.

To return to presumably utilitarian implements, other large points with expanding stem are recorded from Tajumulco, Guatemala (1, chalcedony; Dutton and Hobbs, 1943, fig. 25,a); from Xolalpan (2, jasper and chalcedony; Linné, 1934, figs. 259, 263); from Gualupita (Vaillant, 1934, fig. 32,1,4); and from unknown localities in Mexico (Peñafiel, 1903, pl. 168).

III. Implements of Obsidian

Material. Both black and green obsidian were in use at Uaxactun. The former is for the most part clear, unstreaked stone; always jet-black in thick pieces, still black in some even quite thin chips and flake-blades, almost transparent in others. A relatively few specimens contain gray to black streaks. Green obsidian seems black when thick, but even so can be distinguished from the much commoner black stone by an almost golden sheen, impossible to describe but highly characteristic. When thin it is a clear, always unstreaked green, varying in shade according to the thickness of the piece. Green obsidian is further characterized by its extraordinarily straight cleavage, flake-blades of this material having very little longitudinal curvature and edges that are almost perfectly parallel (see Smith and Kidder, 1943, fig. 56,a).

All obsidian was of course imported into the limestone country of Peten, the black variety doubtless from volcanic ranges farther south in Guatemala. There must have been an active northward flow of this invaluable stone, as it is abundant not only at Uaxactun and Holmul in Peten, but is also common in all ruins that have been excavated in the northern part of the Yucatan peninsula (see also Blom, 1932, p. 543). Although there are probably nearer sources, some of the Uaxactun obsidian may have come from the great deposits about Joya in the Department of Guatemala. The Joya stone, however, is more liberally streaked with black than is most of that found at Uaxactun. Enormous quantities of chips and other workshop debris at the ruins of

Asuncion Mita, in southeastern Guatemala, indicate a source of obsidian near that site.

The provenience of the green obsidian is unknown, but I feel sure that it emanated from Mexico, probably from somewhere in the Valley of Mexico or its vicinity, where it occurs, or at least has been recorded, more commonly in archaeological sites than in any other area. It came into use there in very early times, Vaillant (1935, pp. 241–43) having found it to constitute 5 per cent of all obsidian on his Early Arbolillo I horizon and 22.5 per cent of all specimens from the site. Fewer pieces (6.4 per cent) came to light at Ticoman, another Middle Culture ruin, but at Gualupita they actually outnumbered (52.1 per cent) those of white-gray stone. Green held an even stronger preponderance at the much later site of Tenayuca, where 80 per cent of the 762 knives, flakes, cores, etc. recovered by Noguera (1935a, p. 162) were of that color. These figures and Vaillant's tend to substantiate the belief of Roberto Weitlaner, a keen and careful observer, who, as quoted by Noguera, considers green obsidian to have been more and more frequently employed as time went on. Other counts by Noguera (1935, p. 56) are to the same effect, for in the interior of the Pyramid of the Sun at Teotihuacan green stood at 20 per cent, whereas on the surface of the ruins, and therefore presumably of later deposition, green rose to no less than 84 per cent. At El Cerrito, Tepotzotlan, Valley of Mexico, Mülleried and Winning (1943, table on p. 139) found about 80 per cent of the flake-blade fragments to be green obsidian. I have noticed, but without making statistical counts, that green is common at Tula. A fragment of a flake-blade was found in a deposit of the Mexican Period at the Temple of the Phalli, Chichen Itza (field notes of Carnegie Institution).

I have no information as to the presence or absence of green obsidian in southern Mexico, but in Guatemala it is extremely rare. Dutton and Hobbs (1943, p. 45) found very few fragments at Tajumulco; there are few in Wauchope's collection from Zacualpa. Not a single green chip or fragment of a green flake-blade occurred among the scores of thousands of such objects in Miraflores and Esperanza phase refuse at Kaminaljuyu, although green flake-blades occurred in one tomb and in others there were very fine points, sequins, and a beautiful knife of this stone (Kidder, Jennings, and Shook, 1946, fig. 157,a; this work will hereafter be referred to as KJS). I could find no example in the extensive Burkitt collection from Alta Verapaz in the University of Pennsylvania Museum except the spool-type earplug from Chipal figured by Butler (1940, pl. XI,a). The only specimens from San Agustin Acasaguastlan are a few flake-blades from a Magdalena phase tomb (Smith and Kidder, 1943, fig. 56,a). Even in the Valley of Mexico, according to Vaillant, green obsidian was used principally for well-made implements and for the better sort of flake-blades; in

Guatemala the material seems to have been restricted entirely to the manufacture of such objects, an added indication that it was a highly valued importation.

A third variety of obsidian, not found at Uaxactun and very rarely anywhere south of the Valley of Mexico, is red streaked with black. Only one specimen of this stone appears to have occurred in a controlled excavation, a fragment of a chipped knife found at Chametla, Sinaloa, by Kelly (1938, pl. 21b). But there are pieces from Calixtlahuaca, State of Mexico (fig. 12,c; Amer. Mus. Nat. Hist.) and from San Simon, presumably the Mexico City suburb of that name (fig. 12,b; Amer. Mus. Nat. Hist.); and a crescentic ornament (cf. fig. 13) and a large spearpoint with square shoulders and long, straight stem from Zacoalco, Jalisco; a long narrow chipped point with square butt from Cotija, Michoacan (both in Chicago Nat. Hist. Mus., information from Dr. Paul S. Martin); and a 20-cm. laurel-leaf blade from Colima (Mus. Amer. Ind.). The southernmost specimens I have seen are a small double crescent and a 30-cm. laurel-leaf blade said to be from Oaxaca and Chiapas respectively (Mus. Amer. Ind.).

Although all obsidian must have been brought to Uaxactun in trade, we do not know in what form it arrived. The presence, there, of cores attenuated beyond further serviceability for the striking-off of flake-blades indicates that the making of the latter implements, at least, was carried on locally. And the abundance of small chips (as distinguished from flake-blades) also points toward the local working of obsidian. Large, ready-shaped cores for the production of flake-blades and "blanks" for the manufacture of chipped implements could have been transported conveniently, and it is likely that most obsidian reached Uaxactun in those forms. Whether or not any finished tools were imported is uncertain; possibly those of green stone were, as no cores or chips (as distinguished from flake-blades) of this color were found (see also general comment on obsidian, pp. 29–32).

A. Projectile points or knives, stemmed, 16.

    1. *Straight or tapering stem*, 8 (figs. 64,a,3,4,10–13; 68,d,1,2). The material is so scanty and so imperfect that statistically significant measurements are not obtainable. The only two complete pieces (fig. 64,a,10,12) are 5.5, 5.2 cm. long, but one fragment (fig. 64,a,4) was probably at least 9 cm. long. Two (fig. 64,a,3,4) have rounded shoulders like those of some of the flint points (cf. fig. 65,c,d). Three (figs. 64,a,11,12; 68,d,1) have barbed shoulders, a form not seen in Uaxactun flint specimens. Three (figs. 64,a,10,13; 68,d,2) have square shoulders. The chipping is in no case exceptionally good, the work on the stems being particularly slipshod.

    2. *Expanding stem*, 2 (fig. 64,a,5,9). The only reasonably complete specimen (fig. 64,a,9) is 6.6 cm. long. The stem of this piece, as apparently was that of the other (fig. 64,a,5), is of less width than the right-angled shoulders.

    3. *Unclassifiable fragments, possibly not all stemmed*, 6.

COMMENT. The fact that the Ricketsons report no obsidian points or fragments thereof from the Mamon deposit under the plaza floor in Group E is in accord with the great rarity in that early stratum of the elsewhere abundant bits of obsidian flake-blades and suggests that trade with the southern highlands may not have been brisk in the first days of Uaxactun. Thompson (1939, p. 171) notes the absence of obsidian from Phase I refuse at San Jose, British Honduras, although it was increasingly well represented thereafter. Miraflores phase middens at Kaminaljuyu, approximately contemporaneous with Mamom and San Jose I, are, however, literally full of obsidian. It is also interesting that none of the points under discussion was taken from the superficial deposits at Structure A-V, for these yielded the majority of the flint points. Can it be that toward the close of the occupancy of Uaxactun commerce with the south had been cut off? Most of our obsidian specimens came from Stratum 4 of Pit 2 in Group A, a deposit of the Tzakol phase; others are from Tzakol rooms and only one or two from rooms of the Tepeu phase.

As to the function of the points it is impossible, as always in such cases, to say whether they served as knives or as spearheads. All are almost surely too large to be considered arrowheads and, because of their rather crude workmanship, I doubt if they were used on atlatl darts.

Stemmed points of this large type are recorded from a few sites in Guatemala, Honduras, and Mexico. Examination of museum collections here and abroad would doubtless bring to light many more, as unspectacular material of this sort was seldom thought worthy of illustration by the authors of the earlier reports. With tapering stem: Kaminaljuyu, several sets of from three to eight, one lot of green obsidian; in tombs of the Esperanza phase, i.e. contemporaneous with the Tzakol phase at Uaxactun (KJS, fig. 157,b-d,g); Quiche region, several 6–12 cm. long, rounded shoulders (Rossbach coll., Chichicastenango); Chuitinamit on Lake Atitlan, fragmentary but apparently with tapering stem (Lothrop, 1933, fig. 54,e,f); Chama, rounded shoulders, length about 15 cm. (Carnegie Inst. photo file); Copan, a number of specimens with rounded shoulders resembling the cruder Kaminaljuyu examples (Peabody Mus. Harvard); Teotihuacan, with right-angled shoulders or tending toward barbed form (Peñafiel, 1899, pl. 40; Linné, 1934, figs. 301, 302, 308, 310; 1938, fig. 10). Also from Teotihuacan are points 5–7 cm. long of green obsidian with tapering stem and barbed shoulders. They retain the relatively strong curvature of the original thin flakes from which they were made and the concave side is unworked save for delicate retouching on the edges of the blade (Univ. Calif. Mus. cat. nos. 3-4834-36). From unspecified localities in Mexico are more points with tapering stem (Peñafiel, 1903, pl. 168; these are described as "*cuarzo*," but several are evidently of obsidian); Sierra de las Navajas, Hidalgo, two fine specimens with barbed shoulders, one with wider stem and right-angled shoulders (Holmes, 1919, fig. 226); Tepetitlan, Puebla, barbed shoulders, weight—tip broken off—4.5 grams (Linné, 1942, fig. 94); Tlamimilolpa and Tlaxcala, one with barbed, one with right-angled shoulders (Linné, 1942, figs. 247, 252). Chametla, Sonora, two with tapering stem and rounded shoulders, one 16 cm. long (Kelly, 1938, pl. 21,*c*,*k*). On Roatan, Bay Islands, Honduras, Strong (1935, fig. 15,*d*) found a specimen whose lower end is on the borderline between a tapering stem and a merely pointed termination. With expanding stem: Quiche region, 7–10 cm. long, stem

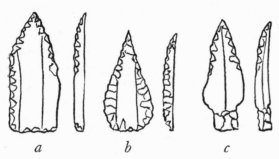

FIG. 4—OBSIDIAN ARROWHEADS

a,*b*: From Chuitinamit, Lake Atitlan, Guatemala. *c*: From present-day Lacandon Indians. Natural size.

somewhat less wide than the square shoulders (Rossbach coll.; fewer than those with tapering stem mentioned above); Lancetilla, Honduras, a well-chipped point, 10.5 cm. long, with side notches (W. and D. H. Popenoe, 1931, fig. 1); San Jose, British Honduras (Thompson, 1939, pl. 25,*b*,2); Chichen Itza, High Priest's Grave (Thompson and Thompson, 1938, fig. 18,*h*). Teotihuacan (Peñafiel, 1899, pl. 40; Linné, 1934, fig. 309); Tenayuca, Valley of Mexico, a relatively late site, produced obsidian points with expanding stem and barbed or right-angled shoulders, perhaps altatl dart points (Noguera, 1935a, pl. LV, 6,7). Alojuca, Puebla, side-notched, fine workmanship (Linné, 1942, fig. 20). Tepetitlan, Puebla, a side-notched point weighing 5.5 grams (Linné, 1942, fig. 95). Chametla, Sonora, a specimen with square shoulders, length about 8 cm. (Kelly, 1938, pl. 21,*d*).

It may have been noted that under the present heading of utilitarian implements there have been included none of obsidian that were pointed at both ends. The reason for this is that the single specimen of that form (fig. 10) was obviously ceremonial, as apparently are most of those found elsewhere in Mesoamerica (see p. 18). The only examples I have seen that were probably put to practical use as knives

or projectile points are from the Quiche region in the Rossbach collection. They are 8–12 cm. long, not exceptionally well chipped, and relatively thick.

Even the smaller of the foregoing examples were presumably not arrowheads. As has been said (p. 9), points which might be considered to have served the latter purpose were not found at Uaxactun, either in flint or obsidian. As far as I know, indeed, the only indication that the Maya of the Classic Period may have had the bow and arrow is furnished by a bow discovered by A. L. Smith (1937, p. 19; pl. 13,*c*) on the floor of a room in Structure A-XVIII. In view of the fact that no other wooden object came to light there or elsewhere at Uaxactun save vault timbers and lintels, whose elevated position preserved them from decay, it is possible that this specimen was left in the room by some wandering hunter long after the abandonment of the city. The Mexicans, however, already had the bow during the Middle Cultures, as will presently be shown; and the Maya were accomplished archers at the time of the conquest. The absence of small stone points does not, of course, prove that the bow was unknown to the Classic Maya, for their arrows might have been tipped with hard wood or with bone. As a matter of fact, my idea (Kidder, 1932, p. 22) that only very small and light heads were suitable for arrows and that larger ones were probably atlatl dartpoints has been challenged by a practical archer (Browne, 1938). But, as far as I am aware, arrows with large, heavy heads are not known to have existed anywhere in the New World; and most authorities still believe, I think, that such relatively weighty specimens as the Signal Butte and Folsom points were mounted on atlatl darts (for discussion of this problem see Vaillant, 1931, pp. 229–304 and tables of weights there given; Linné, 1934, pp. 147, 148; Kidder, 1938). There is need of further measurement and weighing of specimens provably associated with various sorts of projectiles. The following notes on chipped objects, of obsidian or other stones, which I believe to have been arrowheads are here included, more to indicate the paucity of present information than to form a basis for conclusions.

In Guatemala arrowheads seem to be well-nigh absent and it is to be noted that there is not a single example in the great Rossbach collection from the Quiche region, which contains many chipped objects of other forms. At Chuitinamit on Lake Atitlan, the sixteenth-century Zutugil stronghold, I have picked up a very few heads without stems made by retouching the pointed ends broken from obsidian flake-blades (fig. 4,*a*,*b*). These are chipped only on the edges; they thus retain much of both surfaces and also the slight curvature of the parent flake. Modern Lacandon arrowheads of flint and obsidian, also made from flakes, are provided with a short, straight or slightly tapering stem (fig. 4,*c*). In spite of the crudity of their chipping and their curvature, these points, and those from Chuitinamit, are apparently as serviceable as the better-made examples from farther north, for all observers comment on the effectiveness of the Lacandon stone-tipped arrow (for descriptions of Lacandon archery and the manufacture of bows, arrows, and arrowheads, see Maler, 1901; Tozzer, 1907; Soustelle, 1933, 1937). How early the type of arrowhead under discussion came into use in Guatemala and Chiapas is unknown. Those from Chuitinamit probably date from not long before the conquest. It is possible that such inconspicuous little objects, some of which might often not even be recognized as artifacts, have failed to be noted by excavators or included in collections. But none were found at Uaxactun, nor any at Kaminaljuyu, although at the latter site I have been constantly on the lookout for them.

Dutton and Hobbs (1943, fig. 24,k) found at Tajumulco a single carelessly chipped obsidian point with expanding stem, 1.5 cm. long. Boggs (in Longyear, 1944, p. 60) records, but does not illustrate, three specimens from Tazumal in western Salvador, two "leaf-shaped," one "triangular with notched base." It is only when we reach Mexico that well-made arrowheads seem at all common. Whether they occur in the southern part of the country is uncertain, as almost no archaeological work has been done there. But from central Mexico there are numerous records. The earliest examples are of the Middle Cultures. As in the case of scrapers, it would be very interesting to learn what, if any, types of arrowpoints were used by even more ancient Mexican peoples, but no preceramic sites, to say nothing of sites of really remote date, have yet been discovered in the republic. The Middle Culture specimens from Ticoman appear to show a development from simple, unstemmed forms or forms with broad, tapering stem to those with expanding stem and shoulders tending toward barbedness (Vaillant, 1931, pl. LXXXVI; see also pl. XCIII); the same is true of El Arbolillo, where stemmed points were not found before late El Arbolillo I (Vaillant, 1935, p. 240). The Ticoman and El Arbolillo points are all of obsidian, as are those from Zacatenco (Vaillant, 1930, pl. XLII).

Arrowheads seem to be somewhat less abundant at later Valley of Mexico sites, as Linné found relatively few in his extensive excavations in the ruins of Xolalpan and Tlamimilolpa at Teotihuacan. All were of obsidian. From the former site came simple little obsidian points with straight stem (Linné, 1934, figs. 298–300). They are made from flakes and resemble Lacandon arrowheads (fig. 4,c) but are somewhat more carefully chipped. Also from Xolalpan are side-notched examples (Linné, 1934, figs. 307, 311) and several with tapering or straight stem and pointed shoulders that flare widely (Linné, 1934, figs. 303–06, 312). I have not seen specimens of this type from any other locality; whether they are of the Teotihuacan culture or the later

Mazapan is not clear. The Tlamimilolpa arrowheads, of which Linné (1942, p. 136, figs. 265, 266) found six in an infant's grave of Teotihuacan II or III date, are rather crude, tapering stemmed, and with right-angled shoulders flaring slightly.

Undoubtedly post-Teotihuacan, and probably all of Aztec period, are well-made obsidian arrowheads from Tenayuca with broad expanding stems produced by simple side-notching. Their bases are concave (Noguera, 1935a, pl. LVII, 16, 17, 19, 20). There is one of the same side-notched, concave-based type from the surface at Tres Zapotes (Weiant, 1943, pl. 78,4). Also from Tenayuca are cruder examples of flint: barbed with tapering or straight stem, side-notched with expanding stem (Noguera, 1935a, pl. LV, 2–5). Linné (1942, figs. 44, 59) shows two obsidian examples from Aljojuca, Puebla, one with side notches and small expanding stem, the other with tapering stem and right-angled shoulders; Holmes (1919, fig. 101) a point with short, straight stem and right-angled shoulders from Sierra de las Navajas, Hidalgo. From unlocated sites in Mexico are numerous small points illustrated by Peñafiel (1903, pl. 168). Although captioned "cuarzo," most of these are obviously of obsidian. Most of them have tapering stems and are barbed or with right-angled shoulders. Dr. Caso has kindly sent me a photograph of some obsidian specimens collected on the surface in the vicinity of Monte Alban. They are 3–3.7 cm. in length, side-notched and with bases more deeply and sharply concave than those from Tenayuca. Dr. Caso informs me that no arrowheads were found in the excavations at Monte Alban and states that the pieces in question may date from the Mixtec or the even later Aztec occupation of this part of Oaxaca. Batres (1902, fig. 28) figures a flint side-notched point from Monte Alban but gives no data as to provenience. E. H. Thompson (1897, pl. VII, 2,h) shows one from the Loltun cave in Yucatan. Strebel (1885–89, II, pl. XVII) illustrates a fine series of small obsidian points, evidently arrowheads, from Coatlatlan, Veracruz, which have side-notches and straight or concave base. This type appears to be a late one and it is interesting to note that the only record of occurrence I can find south of Mexico is from Lancetilla, on the north coast of Honduras, where the Popenoes (1931, fig. 1) found numerous obsidian specimens, side-notched with straight base; and, as is well known, there was active trade in late prehistoric times between that region and the gulf coast of Mexico. It is also interesting that side-notched, as distinguished from barbed, arrowpoints seem to constitute the latest type in the Southwest and Great Plains areas. Ekholm's excavations at Guasave in Sinaloa yielded no chipped implements of any sort (1942, p. 106); Kelly's at Chametla, in the same state, produced no arrowpoints (1938, p. 61); and Sauer and Brand (1932, p. 32) state that "there are extraordinarily few arrows [in coastal Sinaloa], but these are finely made of obsidian." Ekholm observes (1942, p. 106) that farther north in Sonora arrowheads are "fairly common." I suspect that stone arrowheads may prove to have been more commonly used by the less cultured tribes of northern Mexico than by the peoples of high civilization to the south. In this connection, the apparently greater frequency of arrowheads in early than in late Valley of Mexico sites is interesting. Further data on the chronological and spatial distributions of arrowheads in Mesoamerica might well provide valuable information on the at present little-understood history of the bow and arrow in the New World.

B. Scrapers, "thumbnail," 3 (fig. 5). L 1.9–2.8 cm., W 1.6–2.3 cm., T 0.3–0.6 cm. Thin chips or parts of flakes brought to rounded form and with, in places, neatly retouched edges.

COMMENT. These three nicely made little objects from Stratum 4, Pit 2, Group A, a Tzakol deposit, are the only

being turned out in early times. Well-made examples of the type variously called "snub-nosed," "duck-bill," or "humpbacked" were found with other tools believed to be those of a leatherworker in a grave at Ticoman (Vaillant, 1931, pl. XCI), and there are many snub-nosed obsidian scrapers from the Valley of Mexico in the Mexico National and Chicago Natural History Museums, some, perhaps all, of which may come from equally early sites. Whether this form persisted into later periods is uncertain, for one specimen from Teotihuacan, although of similar outline, seems to be flatter than the true snub-nose (Linné, 1934, fig. 289), as is a rather crude one from Sierra de las Navajas, Hidalgo (Holmes, 1919, fig. 99). Another, more nearly of snub-nose form but of unknown date, is from Tacuba (Gamio, 1909); and there is a neatly chipped two-ended scraper, which might be called a "double snub-nose," from Alojuca, Puebla (Linné, 1942, fig. 43). Most of the scrapers from the Teotihuacan horizon are of a somewhat different type. Like

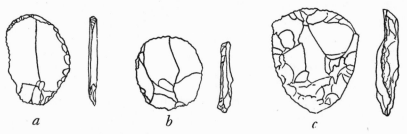

FIG. 5—OBSIDIAN "THUMBNAIL" SCRAPERS
Natural size.

formed scrapers of obsidian found at Uaxactun, the need for scraping tools having evidently been met, as in flint, by the use of raw chips and flakes that were discarded when their originally keen edges had become dulled. Quantities of such worn-out implements were everywhere in the refuse of the later periods. Their edges are characterized by the presence of minute, stubby chip-scars, not uniformly distributed and thus easily distinguishable from the regularly spaced and longer chip-scars produced by retouching.

Formed scrapers of obsidian, as distinguished from amorphous chip-scrapers, seem not to occur anywhere in highland Guatemala or the lowland Maya country, unless a single heavy specimen from Kaminaljuyu be so considered (KJS, fig. 56). The piece from Chuitinamit on Lake Atitlan (Lothrop, 1933, fig. 54,b) and that from San Jose, British Honduras, figured by Thompson (1939, pl. 27,a,13) hardly qualify. None is seen in the great Rossbach collection from the Quiche country. Boggs, however (in Longyear, 1944, p. 60), mentions a "thumbnail" specimen from Tazumal.

In central Mexico, whose pre-Columbian peoples utilized obsidian to a greater extent and in more different ways than any others in the New World, excellent scrapers were already

the snub-nosed specimens, they are end-scrapers made from large flakes; they have the same thick forward end falling abruptly to the working edge, and the same unmodified inner surface of the flake on the under side, but instead of tapering evenly toward the rear end they are constricted in such a way as to provide a more or less straight-sided stem or tail about half the length of the entire implement. Pieces of this sort from Teotihuacan are figured by Gamio (1922, pl. 120,d) and Linné (1942, fig. 267); examples from deposits of the Classic Teotihuacan horizon at El Corral, Azcapotzalco, are in the American Museum of Natural History; one is also reported by Ekholm (1944, fig. 55,z) from a late (Period V) deposit at Las Flores in the Panuco region.

In Gamio's treatise (p. 216) attention is called to the similarity between these tailed scrapers and the iron implements used today in the Valley of Mexico to scrape and freshen the sides of the cavity made in the maguey plant for the collection of pulque juice.

C. Flake-blades (not counted). Fragments of these evidently invaluable little tools were found in quantity throughout the refuse of the later periods, much less commonly in the Mamom deposits below the plaza floor of Group E. The Uaxactun flake-blades of gray obsidian seem to have been both narrower and shorter than those of Kaminaljuyu (KJS, p. 136). The average width of 150 gray fragments from Pit 2 in Group A, the only body of midden material from which all pieces of obsidian were collected, was almost exactly 1 cm. There were many pieces of .7–.8 cm. and a few of .5 cm. Examples approximately 2 cm. wide, so abundant at Kaminaljuyu and other sites in the highlands of Guatemala, constitute less than 4 per cent of the Pit 2 lot. Although, in the case of the broken Pit 2 material, no lengths could exactly be determined, the majority of the specimens seem to have been less than 10 cm. long, which again is far below the dimension attained by most highland flake-blades. That the Pit 2 pieces were utilitarian rather than for special ceremonial or mortuary use is suggested by their abundance, their presence in refuse, and the fact that most of them had work-dulled edges. Those of green stone were even narrower, but seem to have attained greater lengths. Many of them were also work-dulled.

The only complete flake-blades recovered at Uaxactun, being from graves and caches, are described with the other ceremonial objects of chipped stone (p. 20). It may here be noted, however, that they were even more delicate than those from Pit 2. At Kaminaljuyu there was a similar difference between grave and refuse specimens.

COMMENT. The making of flake-blades is discussed at length in the report on Carnegie Institution's work at Kaminaljuyu (KJS, p. 135, fig. 56) in which there is included a translation by J. E. S. Thompson of Torquemada's detailed description of their manufacture in Mexico. This is more accurate than the often-quoted translation of Wilson. (See also Holmes, 1919, ch. 21, for an interesting description of obsidian "mines" and obsidian working; Breton, 1902, lists a number of localities in Mexico from which obsidian was procured.)

The material from Uaxactun yielded no significant new technological data, but some notes on cores may not be amiss. There came to light no large, roughed out, but apparently unused, cores such as that found by Strömsvik (1941, fig. 32,*d*) in a cache at Quirigua, all those recovered at Uaxactun having been of "exhausted" type, reduced beyond further usefulness for the striking-off of flake-blades. Most of these were reworked into ceremonial forms which are described below (p. 19). Study of these secondarily shaped cores and of the relatively few whole and broken examples from the rubbish shows them to be of two types: round and thin-oval (fig. 6). I cannot remember to have

noticed the thin-oval form at other sites; what caused it is unknown, but it may be that by working a core to oval form it was possible to produce from its edges the very narrow, lancetlike flake-blades which occur at Uaxactun. The chip-scars indicate that the flake-blades struck from the sides of the oval cores were somewhat broader and possessed less curvature than those emanating from the round type. Round cores were discarded when the striking table had been brought down to a diameter of about 1 cm.; oval cores, when the striking table had diminished to about 1.5 cm. by .5 cm.

The flake-blade was characteristic of, and almost entirely confined to, the cultures of Mesoamerica. Both Wendell C. Bennett and Alfred Kidder II tell me that they do not know of its occurrence in Peru or Bolivia, but Dr. Bennett informs me that he has seen specimens from the coast of Ecuador, an area in which there are other as yet unexplained evidences of contact with Mesoamerica. No example, so far as I know, has ever been found in the United States. Very small flake-blades, however, were produced from the flint of Flint Ridge, Ohio, and from that of a deposit in Ottawa County, Oklahoma (Holmes, 1919, pp. 181, 207, fig. 87). At a series of small Basket Maker III sites along the eastern foot of First Mesa in the Hopi country of Arizona I have picked up a number of little gray flint flake-blades. Holmes (p. 181) believes that the striking of such blades was not widely practiced in eastern United States; the technique was certainly unknown in most parts of the Southwest, for since finding the above-mentioned specimens I have vainly looked for others, both in the field and in museum collections. Those at First Mesa seem therefore to represent an independent invention which, perhaps because suitable material was not generally available, failed to "take hold."

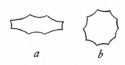

FIG. 6—"EXHAUSTED" OBSIDIAN CORES
Shapes of striking tables. Natural size.

To return to Mesoamerica, the southernmost record I can find of the obsidian flake-blade is from Orosi in Costa Rica, where Hartman (1901, p. 154, fig. 371) discovered part of one in a grave. He states that this was the only piece of obsidian recovered during his extensive excavations in the Costa Rica highlands, that he did not encounter this stone at all on the Pacific Coast, but that obsidian "implements" from Nicoya are in the National Museum at San Jose. Sr. Jorge A. Lines has very kindly sent me a photograph of all the pieces in the museum. They comprise seven points 2–5 cm. long with tapering stems, one of the same form 8.5 cm. long, five fragments of flake-blades, and two cores about 15 cm. long—one from which few if any blades have been struck, the other nearly "exhausted." In Nicaragua flake-blades or other objects of obsidian seem equally rare, as

Bransford (1881, p. 46) states that none came to light in his excavations at Ometepec Island. In eastern Salvador, however, the flake-blade begins to appear in quantity. Long-year (1944) found it to be common at Los Llanitos, and I have observed fragments at Quelepa. In western Salvador, western Honduras, Guatemala, and throughout a large part of Mexico these invaluable little tools were in use from the time of the Middle Cultures onward, not only in the volcanic regions where deposits of obsidian occur, but in areas,

flake-blades is uncertain. Dr. J. A. Mason (personal information) found none during his careful surface examination of sites in Durango and doubts if these tools were a trait of the La Quemada–Chalchuites culture. He also tells me that no trace of them was seen by him in northern Tamaulipas or about Brownsville, Texas. Mr. E. B. Sayles and Dr. E. W. Haury (personal information) state that they do not occur either in Chihuahua or in the Hohokam sites in southern Arizona.

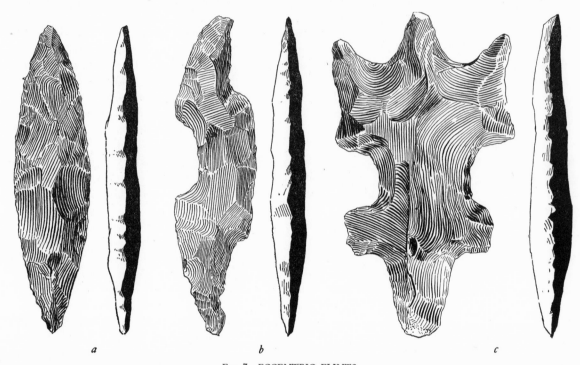

a   *b*   *c*

Fig. 7—ECCENTRIC FLINTS
Note coarse chipping, a characteristic of Uaxactun eccentrics. Scale ½.

such as northern Yucatan, to which they, or the raw material for making them, must have been brought in trade over long distances. Obsidian, indeed, undoubtedly provided many groups with one of their most important export commodities.

The northern range of the flake-blade seems to have coincided, on the two coasts of Mexico, pretty closely with that of higher Mesoamerican culture. Ekholm (1942, p. 106) reports it from Guasave, Sinaloa. He states, however, that no cores have been found in that state. Kelly (1938, p. 61) found obsidian scarce at Chametla, Sinaloa, and flake-blades "apparently a later vogue." Ekholm's northernmost record of the flake-blade on the Pacific side is from Huatambo, Sonora. On the Atlantic Coast it occurs in the Panuco region (Ekholm, 1944, p. 489), but only in the later deposits. Data as to the north-central part of the republic are unsatisfactory. Hrdlička (1903, p. 394) mentions "obsidian knives" at Totoate, Zacatecas. Whether or not these were

CEREMONIAL CHIPPED STONE

I. OBJECTS OF WHITE FLINT

Material. The relatively coarse, presumably local, grayish or pinkish to pure white flint described on p. 5. Mrs. Ricketson (RR, pl. 56,*b*,3) illustrates a trident of black stone. No specimen of the fine dark gray flint used for eccentrics at some other sites (see p. 18, below) occurred at Uaxactun.

A. Eccentric flints, 41.

   1. *Tridents*, 10 (figs. 7,*c*; 66,*a*,4; *b*,2,4; *c*,2,4,5; *d*,3,4; 67,*a*,1; *c*,4; also RR, pls. 56,*b*; 57). L 15–21.7 cm., T 1.5–2.5 cm. Broad end terminates in three points, the central one usually the longest; toward the elongated, tapering end are two lateral projections, usually lightly notched. Aberrant specimen (fig. 66, *d*,4) probably went wrong in the making.

   2. *Disc,* 1 (fig. 67,*a*,3). D 9 cm., T 1.8 cm. Edge sharp, true.

3. *Crescent,* 1 (fig. 67,*a*,2). L 9 cm., T 1 cm. Edge sharp, true.

4. *Laurel-leaf blades,* 15 (figs. 7,*a*; 66,*a*,3,5; *b*,5; *c*,1,3; *d*,1; 67,*b*,*d*-*f*; 67,*c*,1–3; 68,*c*,2,3; 68,*d*,8; also RR, pl. 54,*a*,1–10). L 15.3–20.8 cm., T 1.2–2.3 cm. Workmanship varies from crude to very fine (cf. figs. 66,*c*,1; 68,*c*,2; *d*,8; also RR, pl. 54,*a*,2 and *a*,10), the best examples approaching, in regularity of outline and excellence of chipping, the so-called "sacrificial" knives (see p. 18). There can be no doubt that all should be classed as ceremonial and included with the eccentric flints, as at Uaxactun none were found save in caches also containing truly eccentric specimens.

Cruz of the Mexico-Guatemala Boundary Commission. A. L. Smith, present when some of these were found, reports that from beneath Stela 16 (9.14.0.0.0) came nine flints (fig. 8,*a*-*i*) and nine incised obsidians (fig. 70, see its caption). Under plain Stela A-21, nine flints (figs. 8,*o*-*w*) and nine incised obsidians (fig. 70,*a*-*i*). Under plain Stelae A-16, A-18 and, Mr. Smith believes, A-24, were other flints and incised obsidians. Earlier in 1931, three English treasure hunters, Messrs. Robson, Jolly, and Herron, excavated at Tikal, recovering eccentric flints and incised obsidians from beneath stelae (the flints assigned to Tikal in Joyce, 1932, are some of these, as are the obsidians Joyce figures in pl. VIII and are here reproduced in fig. 71). Mr. Smith, on visiting the site with the Boundary Commission, ob-

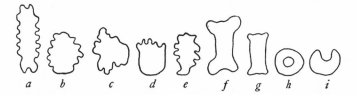

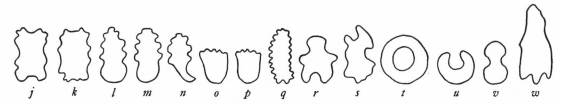

FIG. 8—ECCENTRIC FLINTS FROM TIKAL

a-*i*: Under Stela A-21 with nine eccentric obsidians (fig. 70,*a*-*i*; see its caption). *j*-*w*: Nine of these, but which nine is unknown, were found with nine of the eccentric obsidians shown in fig. 70,*j*-*x*. L of *a*, 11.5 cm.

5. *Notched blades,* 11 (figs. 7,*b*; 66,*a*,1,2; *b*,3; *d*,2; 67,*d*,1–5; 68,*d*,6,7; also RR, pl. 58). L 16.9–19 cm., T 1.8–2.5 cm. Laurel-leaf blades in the edges of which large notches have been chipped: commonest arrangement is two notches near ends on one edge, single notch at middle of other edge. In some cases (e.g. fig. 68,*d*,7) edges have been enough chipped to modify the probably original laurel-leaf form and produce a serpentine effect.

6. *Offset blades,* 2 (fig. 67,*b*,2,3). L 14.8, 13.5 + cm., T 1.3, 1.5 cm.

7. *Rhomboidal,* 1 (fig. 67,*b*,1). L 15 cm., T 1.5 cm.

In addition to the above forms, Uaxactun has yielded but three others: large crescents with pointed protuberances on the convex edge (RR, pl. 59,*b*), some very crude notched pieces (RR, pl. 59,*a*), and well-chipped blades of laurel-leaf form with hiltlike protuberances near one end which give them the appearance of daggers (RR, pl. 60,*a*).

As they have not previously been published, record is here made of 23 eccentric flints from Tikal (fig. 8). They were collected in 1931 by Gen. Eduardo Hay and Sr. Fernando

served signs of recent digging under Stela 5 (9.15.13.0.0) and Stela 10 (9.3.13.0.0 ??; see remarks regarding this find on p. 21). He thinks it probable that the Robson-Jolly-Herron specimens came from below these monuments.

COMMENT. All the Uaxactun eccentric flints occurred in caches whose contents, location, and probable date are discussed in the general comment on eccentric flints and obsidians (pp. 25, 26). In the same section (pp. 26, 27) are listed finds of similar material elsewhere.

The Uaxactun eccentric flints are well shaped but their chipping is bold rather than fine (fig. 7) and their forms are simple and few in number. Other ruins have yielded examples much more carefully fashioned and of many shapes not represented here. An idea of the variety of form exhibited by these strange objects may be gained from the Tikal series (fig. 8) and from the illustrations in the publications listed below (pp. 26, 27), particularly those of Gann. Joyce (1932) presents a useful classification, with outline drawings of the more common types; and photographs of many specimens, ordinary, unusual, and unique.

Most eccentric flints are relatively small and, like those

of Uaxactun and Tikal, were produced by notching the edges of laurel-leaf or discoidal "blanks." The majority of the latter were worked into crescentic forms by chipping out a single large notch on one side (fig. 8,*i,u*); the remainder of the periphery might be plain, as in the Tikal specimens just mentioned, but more commonly was elaborated with smaller notches, serrations, or spiky projections (Joyce, 1932, pls. IV,2,3; V,2). In some cases discs have been centrally perforated (fig. 8,*h*; Joyce, *ibid.*, pl. IV,1). Joyce (*ibid.*, p. xxi) suggests that this was accomplished by taking advantage of one of the natural holes which often occur in the Peten flints, and L. Satterthwaite Jr. informs me that one of the eccentrics from Piedras Negras has such a hole which, although not utilized, might have served to give the artisan a start upon what would otherwise have been a very difficult operation.

What, if any, symbolic significance the eccentric flints may have had, is problematical. Most of them seem to be pure abstractions, and realism was seldom attempted. The scorpion was without doubt represented (fig. 8,*e,n*; Joyce, 1932, pl. III, fig. 1). This identification is confirmed by obsidians of the same hook-tailed shape, upon which details of the creature's body are incised (fig. 69,*e*). Some notched flints might be taken to be renderings of serpents (fig. 66,*b*,3; Joyce, 1932, pl. I, fig. 3), centipedes (fig. 8,*a,q*), human beings (Joyce, 1932, pl. V, fig. 4; Thompson, 1939, pl. 24, *c*,3), animals (Gann, 1918, pl. 15,*a,g*; Thompson, 1939, pl. 24,*a*,3; *c*,1) or birds (Ricketson, 1929, pl. 12,*c*). One would suppose, however, that had they intended to depict these forms, artisans capable of turning out the extraordinary pieces next to be considered would have succeeded much better than they did.

The eccentrics in question are of fine, dark gray flint; large, flamboyantly branching, and with edges in which are chipped what seem to be human faces in profile. One of these, from El Palmar in southern Quintana Roo, is perhaps the most elaborate example of flint working ever discovered (Thompson, 1936, fig. 1). It was found near, but not in direct association with, a cache of rather crude laurel-leaf blades, eccentrics of the ordinary forms, and obsidian cores, beneath Stela 10 (9.15.15.0.0; Thompson informs me that this is the correct reading, rather than 9.14.0.0.0 given in his 1936 article). Another, almost equally fine, came from below Zoomorph O at Quirigua (9.18.0.0.0). With it were a small human head of jade, a quartz crystal, and an unworked lump of jade (Strömsvik, 1941, fig. 32,*a*). A third (Joyce, 1932, pl. VII; Morley, 1935, p. 44, fig. 36), also from Quirigua, formed part of a cache containing 23 other eccentric flints (nature not recorded) in a small temple on a ridge overlooking the Main Group. No date can be assigned to the cache, for although two stelae are associated with the temple, their inscriptions are badly defaced. Morley

(1935) reads one at 9.13.0.0.0 (?), the other at 9.14.0.0.0 (???), but even were these dates more certain they could not safely be applied to a deposit which might have been placed in the temple before or after the erection of the stelae. Finally, there is from Copan a fragment (fig. 73) of a specimen, which may have been as elaborate as that from El Palmar. It was found with other materials, evidently from a cache, in the debris of the Hieroglyphic Stairway (information from G. Strömsvik). If, as Mr. Strömsvik believes, the cache was laid down when the stairway was built, this flint should date from after 9.16.0.0.0. A piece of a cruder example, but also of dark flint, is said to have been found in the Department of Quiche (Mus. Amer. Ind.).

The laurel-leaf blades, which so often accompany the eccentric flints, never, so far as I am aware—and I have examined a number of them—show any sign of use. With the single exception of the beautifully chipped one from Cist 13 at Uaxactun (RR, pl. 54,*a*,10), they are hardly sharp enough to have served as sacrificial knives, and are much too heavy for spearheads. Stemmed points that might have been either spearheads or knives sometimes also occur in caches; as do very fine laurel-leaf blades of dark flint, which have usually, and probably correctly, been referred to as sacrificial knives. None of these has been found at Uaxactun but splendidly shaped specimens, thin and sufficiently keen for the most exacting heart-remover, have come to light in caches at San Agustin Acasaguastlan (Smith and Kidder, 1943, fig. 57,*g*), Quirigua (Strömsvik, 1941, fig. 30), Copan (pink flint, Peabody Mus. Harvard; black flint, Copan Museum, fig. 73), Benque Viejo (Amer. Mus. Nat. Hist.), Tzimin Kax and San Jose (Thompson, 1931, pl. XLVI; 1939, pl. 26,*a-c*), Bay Islands (Strong, 1935, pl. 16), and El Baul (Thompson, 1946, fig. 23). These are comparable to the doubtless sacrificial flint knives found in such quantities in the great Calle de las Escalerillas deposit of ceremonial materials in Mexico City, but the latter differ from the Maya knives in that one end is broader than the other and terminates in a sharp point (Batres, 1902a). Other examples of the same form, said to be from Oaxaca, are illustrated by Joyce (1920, fig. 19,8; 1927, p. 181, nos. II, V). One of the El Baul specimens has the sharp point as do still others from Cerro Montoso and Atotonilco, Veracruz (Strebel, 1885–89, vol. I, pl. XII, 34; vol. II, pl. XXVIII, 9). Because of the close similarity in shape of specimens of the Escalerillas type, it seems likely that they all come from a single center of manufacture. It would be interesting to know whether or not the "sacrificial" flint knife from the Sacred Cenote at Chichen Itza, whose butt is still embedded in its elaborately carved wooden handle, is of this pointed type (Willard, 1926, p. 140). However, it is possible that the "business end," so to speak, of the Escalerillas knives was that which bears the small point, for there is an example from the Valley of Mexico which bears, on the more taper-ing end, a ball apparently of some resinous material, which may have served as a haft (specimen in Mus. Amer. Ind.).

Still another form of flint blade, only two rather crude examples of which have turned up at Uaxactun (RR, pl. 61,*b*,14,15), should also probably be classed as ceremonial, although it may have had secular uses as well. It might be called the stemmed flake-blade, as it was produced from a large flake struck from a core. One side (the inner in relation to the parent core) is therefore without chip-scars, while the other bears the scars of flakes previously struck (see description of obsidian flake-blades in KJS, p. 136). Such a flake has a point so sharp that retouching was seldom necessary. The originally broad proximal or striking-table end was skillfully chipped from both sides to produce a long, tapering stem. Very fine examples of this type from the Belize River region in British Honduras are illustrated by Joyce (1932, pl. VI), there is a splendid series of them from British Honduras (Mus. Amer. Ind.), a set of five fine specimens from a cache at Tayasal (Peabody Mus. Harvard), and somewhat cruder ones are figured by Thomp-son (1939, pl. 27,*d*) from a cache at San Jose. Evidently made from flakes of the same sort are beautiful completely retouched stemmed blades (Joyce, 1932, pl. VI, fig. 4; Thompson, 1939, pl. 25,*d*, the latter from an early burial—San Jose I or II). The very fine stemmed flake-blade ap-pears to be characteristic of central Peten and British Hon-duras, particularly of the latter. The only examples from elsewhere, of which I have knowledge, are a few said to have been found in the Ulua Valley, Honduras (Mus. Amer. Ind.).

II. OBJECTS OF OBSIDIAN

A. Eccentric obsidians

1. *Tridents,* 16 (figs. 9,*c*; 66,*b*,1; 68,*a*; *b*,3; RR, pl. 57,*b*). L 8.2–11.5 cm., T 1–1.5 cm. Broad end terminates in three points. In three cases (fig. 68,*a*, 1,2; RR, pl. 57,*b*) there are lateral projections to-ward the tapering end, similar to those of the flint tridents (cf. fig. 66,*b*,2,4); there is a fourth (fig. 68,*b*,3) with lateral projections, the small end T-shaped rather than tapering; a fifth (fig. 68,*a*,3) with both ends in trident form. The remaining 11 lack lateral projections; these end in a long, taper-ing stem, save in one case (fig. 66,*b*,1) in which the end is a triangular blade. With one exception, the tridents appear to have been made from thick flakes, although they have been so thoroughly chipped on both sides that no part of the flake's original surface remains. The aberrant specimen (figs. 9,*c*; 68,*b*,3), like the two forms next to be described, has been worked from a core.

2. *Notched cores,* 1 only in present collection (fig. 68,*d*,5); about 75 found in earlier excavations at Uaxactun (RR, pl. 60,*b*). L av. 7.6 cm. Small, "exhausted" cores in the sides of which shallow notches have been chipped. Some have been re-duced in thickness before notching, but in no case has all trace of the core's original chip-scars been removed. Three arrangements: one notch on each side, two notches on each side, two notches on one side only.

3. *Core knives,* 3 (figs. 9,*a*,*b*; 68,*b*,1,2; 68,*d*,4; RR, pl. 54,*a*,13–15). L 8.2, 8.5, 9 cm., W 2.3, 2.5, 2.5 cm., T 1, 1, 1.2 cm.; the three RR specimens ap-proximately same size. In each case one side of

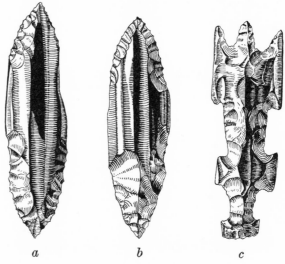

FIG. 9—ECCENTRIC OBSIDIANS

Core knives and trident; for photo see fig. 68,*b*. L of *a*, 9 cm.

an "exhausted" core was so chipped away as to reduce the piece to one half or less its original thickness. On the other side only enough work was done to bring each end to a sharp-edged point. This has left unaltered, on that side, several of the longitudinal chip-scars of the original core (the well-worked side of one specimen is shown in fig. 68,*b*,1; its less-worked side in fig. 9,*a*).

COMMENT. The geographic range of eccentric obsidians seems to lie within that of eccentric flints, for I know of no occurrence in such outlying areas as Yucatan, the Quirigua-Copan region, or the south coast of Guatemala, all of which have yielded flints. They thus appear to be even more closely tied up with Classic Maya ceremonialism than are the flints. They sometimes form the sole contents of a cache, but more often are found with flints and presumably served a similar ceremonial purpose.

Most eccentric obsidians are small and the range of forms

is much more restricted than that of the flints. The trident, as far as I know, has been found only at Uaxactun, the core knife only there and at Piedras Negras. Notched cores are widely distributed: Piedras Negras (information from L. Satterthwaite Jr.), Tikal (Joyce, 1932, pl. I,4*d*,8*d*), Benque Viejo (Gann, 1918, fig. 44,*m-p*), Pusilha (Joyce, Gann, Gruning, Long, 1928, pl. XXXV,2). Forms smaller than but otherwise much like those of the simpler eccentric flints, and like them made from thick flakes rather than from cores, have been found at Benque Viejo, Pusilha, and Piedras Negras. Among them are scorpions, crescents, discs, notched blades, and waisted blades (for shape of the latter see Joyce, 1932, fig. 1,*c*). Only at Piedras Negras, apparently, were small obsidian chips and broken flake-blades notched to produce crude little eccentrics. Of all the above types, Copan has produced only discs. From that site, however, is a large laurel-leaf blade with side notches (Peabody Mus. Harvard). A unique form comes from Mound 10 at Douglas, British Honduras, where Gann found 60 obsidian objects resembling fleurs-de-lis (Gann, 1918, fig. 31; Joyce, 1932, pl. II, fig. 4,4*d*,5*d*). Large obsidian eccentrics are represented only by the above-mentioned notched blade from Copan and a magnificent piece from a Period V cache at San Jose, 29.5 cm. long, in the form of a hafted celt (Thompson, 1939, p. 188, pl. 28,*a*).

Probably not directly connected with the eccentric obsidians from the Maya area, but possibly the result of a distantly related collateral development, are certain evidently ceremonial chipped obsidians from Mexico described on p. 30.

B. Core, 1 (fig. 68,*d*,3; RR, pl. 61,16–18). Cache in Structure A-XV. L 7 cm.; RR specimens L 15–18 cm.

COMMENT. The ceremonial use of cores was not restricted to the making of eccentric forms, for many examples with no secondary working have been found in caches. The one piece in the present collection approaches more nearly than do the large RR specimens the average size of cache cores from other sites and of those used at Uaxactun and elsewhere for making eccentrics. Because of the smallness of most cache cores I have wondered if their ceremonial significance might have been due to prior service as blanks from which to strike the short, delicate, and keen-pointed flake-blades that, as will be shown below, are also often found in aches and graves.

Occurrences of cores in caches. El Palmar, several, with eccentric flints under Stela 10 (9.15.15.0.0; Thompson, 1936); San Agustin Acasaguastlan, two, in pottery cache-box with a flint "sacrificial" knife, obsidian flake-blades, shells, sting-ray spines (Smith and Kidder, 1943, p. 145, fig. 56,*b*); Quirigua, 1, large, in pottery cache-box under Zoomorph G (9.17.15.0.0; Strömsvik, 1941, fig. 32,*d*). Quen Santo, one, in pottery jar with stone beads (Seler, 1901, p.

107, figs. 134–136). *British Honduras*: Baking Pot, one, cached with worked pieces of human skull (Ricketson, 1929, p. 14, pl. 15,*a*); Nohmul, Mound 1, several in tomb (Gann and Gann, 1939, p. 10); Douglas, Mound 10, 60, unusually small (2.5–7.5 cm. long), in caches with eccentric flints and obsidians (Gann, 1918, pp. 86, 88); Pusilha, in caches with eccentric flints and obsidians, under stelae (see p. 26). Strebel (1885–89, II, p. 14 and pl. VII, 14, 27) reports the finding of a core and a fine carved jade plaque cached together near Misantla, Veracruz.

C. Flake-blades, 15 (three sets of five each; see also RR, p. 187; pl. 61,1–11). (1) From Burial A-31 (fig. 64,*b*), L 4.3–8.5 cm. The tips of the three broader specimens have been retouched with unbelievably fine chipping, one of the very few cases I have seen from anywhere in Mesoamerica of the retouching of flake-blades. The other two have the naturally keen points characteristic of the lancet type. (2) From Burial B-2, L 10–11 cm. Extremely sharp points, translucent gray obsidian. (3) From below plain Stela A-15, L 5–6 cm. Very keen points, almost transparent gray obsidian. These are the finest lancet-type flake-blades that I have seen.

COMMENT. The ceremonial use of obsidian flake-blades, as indicated by their inclusion in caches and in mortuary equipment, was both frequent and widespread. There are, generally speaking, two sorts: short (4–10 cm.), lancetlike, with very sharp points; long (14–18 cm.), usually with less keen points. All are extra-fine pieces, narrower, straighter-edged, and of clearer stone than the utilitarian flake-blades whose work-dulled fragments abound at Guatemalan and Mexican sites.

The Maya doubtless employed the lancet type of obsidian flake-blade for ritual bloodletting, as did the Aztecs. Of the latter, Motolinia (1858, trat. 1, ch. 10) states:

[Then] came the master craftsman who detached [struck from a core] the knives, they also fasted and prayed, and they detached many knives with which the tongues had to be opened, and as they kept detaching them they kept placing them upon a clean mantle. And if one should break while being detached, they said that they had not fasted properly. . . . And they will detach from a stone more than two hundred knives and some bloodletting lancets. And having placed the knives on a clean mantle, they perfume them with their incense, and when the sun has completely set, all the priests being together, four of them sing songs of the devil to the knives, beating their drums. [Translation by J. E. S. Thompson; for notes on bloodletting by the Maya and other Mesoamericans, see Tozzer, 1941, p. 114.]

To make clear the nature and range of the ritual employment of flake-blades, there follows a list of typical occurrences selected from the many recorded in the literature and noted in museum collections. *Costa Rica*: Orosi, 1, in grave; the only one recovered from the many interments excavated by Hartman (1901, p. 154, fig. 371) and the only object of obsidian found by him in the Costa Rican highlands. *Nicaragua*: no records. *Salvador*: Los Llanitos, 1, fragmentary, in cache with tanged obsidian point and obsidian chip-scraper (Longyear, 1944, p. 41; pl. VI,11). The lack of other Salvador records is doubtless due to paucity of controlled excavation, for obsidian was much used in that area. *Honduras*: Las Flores, 16, very fine, long, with bundle burial (Strong, Kidder, and Paul, 1928, p. 41); Playa de los Muertos, 6, short, strongly curved, in grave (Peabody Mus. Harvard), Middle Culture; Copan, 1, lancet type, Tomb 1, Late Classic Period (Peabody Mus. Harvard). *British Honduras*: Nohmul, "nearly 200," tomb in Mound 1, Late Classic Period (Gann and Gann, 1939, p. 10); Douglas, "a number," deeply notched at each side of blunt end, Mound 10, in cache with cores and eccentric obsidians; 12, cached farther down in same mound, with cores and eccentric flints (Gann, 1918, pp. 86, 88); San Jose, many, av. L 7 cm., apparently lancet type, in lots of from 1 to 22 in graves, caches, and ceremonial (?) ash deposits, San Jose II to V (Thompson, 1939, p. 171; the U-shaped nick in the points of the Cache A1 specimens was not intentionally produced, but was the result of a "throw-off" of the blade short of the lower end of the core. It is not uncommonly seen in utilitarian blades but this is the only case I know of in which such pieces were selected for caching). *Guatemala*: Holmul, 3, lancet type, cached in 2 bowls set lip-to-lip, Early Classic Period (Merwin and Vaillant, 1932, pp. 24, 28; pl. 30,*o-q*); San Agustin Acasaguastlan, many, in tombs, probably originally in sets disturbed by subsequent interments, some with notched butts, a few of green obsidian, Late Classic or early post-Classic Period (Smith and Kidder, 1943, p. 164, fig. 56*a*); Santa Cruz Verapaz, a flake-blade with bones of a human finger found in each of three anthropomorphic vessels (Dieseldorff, 1926, pl. 6), an extremely interesting occurrence; Kaminaljuyu, many, in tombs, in sets of fine long specimens, butts often slightly rounded by retouching—no examples of lancet-type—a very few of green obsidian (KJS, p. 136, fig. 157,*e*); Tajumulco, one or two in several graves, post-Classic Period (Dutton and Hobbs, 1943, pp. 26–28). *Mexico*: Ticoman, Gualupita, Middle Culture sites, use during that period as nonutilitarian mortuary offerings not clearly indicated as only a few single flake-blades, not extra-fine, were found in graves (Vaillant, 1931, pp. 404, 420; 1934, p. 106); Loltun Cave, Yucatan, "several," in cache (E. H. Thompson, 1897, p. 18, pl. VII, 2,*a*); Chichen Itza, Sacred Cenote, a fine lancet (from Peabody Mus., Harvard); Teotihuacan, 39 in grave at Tlamimilolpa, very fine long specimens of green obsidian and 2 with notched base, in other graves less fine pieces (Linné, 1942, figs. 240, 241, 245,

250, 251); Monte Alban, Tomb 7 (Caso, 1932, p. 4); Guasave, several, L 14–15 cm., in graves (Ekholm, 1942, p. 106); Totoate, found with cremations (Hrdlička, 1903, p. 394).

The foregoing flake-blades are either entirely unworked—the vast majority—or with bases very slightly retouched or side-notched. Specimens whose original form has been more radically altered are of extreme rarity. In a grave at Alojuca, Puebla, Linné (1942, figs. 28, 29) found blades with retouched edges, their points chipped to triangular form; and in a grave at Tlamimilolpa examples reduced by chipping to slender, rodlike shape, pointed at both ends (*ibid.*, figs. 243, 244). Specimens of the latter sort also occurred in caches with small jade figurines beneath the stairways of pyramids in the Ciudadela at Teotihuacan (information from Dr. Caso). Lastly, and classed as ceremonial because obviously too delicate for practical service, are flake-blades 8–12 cm. long, with naturally very keen points, which have been given the appearance of projectile points by chipping a notch on either side close to the shallowly notched base (Zocoalco, Jalisco, Chicago Nat. Hist. Mus.).

D. Incised obsidians, 9 (fig. 69). Cached in Structure A-V with vessels of the Tepeu 2 ceramic phase in construction of Phase 2d of the vault. Flakes of black obsidian, each one retaining a portion of the parent core's striking table. Because of the thickness of all the specimens and the stubbiness of some of them, it would seem that they were produced during the preliminary trimming of a core that might later have been used for the striking of flake-blades. The incising, in each case, is on the inner side, which offers a surface unbroken by the scars of flakes previously struck. This surface is in general concave, but toward the striking table the bulb of percussion renders it slightly convex (see fig. 69,*e'*). The various depictions were scratched in with a sharp point which sometimes slipped a little, necessitating multiple strokes to establish the desired line. The work was presumably done with a splinter of quartz, whose hardness (7 in Mohs' scale) is slightly greater than that of obsidian (6). Joyce (1932, p. xxiii) states that he was able to produce on obsidian lines similar to these with a bit of Peten flint. The naturally sharp edges of the Uaxactun specimens are unaltered, save in the case of the scorpion (fig. 69,*e*), the sides of whose tail have been notched and its tip worked into a slight lateral hook (cf. eccentric flint scorpions, fig. 8,*e,n*).

Specimens from Tikal. As stated in discussion of the eccentric flints, several lots of inscribed obsidians were found at Tikal in 1931. Those illustrated in figure 70 were taken from beneath stelae by the Mexico-Guatemala Boundary Commission; others, number unknown, were also in substela caches opened by Robson, Jolly, and Herron. Some of the latter are figured by Joyce (1932, pl. VIII and reproduced in our fig. 71). The Tikal specimens correspond closely in treatment and in subject matter to those from Uaxactun, but a greater number of them have edges chipped to follow more or less accurately the outline of the incised drawing. In most cases (e.g. figs. 70,*r*; 72,*c*) this was obviously done after the incising.

COMMENT. These remarkable objects have, to date, been found only at Uaxactun and Tikal. It seems probable that they were always deposited in sets of nine, as that number were in the Uaxactun cache and nine were in each of two caches at Tikal (Stelae 16, A-21). Unfortunately A. L. Smith was not able to observe all the excavations by the Boundary Commission; and because some of the specimens are fragmentary and one (fig. 72,*c*) was found by Mr. Smith some months later in the back-dirt, it would appear that the digging under the other stelae which produced obsidians had not been thorough. Neither the provenience nor the number of the Robson-Jolly-Herron pieces is certain, but Mr. Smith thinks they probably came from Stelae 5 and 10.

Mr. J. E. S. Thompson has been good enough to supply the following notes on the incised obsidians:

The designs incised on the obsidian flakes, with three exceptions, depict gods or symbolic attributes of gods. The three exceptions, of very superior workmanship, almost surely represent sections of planetary bands. The nine incised flakes in each of the two segregated caches carry designs which represent deities or their symbols, and the same group of deities seems to occur in both caches. Most of these are also recognizable in the remaining obsidian flakes from Tikal, including those illustrated by Joyce, which are without information as to exact provenance. In the illustrations the material has been arranged as far as possible so that the same deity occupies the same position in each series. Such identifications as can be made are given below.

Young sun god in celestial disk. Figure 69,*a* is a disc which frames the portrait of a deity. The same design occurs on five other obsidian flakes (figs. 70,*a,j,s*; 71,*a,j*). Almost identical cartouches enclose deities on Stelae 1, 4, 6, 10, and 11 at Yaxchilan. These frames on the Yaxchilan stelae are placed at the top of each monument immediately above celestial monsters with planetary symbols. Each is paired with a second frame which is open at the top and represents a moon sign, easily recognizable as such because of its resemblance to lunar glyphs. Between each pair of frames there is a portrait of an aged god, Schellhas' God D with solar attributes (probably the sky god, the supreme deity), or the aged sun god himself.

The frames at Yaxchilan resembling those on the obsidian flakes also have semicircular indentations at the four cor-

ners, but these indentations hold figures which in some cases are recognizable as the heads of celestial dragons. The indistinct elements which emerge from the semicircles of figure 69,*a* are presumably attempts to reproduce the same design. Similar cartouches with celestial dragons emerging at each corner, but without the semicircular indentations, are set along the wall of the front room of Structure A of the Palace Group at Palenque. These are modeled in stucco and enclose damaged but still recognizable kin (sun) glyphs.

I think that there can be little doubt that the enclosed frames represent solar discs, partly because they are paired with obvious lunar cartouches at Yaxchilan, and partly because a similar disc, surmounted by a sun glyph, is one of the series of pictures in the eclipse tables of Codex Dresden (p. 56). The only other possibility is that the frame is formed of a segment of the celestial snake-monster (cf. the design on the top of Stela 4, Ucanal). The pairs of cross-hatched semicircles on the discs in that case would represent the markings of the snake's skin, as was customary in Maya art. This, however, is not a contradictory assumption since the Maya sun disc appears to be derived from the celestial serpent-monster which carried the sun across the skies in his capacious jaws.

With one exception the deities inside the discs are not surely recognizable either on the incised obsidians or on the Yaxchilan stelae. They are not portraits of the aged sun god with his squarish eyes with pupil in top inner corner, filed teeth, Roman nose, lock of hair or frontlet on forehead, hollow at top of head, and fang in corner of mouth. The exception is one illustrated by Joyce (fig. 71,*j*) which is either the old sun god or Schellhas' God D. The former, however, is merely a manifestation of the latter.

The other deities in the discs are youthful with straight noses and almond-shaped eyes. However, the sun is sometimes pictured as a handsome young man in memory of his life on earth as a youth before he ascended to the skies to assume his solar duties (or perhaps the morning sun was depicted as a youth, the afternoon sun as a god). This youthful sun god is represented very clearly in the head variants of the day Ahau, the sun god's day (Bowditch, 1910, pl. 6, Ahau, nos. 21–34). He is also depicted emerging from the jaws of the celestial dragon at the top of Stela 4, Ucanal.

Figure 70,*s* clinches the identification of the deity inside the cartouche as the youthful sun god, for in this design the cartouche encloses not the portrait of a deity, but, like the stucco medallions of Palenque, the sun glyph itself. This group therefore represents without much doubt the sun god in his celestial cartouche.

Maize deity. Figures 69,*b*; 71,*b*, and probably 70,*b* represent the maize deity, Schellhas' God E. He (for feminine portraits, as in fig. 71,*b*, are rare) is one of the most easily recognized of Maya deities. His characteristics are extreme youthfulness, almond-shaped eye, straight nose, drooping lower lip, receding chin, and a string of grains of corn around his neck or falling from the ear. Usually the top of his head is shaped as the conventionalized top of a cornstalk with one leaf falling forward, the other to the rear. This last feature is very clear in figures 69,*b* and 71,*b*, and the grains of corn are prominent in the latter portrait. Figure 71,*b*, I think, must also represent the maize god because of the way the crown of the head is prolonged upward and back. The element representing the forward leaf appears rather faintly in front of the forehead. Figure 70,*k*,*t* shows perhaps additional portraits of the maize god, although this is uncertain because the top of each is missing.

Moon goddess in lunar frame. Figures 69,*c*; 70,*c*; 71,*c* undoubtedly represent the moon goddess within the crescent moon. In the first case the oval areas on the inner edge of the crescent, typical of the moon glyph, are clearly visible. In addition the head of 71,*c* is clearly recognizable as that of the moon goddess (used also as the head form of the number one). The youthful features and the rod projecting from the earplug which are characteristic of that deity are very apparent, and, immediately above the earplug, the lock of hair on the cheek, one of the most characteristic attributes of the moon goddess (and the head for one) can, I think, be distinguished.

The corresponding figure from the Uaxactun cache (fig. 69,*c*) holds in her arms a rabbit, which in the mythology of the Mexican plateau is the symbol of the moon. I know of no other representation in the Maya area which associates the rabbit with the moon, but the idea is still current among the Mopan Maya of southern British Honduras (Thompson, 1930, p. 64). At the time I gathered that tag of folklore, I had supposed it to have been a survival of late contact with the peoples of the Mexican plateau, but this obsidian is evidence that the association goes back far in Maya history.

Agricultural deity. Figures 69,*d*, 71,*d* and almost surely 70,*d* portray an unidentified deity. The form of the top of the head (particularly in fig. 71,*d*) suggests an animal. This identification is strengthened by the prominent fang in the upper jaw. The snout is long and turns up at the point. The example from the Uaxactun cache rather resembles glyphs of the leaf-nosed bat, but that animal has no connection with agriculture and symbolizes death. The pointed ears suggest a dog, which has an agricultural role in Codex Madrid, but the upturned snout is against that identification.

On the other hand, a deity who is almost certainly the earth crocodile, the Imix monster, has the same snout and curved fang, and sometimes has maize leaves issuing from the crown of his head and occipital region although more commonly the water lily grows from his head. This god is the personification of the earth, and consequently a deity of agriculture. The doubt about this identification lies in the fact that the latter deity has a fleshless lower jaw when decked with foliage (like many earth gods because the land of the dead was in the earth), whereas the deity incised on the obsidians appears to have a normal lower jaw.

The scorpion. Figures 69,*e* and 70,*n* are rather conventionalized scorpions. There is no scorpion in the Tikal cache, but if our assumption that the same group of deities is depicted in both caches is right, the scorpion is probably represented in an anthropomorphized form.

In Codex Madrid, Schellhas' God M is frequently depicted wearing a scorpion's tail, and elsewhere in that codex God B, painted black, also has a scorpion's tail. On page 7 of the same codex, in a passage dealing with rain, a large scorpion descends amid a stream of water. Elsewhere in this codex and in Codex Paris the scorpion is pendant from constellation bands. In fact, the scorpion is the name of a constellation (*signo del cielo*), according to the Motul dictionary. There are, accordingly, precedents from the identification of a deity with the attributes of a scorpion.

Figure 70,*e* has on the forehead a prominent ornament which terminates in a clawlike element. This last is represented in the way in which both the claws and the sting of the scorpion are normally depicted in Maya and Mexican representations of that creature (cf. Seler, 1902–23, vol. 4, figs. 960–75). I think, therefore, that it is highly probable that this figure is an anthropomorphized scorpion or a god with scorpion attributes, and therefore corresponds to the fairly naturalistic scorpion of the Uaxactun cache.

Unidentified deity. Figure 69,*f* has no characteristics that aid greatly in his identification. The corresponding figure in the Tikal cache should be figure 70,*f*.

God with foliated ornament projecting from forehead. Figures 69,*g*; 70,*g*,*p*,*u*; 71,*g* represent a very well known deity, common in monumental sculpture, but unrepresented in the codices. The haft of the foliated element is set in a hole in the god's forehead. The head is that which adorns the so-called manikin scepter carried by the principal personage on many stelae (Spinden, 1913, figs. 47–51, 57, 60). The head of this deity sometimes emerges from the open jaws of celestial monsters (Spinden, 1913, figs. 23, 62, 80). It is also the subject of many hieroglyphs, including Glyph G7 and a rare full-figure glyph (Thompson, 1932, fig. 23, *c-g*).

Unidentified deity. Figure 69,*h* has no particular characteristics unless it be the curved line from nose to chin. The deity is youthful with almond-shaped eye and straight nose. The rather poorly delineated person of small stature in the Tikal group (fig. 70,*h*) presumably is the same deity and in the Joyce series (fig. 71,*h*) there is a nondescript individual with line from nose to chin who may belong with the group.

Plaited band. This decorative element occurs on no less than five of the obsidian flakes (figs. 69,*i*; 70,*i,r*; 71,*i,l*). From what has been said, one must suppose that this is the symbol of some deity. Actually this design is rather intimately associated with the celestial dragon. It occurs frequently as a sort of collar of the celestial monster when this is used as a ceremonial bar (Spinden, 1913, figs. 58, 61, 64) or it is placed horizontally along the whole length of the ceremonial bar (Stelae A, D, H, and 11, Copan) or it is on the inside of the throat of one of the celestial monsters (Stela N, Copan). It almost always forms part of the elaborated end of the loincloth which combines frets with masks

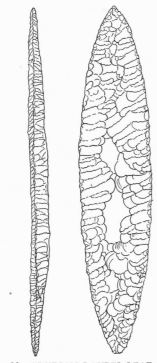

FIG. 10—OBSIDIAN LAUREL-LEAF BLADE
For photo see fig. 68,*c*. Natural size.

of a deity, perhaps God D. However, it is not present in the more naturalistic portraits of the sky monster. Examples at Uaxactun are to be seen on the Initial Series vase (A. L. Smith, 1932, pl. 5). It is combined with the Cauac element (a symbol of water) to form a specialized glyph of unknown meaning.

In a previous paper (Thompson, 1939a, pp. 152–62) I have produced evidence that these ceremonial bars and two-headed altars are representations of the rain-giving celestial monsters set at each corner of the sky, and that these are the god Itzamna (Schellhas' God D?). I think it is a fairly safe assumption that these plaited designs incised on the obsidian symbolize the god Itzamna.

The foregoing discussion would seem to indicate that the

two series of cache material duplicate each other, although this point cannot be established beyond question perhaps because of the inferior delineation of the Tikal flakes. Six deities definitely appear in both series. They are the young sun god in his solar disk; the moon goddess in the lunar crescent; the maize god; the deity with the foliated emblem projecting from his forehead; Itzamna, the celestial dragon (the plaited symbol); and a deity with upturned snout who is associated with plant life, perhaps the Imix monster, the terrestrial crocodile (figs. 69,*d*; 70,*d*). Of the remaining three, the scorpion of Uaxactun probably has his counterpart in a deity with what is probably a scorpion sting or claw projecting from his forehead (fig. 70,*e*). The other two are not delineated with sufficient attention to detail in the Tikal series to permit of certain identification.

The various incised flakes of unknown provenience for the most part correspond to those in the two caches. There are a couple of heads of the long-nosed snake god (God B) in the series illustrated by Joyce, but this deity is merely the anthropomorphised head of the celestial monster or a closely allied group of gods. A few are too damaged or too carelessly incised to be placed, and three are of a quite different class.

The three incised flakes which do not fall into the above classification (fig. 72) bear the head of a deity who is probably God D with a glyph in front of the face. The designs are incised with great care and resemble the best glyphic work. The three glyphs are easily recognizable. The first is a moon sign; the second, the glyph of the planet Venus; the third, the kin or sun glyph. All three signs occur frequently on planetary bands, but these in turn are merely the conventionalized bodies of the celestial monsters, the Itzamnas. Accordingly, the association of these planetary symbols with the head of the sky god was for the Maya a perfectly understandable symbolism.

It is interesting to note that the nine deities of the two caches do not appear to correspond to the nine lords of the night so far as one can tell from the glyphs for those gods, but several of the identified deities are among the lords of the night. Unfortunately, some of the glyphs of that series of gods are not easily matched with known Maya deities, and it is possible that fuller information might identify the series of the nine gods of the obsidians with the nine gods of the underworld and of the night.

E. Laurel-leaf blade, 1 (figs. 10; 68,*c*,1). Pit 1 cache, Structure B-XI. L 18.3 cm., W 4.2 cm., T 1 cm. Green obsidian, beautifully chipped; its slight curvature and bits of plane surface indicate that it was made from a flake (fig. 10).

COMMENT. Large laurel-leaf blades of obsidian such as this and the closely similar one recorded by the Ricketsons

(RR, pl. 54,*a*,11) rank with those of flint (p. 18) in symmetry of form, keenness of edge, and excellence of chipping. They had a wide Mesoamerican distribution, both in time and in space. The earliest example of this general type is from El Arbolillo in a grave of Middle Zacatenco period (Vaillant, 1935, fig. 27). Later horizons: Kaminaljuyu, green obsidian (KJS, fig. 157,*a*); Quen Santo (Seler, 1901, fig. 121); Chacula (Burkitt, 1924, p. 142); Copan (Peabody Mus. Harvard); Dixon Site, Roatan, Bay Islands (Strong, 1935, fig. 15,*d*); Monte Alban (Caso, 1938, p. 65); Tlamimilolpa, Teotihuacan (Linné, 1942, fig. 270); Chametla, Sonora (Kelly, 1938, pl. 21,*a*); Quimistlan and San Elegio, Veracruz (Strebel, 1885–89, II, pls. VII, XXVII); Valley of Mexico (Amer. Mus. Nat. Hist.); Tehuantepec (Amer. Mus. Nat. Hist., cat. no. 30–7447; this measures some 35 cm. and is the longest example I have seen); Chichen Itza, Temple of the Cones (see p. 10); Hervideros, Durango (Mason, 1937, p. 138). Of the above, all whose exact provenience is known were found in graves or caches. Laurel-leaf blades of red obsidian, whose chronological horizon is unknown, are from Colima and Chiapas (Mus. Amer. Ind.).

GENERAL COMMENT ON CEREMONIAL CHIPPED STONE OBJECTS. Although certain of the Uaxactun caches containing specimens of this sort have been recorded by the Ricketsons and the remainder will be listed by A. L. Smith, it seems well to assemble here all the data concerning such deposits for more ready comparison and for reference to illustrations. The following list of cache contents has been prepared *de novo* from the original field notes and photographs because in some cases the descriptions by the Ricketsons (RR) and Morley (1938) do not agree. They are followed by a list of occurrences of similar material from other sites. Dates of stelae are those of Morley (1938). In cases of doubtful readings Morley expresses the degree of uncertainty by one, two, or three points of interrogation. Stelae to whose numerical designation there is prefixed a capital letter bear no inscription and the dates of their erection are unknown.

OCCURRENCES AT UAXACTUN

Cache B-10. Under Stela 1 (9.14.0.0.0). Tepeu.
Obsidian flake-blades, fragments . . . . "few"

Cache B-8. Under Stela 4 (8.18.0.0.0?) (RR, p. 159). Probably Tzakol.
Eccentric flints 8
    Tridents (RR, pl. 57,*a*,*c*) 2
    Notched crescents (RR, pl. 59,*b*) 3
    Notched blades (RR, pl. 58,*b*) 3
Eccentric obsidian, trident (RR, pl. 57,*b*) 1
Obsidian core (RR, pl. 61,16) 1
Obsidian flake-blades, fragmentary (RR, pl. 67,*e*,10,11) 2
Shell 8
    Human figurines (RR, fig. 128,*a*,*b*; pl. 67,*e*,5,6) 2
    Small univalves, unworked (RR, pl. 67,*e*,15,16) . . . 2
    Fragments worked shell (RR, pl. 67,*e*,4,9,20,21) . . . 4

Jade 9
    Human figurine and fragment of another (RR, pl. 67,*e*,7,8) 2
    Animal-head pendant (RR, pl. 67,*e*,12) 1
    Polished cylinder (RR, pl. 67,*e*,2) 1
    Partly worked fragments (RR, pl. 67,*e*,1,3,17–19 . . . 5
Crystalline hematite, fragments 2
Coral, pieces of 2

Cache A-19. Under Stela 22 (9.3.10.0.0). Tzakol.
Eccentric flints 9
    Trident (fig. 67,*a*,1) 1
    Crescent (fig. 67,*a*,2) 1
    Disc (fig. 67,*a*,3) 1
    Skewed blades (fig. 67,*b*,a-c) 3
    Laurel-leaf blades (fig. 67,*b*,d-f) 3

Cache A-25. Under Stela 26 (9.0.10.0.0). Not "above the stela," as stated in RR, p. 166. Tzakol.
Eccentric flints 5
    Trident (fig. 66,*a*,4) 1
    Notched blades (fig. 66,*a*,1,2) 2
    Laurel-leaf blades (fig. 66,*a*,3,5) 2
Sting-ray spines 3
Oliva shell 1

Cache A-40. Under Stela A-1. Period?
Obsidian and flint chips

Cache A-39. Under Stela A-6. Undated, but almost certainly Tepeu, as stela set through floors of that period (see RR, p. 167, fig. 108).
Obsidian cores, some notched (cf. RR, pl. 60,*b*) 38
Obsidian flake-blades small (RR, pl. 61,5–11) 50
Obsidian chips 6

Cache A-38. Under Stela A-7. Probably Tepeu (see note on Cache A-38 and RR, fig. 108).
Eccentric obsidians, mostly notched cores (RR, pl. 60,*b*) 30
Obsidian flake-blades, fragments . . . . "many"

Cache A-36. Under Stela A-11. Period?
Eccentric flints 8
    Tridents (RR, pl. 56,*b*,4,5) 2
    Notched blades (RR, pl. 58,*a*,3–6) 4
    Laurel-leaf blades (cf. RR, pl. 54,*a*, 1–7) 2
Eccentric obsidians 4
    Notched cores (RR, pl. 60,*b*,1, second, third from bottom) 2
    Core-knives (RR, pl. 54,*a*,14,15) 2
Shell 2
    Cardium muricatum 1
    Worked fragment 1

Cache A-37. Under Stela A-15. Period?
Eccentric flints 4
    Tridents (fig. 66,*b*,2,4) 2
    Notched blade (fig. 66,*b*,3) 1
    Laurel-leaf blade (fig. 66,*b*,5) 1
Eccentric obsidian, trident (fig. 66,*b*,1) 1
Obsidian flake-blades 5
Jade beads, subspherical (fig. 80,*b*,18,19,21,24) 4
Shell bead, large, subspherical (fig. 85,*c*,12) 1
Shell disc, perforated (fig. 85,*a*,3) 1
Bone needle, fragmentary (cf. fig. 43) 1

Cache B-9. Under Stela B-2. Period?
"Flint chips"

Cache D-3. Under Stela D-3. Period?
Eccentric flints, all very crude 30
    Tridents (RR, pl. 57,*d*-g) 4
    Notched flakes (RR, pl. 59,*a*) 16
    Laurel-leaf blades (of type shown in RR, pl. 54,*a*,1–7) 10
Flint nodules 3
Obsidian cores 5
    Plain 1
    Notched (of type shown in RR, pl. 60,*b*) 4
Obsidian flake, large 1
Obsidian flake-blades 15
Obsidian discs 2
Shells (*Ostrea* sp. [?], *Crepidula* sp.) 2

Cache A-29. In cist below floor, Structure A-XV. Tzakol.
Eccentric flints (fig. 66,c) 5
    Tridents 3
    Laurel-leaf blades 2
Eccentric obsidians 5
    Tridents (fig. 68,a,1–3,5,9) 5
    Notched core (fig. 68,d,5) 1
Obsidian core (fig. 68,d,3) 1
Obsidian core-knife (fig. 68,d,4) 1
Obsidian projectile points (fig. 68,d,1,2) 2

Cache A-30. Directly above A-29. Tzakol.
Eccentric flints 3
    Notched blades (fig. 68,d,6,7) 2
    Laurel-leaf blade (fig. 68,d,8) 1
Eccentric obsidians, tridents (fig. 68,a,4,6–8,10–13) 8
Antler, burned, fragment 1

Cache A-31. Under upper stairway, Structure A-XVIII. Tzakol.
Eccentric flints (fig. 66,d) 4
    Tridents 2
    Notched blade 1
    Laurel-leaf blade 1
Eccentric obsidian, trident (fig. 68,b,3) 1
Obsidian core-knives (fig. 68,b,1,2) 2
Jade 5
    Human effigy (figs. 37; 74) 1
    Earplug flares (fig. 79,e,f) 2
    Subspherical beads (figs. 80,b,26; 85,c,11) 2
Incised cylindrical tripod lacking legs, Tzakol 1
Eccentric flints were placed around this vessel, which con-
    tained all other objects.

Cache A-20. Under floor of Room 14, Structure A-V. Late Tzakol.
Eccentric flints 9
    Trident (fig. 67,c,4) 1
    Notched blades (fig. 67,d) 5
    Laurel-leaf blades (fig. 67,c,1–3) 3

Cache E-7. Cist 13, Pyramid E-VII platform (shown in situ, RR,
pl. 39). Tzakol.
Eccentric flints 5
    Tridents (RR, pl. 56,b,1,2) 2
    Notched blades (RR, pl. 58,a,1,2) 2
    Laurel-leaf blade, fine (RR, pl. 54,a,10) 1
Flint chips 74
Obsidian laurel-leaf, blade, green, very fine (RR, pl. 54,a,11) . 1
For pottery in this cist see RR, p. 152.

Cache E-8. Cist 14, Pyramid E-IX (RR, p. 152). Probably Tzakol.
Eccentric flints 3
    Trident (RR, pl. 56,b,3) 1
    "Daggers" (RR, pl. 60,a) 2
"Scraper knives" (RR, pl. 56,a,4–10) 7
Obsidian cores (RR, pl. 61,17,18) 2
For pottery in this cist see RR, p. 152.

OCCURRENCES OF ECCENTRICS AT OTHER SITES

(Flint unless otherwise noted)

BRITISH HONDURAS

Pusilha. Stela E (9.15.0.0.0): buried in foundations on side facing plaza, nearly 100 flints, obsidians: rings, crosses, crescents, scorpions, notched blades, latter almost identical to Uaxactun specimens (Joyce, Gann, Gruning and Long, 1928, p. 333, pl. XXXV, fig. 1). Joyce (1932) illustrates some of the above as from Stela D, but they are mentioned in the text as from E. Stela F (9.9.13.0.0??): some 600 flints, obsidians (Joyce, Gann, Gruning, and Long, 1928, p. 333). Stela K (9.12.0.0.0): nearly 100 obsidian flake-blades, cores, eccentrics (*ibid.*, p. 335). Terrace 3: "many," accompanied by obsidians, apparently deposited in rough

pottery jars (Gruning, 1930, p. 478, pl. XXII, fig. 3). Mound 1: number and circumstances of find not recorded, some illustrated in Gruning, 1930, pl. XXII, figs. 1, 2 and in Joyce, 1932.

Lubaantun. Structure D: summit, 2 fragmentary specimens, large (Joyce, Cooper-Clark, and Thompson, 1927, p. 312, pl. XXI, fig. 3; Joyce, 1932, pl. I, fig. 2, 1b; pl. VI, fig. 1, 4a).

Seven Hills. On summit of natural hill: 1 large (Gann, 1918, p. 100, fig. 46).

Kendal. Under rough altar (?): 2 large, 1 small; with 3 laurel-leaf blades (Gann, 1918, p. 94, figs. 37, 38).

Benque Viejo. Summit of mound in Group A: just under surface in area 1 m. sq.; 64 flints, obsidians (Gann, 1918, p. 96, figs. 40, 44). At base of Stela 1 (10.1.0.0.0): 2 (Gann, 1918, fig. 41). Some of the above specimens also figured by Joyce (1932, see plate captions).

Tzimin Kax. Burial VII: 1 small, crude (Thompson, 1931, fig. 15,g). Only eccentric flint found by Thompson in Mountain Cow district.

Cayo District. 1 very fine stemmed ring, 1 large serrated crescent (Joyce, 1932, fig. 2; pl. IV, fig. 4, 2d).

Baking Pot. Summit of Mound E: 9, rather crude (Ricketson, 1929, p. 5, pls. 12, 13).

Santa Rita. Summit of Mound 4: 2, in cache with flint spearhead (Gann, 1918, fig. 19).

Douglas. Mound 10: 5, with 7 spearheads below deposit of 40 human skulls. Higher in the mound, 20 small obsidian cores, notched flake-blades, and 80 obsidian "fleurs-de-lis" (Gann, 1918, pp. 86–88, fig. 31, pl. 15). Two apparently from burial chamber in another mound, probably associated with Early Classic pottery (Anderson and Cook, 1944, fig. 2,l,n).

Rio Hondo, headwaters. Summit of mound: 1 rough "stellate disc," in cache with celts and spearheads (Gann, 1918, p. 99).

San Antonio. Summit of mound: 1 spiked crescent (Gann, 1918, fig. 47).

Nohmul. Mound 1: 1, with 10 crude spearheads and obsidian cores at head of skeleton in burial chamber (Gann and Gann, 1939, pl. 1,1); accompanying pottery of Late Classic Period. Mound 8: 1, "halberd shaped," with knives and spearheads accompanying a burial (Gann and Gann, 1939, pl. 1,4), closely similar to specimen from Douglas (Gann, 1918, pl. 15,b). In chultun below Mound 22: 1, large crescentic, with 20 triangular-bladed flint knives (Gann and Gann, 1939, pl. 1,5); accompanying pottery of Early Classic Period.

San Jose. Cache A1, San Jose IV or later: 14, very fine, including scorpion, cat (?). Cache A4, San Jose IV: 3, 1 a human figure. Burial A4, San Jose V: 1, dog (?). Cache C1, San Jose V: monolithic obsidian hafted celt, obsidian points, copper, shell, and many other objects (Thompson, 1939, pls. 24; 28,*a*).

Wild Cave Key. One, large, "halberd shaped." Amer. Mus. Nat. Hist.

British Honduras, unlocated. Serrated crescent, large notched blade (Heye, 1925); serrated blade, spiked crescent, notched blade, human figure (Joyce, 1932, pl. III, fig. 4, *3d*; pl. V, fig. 2, *2b*; fig. 4, *1d, 2d*—the specimen in pl. V, fig. 3, appears to be of obsidian).

GUATEMALA

Naranjo. Under Stela 13 (9.17.10.0.0): 1 crescent. Under Stela 15 (9.13.0.0.0???): upwards of 20 eccentric flints and flint knives (presumably laurel-leaf). The eccentrics small, similar to, but rather finer than, the Tikal specimens (cf. fig. 21) (Maler, 1908, pp. 97, 100; fig. 19. Gann, 1918, fig. 48, reproduces some of these).

Piedras Negras. During excavations by University of Pennsylvania under J. A. Mason and L. Satterthwaite Jr., a great number of eccentric flints and obsidians came to light. The flints are of light-colored stone and in the same size-range as those from Uaxactun and Tikal, but are of much finer workmanship. A few typical examples have been figured by Mason (1935, p. 542). There are scorpions, highly conventional human and animal figures, very beautiful thin crescents both plain and serrate, and three-pointed objects much like those held in the hands of Maya notables depicted in sculpture, graffiti, and vase-painting (see p. 28, and Follett, 1932, figs. 29–33), laurel-leaf blades, notched blades, and a single trident closely similar to those from Uaxactun. These will be illustrated and the circumstances of their discovery and their probable dates will be discussed in forthcoming reports on Piedras Negras. Mr. Satterthwaite informs me that the great majority were found in caches, usually in a special type of plain bowl with cover. As at Uaxactun, many of the caches were in the heartings of structures, frequently under the columnar altars so characteristic of Piedras Negras. One lot occurred in the fill at the approximate standing position of Stela 29 (9.12.5.0.0) and, pending a final check of all relevant data, Mr. Satterthwaite feels certain that eccentrics were being deposited at about this time, but that the practice had surely been inaugurated considerably earlier. Although no positive upper or lower date can yet be determined, Mr. Satterthwaite has no reason to believe that the placing of such caches did not continue throughout the later history of the site.

Quirigua. In floor or wall (?) of temple, Group A: 24, all but one apparently of ordinary forms, the latter a large, flamboyant specimen of dark flint (Joyce, 1932, pl. VII; Morley, 1935, p. 44, fig. 36). Zoomorph B (9.17.10.0.0): 7 very fine laurel-leaf blades of dark flint (Strömsvik, 1941, fig. 30). Zoomorph O (9.18.0.0.0): 1, very fine, flamboyant, dark flint (*ibid.,* fig. 32,*a*).

El Baul. Cache in front of colossal head: 2 very fine crescents with spikes, 36 laurel-leaf blades of "sacrificial" type, 2 of obsidian (Thompson, 1946, fig. 23).

HONDURAS

Copan. Fragments of a large, dark-colored eccentric flint of flamboyant type (fig. 73), from debris of the Hieroglyphic Stairway on the west slope of the pyramid supporting Temple 26. Near them was found a jade plaque, a trident eccentric of white flint, a laurel-leaf knife of black flint, cinnabar, and shells (fig. 73). Mr. Strömsvik believes these objects to have come from a cache in the hearting behind the upper part of the Hieroglyphic Stairway, perhaps in an elaborately sculptured stone urn of which pieces were also scattered down the face of the pyramid. Morley (1920) dates the Hieroglyphic Stairway and Temple 26 at 9.16.5.0.0. It should be noted that no eccentric flints occurred in the many substela caches examined at Copan (Strömsvik, 1941).

MEXICO

El Palmar. Beneath Stela 10 (9.15.15.0.0): 9 eccentric flints of ordinary types and one remarkable foliated specimen (Thompson, 1936, fig. 1); 19 obsidian cores.

Chichen Itza. High Priest's Grave: 1, fragment of plain crescent; "Mexican" period (Thompson and Thompson, 1938, fig. 18,*j*).

Yucatan (?). Nine eccentric flints: a trident, spiked and serrated crescents, notched blade, laurel-leaf blade etc. In Amer. Mus. Nat. Hist., catalogued as from Ticul. Four of them figured by Maler (1912, pl. 2) over the caption "Yucatan." As these are strikingly similar to examples from Piedras Negras, I think it possible that they were collected by Maler during his explorations on the Usumacintla.

Distribution. It is evident from the foregoing that eccentric flints were most common in the Department of the Peten, Guatemala, and in British Honduras—in other words in the heart of the Classic Maya area. Their apparent greater abundance in British Honduras is perhaps due to the large amount of digging done by Gann and to his keenness in running down all finds made by others, or may be evidence of a particularly intense local development of whatever cult required their use. In any case, specialization in the Peten–British Honduras region seems to be indicated by their rarity in the east, only two occurrences having been noted at Quirigua and but one at Copan, in spite of the fact that excavation under all stelae has been done at both those sites and in many buildings at Copan. Outside the Classic area there are few records: none from Alta Verapaz or the southern Guatemala highlands, none from Salvador, only one (El Baul) on the Pacific slope, very scattering in the northern part of the Yucatan peninsula. Eccentric flints fail to appear in Mexican cultures contemporaneous with

Classic Maya, such as that of Monte Alban, Tajin, or Teotihuacan, although the obsidian lizardlike objects, small human figures, and other oddly shaped specimens from the latter site may, as suggested above (p. 20), be a distantly related development.

Location of deposits. Eccentric flints and obsidians were most commonly deposited in buildings, usually, it would seem, at the time of construction. They were also often placed under stelae. The number of substela records is probably disproportionately large, however, for archaeologists have learned to look for the easily accessible caches under these monuments, but as yet have seldom had opportunity to do the much heavier digging necessary for the examination of the heartings of stairways, terraces, and the summit platforms of mounds, in which, according to the experience of A. L. Smith and Ricketson at Uaxactun, Mason and Satterthwaite at Piedras Negras, and Gann in British Honduras, caches are even more likely to be found.

Use of eccentrics. It is obvious that these flints and obsidians served no practical purpose. But their ritual significance and the method of their use in ceremonies are unknown. There is no mention of them by Landa, or other early writers on the Maya. They seem, indeed, to have gone out of use well before the conquest, for with the exception of one broken crescent from the High Priest's Grave at Chichen Itza (Thompson and Thompson, 1938, fig. 18,*j*) and a single specimen from Burial A4 at San Jose, British Honduras (Thompson, 1939, p. 195, pl. 25,*c*,1), none, so far as I know, has been recorded from any site of the Mexican Period or later. Their entire absence from the rich sacrificial offerings in the Sacred Cenote at Chichen Itza is noteworthy.

Gann (1918, p. 103) certainly errs in considering that eccentrics were made solely for mortuary purposes. As is shown by the foregoing list of occurrences, they have seldom been found, and never in quantity, in graves. There is no basis for Gann's belief that stelae were memorials to the dead; and the caches which he so often encountered in summit platforms would seem to have been associated, as dedicatory offerings, with buildings once crowning the mounds, rather than to have had any direct connection with interments at deeper levels.

The larger and more elaborate flints—all the obsidians save a monolithic axe (see p. 26) are small—might have been *bâtons de commandement* or insignia of priesthoods, although none seem to appear in the sculptures. Smaller, three- or four-pronged objects, are carried in the hands of personages shown on monuments, in graffiti, and in vase-painting (Follett, 1932, figs. 29–33; A. L. Smith, 1932, pl. 5). These are probably eccentric flints, and examples of just this shape come from Piedras Negras, El Palmar, and El Baul.

Follett (1932, p. 388), considers them to have been weapons; this seems to me very improbable.

There are several occurrences of eccentric flints and at least two of incised obsidians in sets of nine, which may indicate connection with the Nine Lords of the Night, so important in Mexican, and apparently also in Maya, theology (Thompson, 1929).

Dating. Specimens encountered below a Maya stela are, beyond reasonable doubt, to be considered as having been placed there at the time of its erection. It is conceivable that they could subsequently have been introduced by burrowing down and in, but in that unlikely case one would expect them to be closely clustered, whereas they appear usually to have been found more or less scattered through the fill surrounding and underlying the butt of the monument. And as the inscription on a stela normally records the day of its dedication, one is provided with a minimum date for objects occurring beneath it—always granted that it had not been reset in a new position at some later time. The following caches of eccentrics or of inscribed obsidians have been taken from beneath monuments whose dates are regarded by Morley as certain:

9.0.10.0.0	Stela 26, Uaxactun	Ecc. flints
9.3.10.0.0	Stela 22, Uaxactun	Ecc. flints
9.12.0.0.0	Stela K, Pusilha	Ecc. obsids., cores
9.12.5.0.0	Stela 29, Piedras Negras	Ecc. flints
9.14.0.0.0	Stela 16, Tikal	Ecc. flints and incised obsids.
9.15.0.0.0	Stela E, Pusilha	Ecc. flints, obsids.
9.15.15.0.0	Stela 10, El Palmar	Ecc. flints, obsid. cores
9.17.0.0.0	Stela 13, Naranjo	Ecc. flints
9.18.0.0.0	Zoomorph O, Quirigua	Ecc. flints
10.1.0.0.0	Stela 1, Benque Viejo	Ecc. flints

Eccentric flints and obsidians, a very typical lot, formed part of a cache under Stela 4 at Uaxactun (see p. 25), to which Morley gives, with one point of interrogation, the date 8.18.0.0.0.

All other Uaxactun deposits of this sort are from the fill of buildings and were unassociated with dated stelae. They are all assigned by the Smiths to Subphases 2 or 3 of the Tzakol ceramic phase (i.e., according to their reckoning, from about 9.0.0.0.0 to 9.8.0.0.0). The San Jose caches containing eccentric flints are believed by Thompson (1939, p. 168) to date from San Jose IV or later, i.e. not before about 10.0.0.0.0. The earliest datable eccentric flints at Piedras Negras, according to Satterthwaite, are of about 9.12.0.0.0, although he thinks it quite possible that others may be older (see p. 27).

These data are somewhat puzzling. There can be no question that the Uaxactun caches in the fills of buildings all date from the Tzakol phase. The Uaxactun substela caches were beneath monuments dated at 8.18.0.0.0 (?), 9.0.10.0.0, and 9.3.10.0.0. There is no Uaxactun occurrence under a stela of known later date nor any in construction of the Tepeu phase. Therefore, were no other information available, one would conclude that the cult of eccentrics was confined to the early part of the Classic Period. But at all other sites the situation is exactly reversed: there are no substela records prior to 9.12.0.0.0; and while the architectural and ceramic associations of eccentric at such sites are in most cases uncertain, the majority, at least of the nonstela finds, would seem to equate chronologically with the Tepeu phase of Uaxactun. Thus, were it not for the Uaxactun data it would seem evident that the cult was confined to the later part of the Classic Period. More information is needed.

GENERAL COMMENT ON OBSIDIAN. As was shown in discussing the varieties of obsidian occurring at Uaxactun (p. 10), this material was most commonly used, in Mesoamerica, from Salvador to north-central Mexico. Throughout that range it played important roles, both practical and ceremonial; and at the hands of the supremely skillful Aztec lapidaries and those of neighboring peoples of late prehistoric times it was worked into cult objects and personal adornments of marvelous delicacy. When these and other types of obsidian implements and ornaments have been accurately defined and their spatial and chronological distributions worked out, they will unquestionably prove a valuable aid in tracing the development and interaction of Mesoamerican cultures. It therefore seems worthwhile to include here notes on certain classes of obsidians not represented at Uaxactun.

Drills. Because of its brittleness, obsidian would appear to have been a poor material for drills and I can find, indeed, only a very few records, all from in or near the Valley of Mexico. Middle Cultures: Gualupita I, fragment of thin shaft (Vaillant and Vaillant, 1934, fig. 32); Middle Zacatenco, two, expanded base, points missing (Vaillant, 1930, pl. XLII). Teotihuacan horizon: Tlamimilolpa, Burial 4, one with expanded base, one straight-shafted (Linné, 1942, figs. 268, 269). Aztec horizon: Tenayuca, Grave 1, straight shaft (Noguera, 1935, pl. LVII). Period uncertain: two fine small specimens with expanded base (Mus. Amer. Ind.).

Cores. Cores were occasionally put to use as rubbing tools. I have seen such specimens from the Quiche region (Rossbach coll.), Kaminaljuyu (surface find, Guatemala Nat. Mus.), Chichen Itza (Merida Mus.), Texcoco (Chicago Nat. Hist. Mus.). There is an excellent example from the Valley of Mexico (Univ. Cal. Mus.) in which the striking table of a small core has been rounded and polished and the flake-scars at that end softened by long service, possibly as a pot polisher. Also from the Valley of Mexico is a small core with both ends worn to very even, tapering, truncated conical form, apparently by use as a reamer (fig. 11) (Amer. Mus. Nat. Hist.).

Macuahuitl blades. Accounts of the conquest of Mexico contain many respectful references to the efficacy of the natives' wooden swords in both edges of which were set pieces of obsidian. From representations in the Codex Mendoza and other picture-writings it appears that these were rectangular and it is probable that they were short segments broken from large flake-blades which, being naturally razor-edged, would have required no modification prior to mounting. Had macuahuitl blades been specially shaped in any way it seems certain that many would have come to light and have been identified as such. Gann (1918, p. 89, fig. 34) does indeed suggest that some 300 small triangular obsidians cached in a mound on Rio Hondo in British Honduras may have been designed for such use, but no similar specimens have been reported from elsewhere in Mesoamerica (in this connection see Follett, 1932, pp. 385–87).

Celts. Brittle obsidian would have been of little service for the manufacture of chopping tools so, like drills, celts of this material are very rare. The four specimens I have seen are beautifully shaped, well polished, and show no signs of use. If not forgeries, they would seem to have been

FIG. 11—REAMER (?)

Made from "exhausted" obsidian core. (Courtesy American Museum of Natural History.) Natural size.

ceremonial objects or weapons. All are from the Valley of Mexico (Mus. Amer. Ind., Amer. Mus. Nat. Hist., Brooklyn Mus., Chicago Nat. Hist. Mus.; the latter is labeled "possible forgery"). Batres (n.d.) illustrates an obsidian celt which he considers a falsification.

Vessels. I know of but two certainly authentic containers of obsidian. One is the magnificent vessel from Texcoco in the Mexican National Museum in the form of a monkey, its tail curled over its head and grasped by its uplifted hands (Toscano, 1944, p. 299). As very similar pieces in tecali are known (Batres, 1906, pl. X), and as elaborate tecali vessels are apparently all post-Classic (Thompson, 1941, p. 43), it is probable that this obsidian example is also late. The other, surely genuine because it is not perfectly cylindrical and therefore could not have been turned on a modern lathe, is a thick-walled cup 7.5 cm. high, said to be from the Valley of Mexico (Brooklyn Mus.). The Chicago Natural History Museum owns a small obsidian bowl with an animal head on one side. It is labeled as of doubtful antiquity. Certainly a forgery is an obsidian cup, its exterior covered with elaborate low-relief carving incorporating Maya-style glyphs and human figures from whose mouths issue multiple speech-scrolls. This was recently being offered for sale in Guatemala at a very high price. It is undoubtedly the work of a lapidary in Quetzaltenango, who has producd a number of fraudulent jade carvings in the same style. Batres (n.d.) includes an obsidian cup among forgeries from Mexico.

Sculptures. All obsidian carvings are naturally small. There is a little figurine in La Venta style, said to be from Guerrero (Amer. Mus. Nat. Hist.) and a monkey head reported to have been found in Puebla. The latter (Danzel and Fuhrmann, 1922–23, III, pl. 25; Kelemen, 1943, pl. 251,*b*) once had inlaid eyes, perhaps of turquoise. Another little monkey head comes from the Valley of Mexico; it is of red obsidian (Mus. Amer. Ind.). A small obsidian amulet, perhaps representing the head of a bird, is from Tenayuca (Noguera, 1935a, pl. LV, 9). From Tepoztlan there is a beautiful little dog head with turquoise eyes (Amer. Mus. Nat. Hist.); said to be from Yucatan, a small turtle effigy (Mus. Amer. Ind.). There are also a few examples in obsidian of the so-called "masks," full-front representations of the human face, usually somewhat less than life-size, which were normally made of other stones. Several of obsidian are believed to be forgeries (e.g., Batres, n.d., pls. 39, 40), but presumably the following specimens are ancient, although none seems to have been found in a controlled excavation: Tlalteloco, "Toltec" (i.e. Teotihuacan) type, according to Palacios (1937, fig. 17); two specimens of unknown provenience classed as Aztec (Joyce, 1927, p. 182; Sociedad de Arte Moderna, 1945, fig. 63); a fine piece, said to be from the Valley of Mexico (Chicago Nat. Hist. Mus.— its label calls attention to the fact that many forgeries exist, but expresses belief in the genuineness of this one). The foregoing should not be confused with much smaller faces crudely executed on waterworn lumps of obsidian. These obvious frauds are for sale in almost every curio store in Guatemala City and have begun to appear in museums. I think they are made in Baja Verapaz. Batres (n.d., pls. 38–49) shows photographs of many fraudulent obsidian sculptures.

Eyepieces. Discs of obsidian 2–12 cm. in diameter, one side chipped, the other retaining the smooth surface of the parent flake, have been found at La Venta (Stirling and Stirling, 1941, p. 642); Teotihuacan (Linné, 1934, figs. 320, 321, 323, 324—two of these lay at the head of a burial and Linné believes that they may have been set in a mask covering the face of the corpse) and from unknown localities in Mexico (Joyce, 1920, fig. 19, 6, 7); Copan (Peabody Mus. Harvard, Amer. Mus. Nat. Hist.); Platon, British Honduras (Gann, 1893–95). It is probable that most, if not all, were mounted in wooden or stone sculptures to represent the eyes, as was done in the case of the colossal serpent heads of the Temple of Quetzalcoatl at Teotihuacan.

Tooth inlay (?). Strebel (1885–89, II, pl. IX, 14) reports from Quilate, Veracruz, a human incisor with a small, round obsidian inlay and Gann (1918, p. 109, fig. 58) another,

from the Rio Hondo in Quintana Roo. As these are the only records of such use of obsidian, one wonders if the stone in question may not have been crystalline hematite, which is black and shiny and which sometimes served for ornamental inlays. Rubin de la Borbolla (1940, p. 360) states that no obsidian inlays have been found in Mexico.

Mirrors. One of the treasures of the American Museum of Natural History is an obsidian disc 27 cm. in diameter, 2 cm. thick, highly polished on both sides. It is set in a narrow frame of carved wood covered with thin gold leaf. It was purchased in Spain, and Saville (1925, p. 87, pl. LI) believes that it may have been one of the presents sent by Cortez to Charles V. Its reflecting qualities are well brought out in a photograph published by Kelemen (1943, pl. 298,*a*). Nordenskiöld (1926) records a disc-shaped mirror from Mexico, diameter 16.5 cm. (Musée du Trocadéro, Paris); and there is another, but with a short perforated handle, from the Valley of Mexico (Mus. Amer. Ind.). Rectangular mirrors are more common. They average about 30 cm. long by 20 cm. wide and 5 cm. thick. Examples are from Azcapotzalco (Chicago Nat. Hist. Mus.), unknown localities in the Valley of Mexico (Mex. Nat. Mus., Mus. Amer. Ind.), Morelos (Brooklyn Mus.), Michoacan (Mus. Amer. Ind.).

Odd forms. I do not call the following objects eccentrics because, as was stated on p. 20, they should not be confused with the differently shaped and perhaps entirely unrelated eccentric obsidians of the Maya area. The Mexican odd forms, however, seem to make their first appearance at about the same time as do the eccentrics of Peten–British Honduras, for the earliest of them so far reported are of the classic Teotihuacan, i.e. II–III, period. Conceivably, both groups may have had a common origin in some phase of Middle Culture that has not yet come to light. The Teotihuacan examples are lizard- and snakelike forms, a ring, a crescent, and numerous small human figures (Gamio, 1922, pl. 102; Linné, 1934, figs. 313–18; 1942, fig. 289; Noguera, 1935, pl. XXIV). A human figure identical to those from Teotihuacan is said to come from Oaxaca (Mus. Amer. Ind.). On a later, presumably Aztec, horizon are little crescents from Tenayuca (Noguera, 1935a, pl. LVI); and from an Upper Tres Zapotes deposit a pair of crescents (Weiant, 1943, pl. 78, 1, 2). Of unknown date are large sickle-shaped pieces from Teopanzalco, Tlaxcala (Chicago Nat. Hist. Mus.) and a large hook-ended object variously stated to be from Yucatan and the *antiplanicie* (Nuñez y Dominguez, 1942, fig. 12). A smaller example of the same general shape is said to be from the Valley of Mexico (Mus. Amer. Ind.). There are many small crescents and specimens of the forms shown in figure 12,*a,b* (Amer. Mus. Nat. Hist., mostly from old collections labelled "Valley of Mexico"); from Oaxaca comes a small double crescent (Mus. Amer. Ind.).

Breast ornaments? Much larger than the above-mentioned crescents are certain crescentic objects from Jalisco (fig. 13). They were made from very large, thin flakes, the original plane surfaces of which form the two surfaces of the specimens, the edges being in one lot merely chipped (Chicago

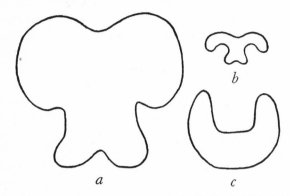

FIG. 12—OBJECTS OF OBSIDIAN FROM VALLEY OF MEXICO
a: Black. *b,c*: Red streaked with black. (Courtesy American Museum of Natural History.) Natural size.

Nat. Hist. Mus.), in the other (Amer. Mus. Nat. Hist.) first chipped and then ground almost smooth. At each end of each piece is a small drilled hole. They occur in graded sizes and are said, in the Chicago catalogue, presumably on the authority of their collector Frederick Starr, to have been worn in series on the breast, the smallest at the top.

Sequins. In tombs of the Esperanza phase at Kaminaljuyu (KJS, p. 138, fig. 157,*f*) were found small discs made from very thin flake-blades. They have chipped edges and an apparently punched central perforation. Others of identical form and fashioning are in the Regional Museum at Teotihuacan. From Jalisco there is another, finely chipped to an almost perfect circle 1.5 cm. in diameter, the central perforation drilled (Chicago Nat. Hist. Mus.); and from the Valley of Mexico still another of the same size with drilled perforation, the periphery rubbed smooth. Vaillant (1935, p. 245) mentions a fragment of an apparently similar disc, from El Arbolillo, which he believes to be of Teotihuacan date. As these little objects would have no attractiveness if strung together, they were probably sewed or otherwise attached to garments in such a way as to present their lustrous black surface.

Pendants. From Jalisco come pendants made from thin flakes, bits of which have been chipped to ovals some 3 cm. long; there is a small drilled suspension hole at one end of each (Chicago Nat. Hist. Mus.). In Grave 1 at Tenayuca, Noguera (1935, pl. LVII,5–7) found three banjo-shaped obsidian pendants about 4 cm. long. A little perforated flange rises from the small end, permitting them to hang flat; several almost identical specimens are said to be from the Valley of Mexico (Amer. Mus. Nat. Hist., Mus. Amer. Ind.).

Labrets. Usually and probably correctly classed as lip plugs are carefully shaped and highly polished little objects that in section resemble a top hat (fig. 14). These are both of obsidian and rock crystal. Of those of obsidian, Gamio (1922, pl. 119,*a*) illustrates a number from Teotihuacan, some with unusually narrow "crowns." Linné (1932, p. 151, fig. 319) recovered one at the Teotihuacan suburb of Xolalpan. He thinks it probable that it is of post-Teotihuacan date, and those of Gamio are chronologically unplaced. The same is true of a number of obsidian examples of the "top hat" variety from unknown localities in the Mexico National Museum, the Museum of the American Indian, Museum of the University of Pennsylvania (Mason, 1943, fig. 9), American Museum of Natural History, and Brooklyn Museum (one with a silver base). One from Quilate, Veracruz, is figured by Strebel (1885–89, II, pl. VII,10). Lastly, there must be noted the two magnificent labrets found at the Tarascan site of Tzintzuntzan by Rubin de la Borbolla (1944, p. 132, fig. 13). Like some of the obsidian earplugs next to be listed, these are marvels of

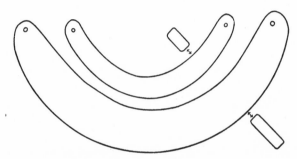

FIG. 13—OBSIDIAN BREAST ORNAMENT (?), JALISCO
(Courtesy American Museum of Natural History.) Scale ½.

craftsmanship. They are of the same general shape as the "top hat" labrets, but much larger, and the top of the "crown" flares and is cupped to receive an incrustation of turquoise mosaic, in one case framed with a narrow, beaded gold border. That they were worn in the lower lip is indicated by the fact that each lay on the center of the lower jaw of a male skeleton. It was doubtless labrets set like these with turquoise, to which Bernal Diaz (1908–16, vol. 1, p. 151) refers: "These men [ambassadors from Tlaxcala] had large holes in their lower lips, some with stone discs in them spotted with blue."

FIG. 14—OBSIDIAN LABRET

Teotihuacan (section, after Linné). Some specimens from Valley of Mexico are cupped, as shown by dotted line. Scale 2/3.

Earplugs. For accurate and delicate working of hard and brittle stone nothing made by any people at any time can, I think, surpass the obsidian earplugs produced during the post-Classic period in Mexico. They constitute one of the supreme achievements of lapidary art. As a rule they are spool-shaped, the central column usually cylindrical, but in the case of a Tzintzuntzan specimen and some from Monte Alban (Rubin de la Borbolla, 1944, fig. 10; Caso, 1932, fig. 36) wider at one end than the other; the flaring front and back lips are at right angles to the central column. All parts were ground almost incredibly thin, sometimes no more than .75 mm. Orchard (1927) figures a typical example from Tlatiluco (*sic*) in the valley of Mexico and describes another which, apparently having been marred during manufacture and therefore left unfinished, illustrates the chipping and grinding techniques employed by the craftsman. Most, if not all, such earplugs were of green obsidian. Over how long a period they were made is uncertain. Those from the controlled excavations at Tzintzuntzan and Monte Alban, where Caso (1932, 1932a) recovered no less than 10 in the fabulously rich Tomb 7, were associated with metal and probably date from not long before the conquest. One found at Xolalpan by Linné (1934, p. 151, fig. 322) was in a disturbed superficial deposit and therefore cannot surely be assigned to a Teotihuacan horizon. In addition to those mentioned above, there are examples from Quilate, Veracruz (Strebel, 1885–89, II, pl. VII, 6, 7) a number of unknown provenience in the Mexico National Museum, and unusually small specimens in the American Museum of Natural History and Museum of the American Indian. The only record other than Mexican is from Chipal, Guatemala, in a late, Chipal 3, context (Butler, 1940, pl. XI,*a*). There are a number of small earplugs of this general type, from unknown localities in Mexico (Univ. Pa. Mus., Mason, 1943, fig. 9; Amer. Mus. Nat. Hist.; Mus. Amer. Ind.); and a

still smaller one, shaped like a little pulley-wheel, was found at Tenayuca (Noguera, 1935a, pl. LV,8; this may perhaps have been a nose- or lip-plug). Differing from the spool-shaped specimens, which are complete earplugs, are stemless flares that evidently formed the frontal elements of plugs with stem and backing of perishable material. They are only slightly thicker than the foregoing and are about 7 cm. in diameter (Texmilincan, Guerrero; Mexico Nat. Mus.; there are metal objects in the collection from the site).

Beads. Although the Mesoamericans of all periods were inordinately fond of beads, they very seldom made them of obsidian, in spite of the fact that even harder stones, such as rock crystal, were often utilized. A single subspherical, five-lobed specimen about 1.5 cm. in diameter is from Tenayuca (Noguera, 1935a, pl. LVII,8). There are very handsome, spirally grooved, tubular beads from Teotihuacan (Templo los Sacerdotes; Batres, 1906, p. 18, fig. 12); Texmilincan, Guerrero (Garcia Payon, 1941, p. 353); Chichen Itza (Sacred Cenote; Peabody Mus. Harvard). Although none appears to be complete, they must have attained considerable size, as the Teotihuacan fragment is 10 cm. long. Those from Texmilincan were associated with metal, the Chichen Itza examples are also probably late. That from Teotihuacan, if the provenience was correctly reported, should be several centuries older, but it must be remembered that elaborate grinding and carving of obsidian was more characteristic of post-Classic times, and that any unusual find reported by Batres is unfortunately open to suspicion.

GROUND STONE

Metates		15
Large	13	
Small	2	
Manos		55
Quadrangular in section	36	
Flat in section	12	
Aberrant	7	
Stone vessels		4
Mortar (?)	1	
Lava paint (?) dish	1	
Alabaster bowl	1	
Marble vase	1	
Hammerstones		17
Spherical	17	
Amorphous	?	
Rubbing stones		6
Troughed stone		1
Perforated disc		1
Bark beaters		8
Celts		11
Spheres and hemispheres		7
Incised sphere	1	
Cupped subspherical objects	2	
Cupped and uncupped hemispheres	4	
Spindle whorls		5
Stamp (?)		1
Cylindrical stone		1
Ear (?) ornament		1
Minor sculptures		2

Jades		171
Earplugs		10
Jade and slate	2	
Jade, slate, and shell	2	
Flares	2	
Discs	2	
Shell, jade incrustation	2	
(Shell earplugs	2)	
Miniature flares		11
With neck	5	
Neck removed	3	
Without neck	3	
Pendants, carved		5
Human face	3	
Alligator (?) head	1	
Small carved pendant	1	
Miscellaneous small jades		7
Plain pendant	1	
Human hand	1	
Loaf-shaped objects	2	
Adorno	1	
Fragment	1	
Jointed object	1	
Human effigy		1
Mosaic, assemblages and single elements		8
Beads		129
Subspherical	118	
Barrel-shaped	10	
Tubular, flared end	1	

METATES AND MANOS

LARGE METATES

Legless, 8 (figs. 15; 76,*g*; RR, pl. 65). Limestone, 4; granite, 3; conglomerate, 1. L *ca.* 40–50 cm., W *ca.* 25–35 cm. Grinding surface strongly curved laterally, more gently from end to end. Depth of trough depends on amount of wear, surface of new specimens (fig. 15,*d*) being flat. Both ends even in long-used metates (as figs. 15,*b*; 76,*g*) are always "open," i.e. have no raised border such as developed along the sides. Bottoms usually well shaped by pecking to a form so strongly curved both laterally and longitudinally that it would seem that these metates, to be kept from

L 24 cm., W 15 cm., T 1.5 cm. Unused, all surfaces show pecking-marks. Grinding surface very faintly cupped both laterally and longitudinally. Two rounded boss-legs, 1.5 cm. high, set in from corners at one end; single rectangular leg, 3 cm. high, set in from edge at other end. Schist specimen, fragment (fig. 76,*a*). T 2 cm. Grinding surface flat, polished by wear. Shallow groove surrounds grinding surface 1 cm. from edge. Bottom flat, well finished. Single remaining leg mammiform, H 3 cm.; may have been single leg at one end or one of two set well in from corners at other end.

MANOS

Quadrangular in section, 36 (figs. 16; 77,*b,c*). Granite, 16; limestone, 20. L 15–22 cm. (22 cm. seems to have been a standard size, as there are five whole specimens of exactly

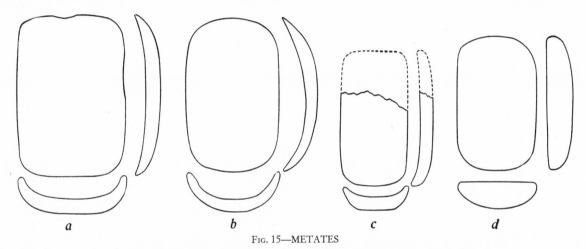

FIG. 15—METATES

Common legless type. *a*: Limestone. *b,d*: Granite. *c*: Conglomerate. Scale 1/12.

rocking, must have been set in a depression in the floor or the ground or, perhaps more probably, steadied and held at the proper angle with stones, as was done in the case of not dissimilar metates in the Southwest (see Bartlett, 1933). There are fragments, however, with flat bottoms (fig. 15,*c*). Limestone examples, less carefully finished than those of granite, are of hard, flinty material with many small pores (fig. 76,*g*). This type of stone is not seen in manos, which are all poreless.

Legged, 5 (fig. 76,*c-f*). Vesicular lava, 4; granite, 1. All small fragments. No over-all measurements obtainable: T 3–4 cm., W of one fragment *ca.* 22 cm. Grinding surface flat or very faintly curved, no side or end ridges. Bottom also flat. Lava specimens: two tall (8–10 cm.) legs at corners of one end, single similar leg in center of other end; all legs set at edge of metate. Granite specimen: legs at two-leg end are low, rounded bosses set in 3 cm. from end and side; third leg missing.

SMALL METATES, 2

Greenish sandstone specimen (fig. 76,*b*; cf. RR, pl. 64).

that length and several fragments that were probably of similar size; there are three at 17–18 cm., two at 15 cm.). T varies, probably because of wear, much more than length, from 4 by 5 cm. to 7 by 7.5 cm.; commonest T 5 by 5.5 cm. These manos have four distinct faces, gently convex both laterally and longitudinally. Junctions of faces usually rounded, but occasionally more nearly angular (fig. 16,*c,d*). Seldom are two opposite faces exactly parallel to each other, or any two adjoining faces at right-angles; in section, therefore, the manos are rarely either truly square or rhomboidal (see fig. 16). The two ends are normally blunt. All four faces generally show wear-polish, but this tends to be greater on one pair of adjoining faces than on the other two. In some cases the wear on such a pair of faces has been so severe as entirely to have obliterated their junction and to have produced a single rounded surface (fig. 16,*n*). There seem to be no significant differences in size or shape between the granite and limestone examples. The former are of a handsome gray or pink and white stone; the latter are of hard, close-grained material that takes a glassy polish.

There is but a single fragment of a lava mano in the collection. It appears to have been quadrangular in section.

Flat in section, 12 (figs. 17; 77,*a*). Limestone, 11; granite, 1. Only two complete specimens, but these seem typical: L 15.5, 13 cm.; W 7.8, 6 cm.; T 4.5, 3.7 cm. The two grinding

of this type), are waterworn pebbles one face of which has been used as a grinding surface (fig. 18,*a,c*). The granite specimen (fig. 18,*b*) is a thick oval in section, ends squared.

COMMENT ON METATES AND MANOS. The present collection is unsatisfactory, not only because of the scarcity of

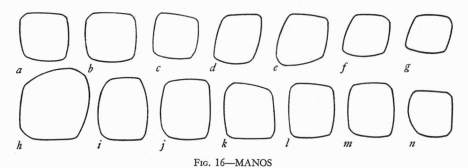

FIG. 16—MANOS

Quadrangular in section. *a,d,g,j,k,n*: Granite. *b,c,e,f,h,i,l,m*: Limestone. Polish from use on metate on all four sides of all but *i*, which is polished only on two longer faces, and *n*, in which excessive wear has produced rounded coalescence of two adjacent faces. For photos of *a,c,f,g,i,l* see figs. 77,*b*,1; 77,*b*,4; 77,*c*,2; 77,*b*,3; 77,*c*,1; 77,*c*,4. Scale ¼.

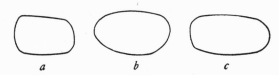

FIG. 17—MANOS

Flat in section. Limestone. Wear-polish only on long faces. For photos of *a,b* see fig. 77,*a*,1,2. Scale ¼.

material for study of metates, but also because, with very few exceptions, both metates and manos came from above the uppermost floors in Structure A-V or from the surface of other buildings. Thus the majority are certainly very late and, indeed, probably date from a time when Group A had ceased to be a ceremonial precinct and its temples were being occupied as dwelling places. That such conditions existed for at least a short period before the final abandon-

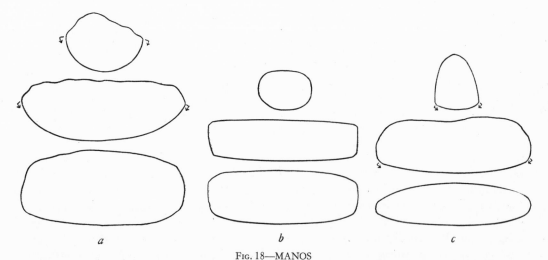

FIG. 18—MANOS

Aberrant specimens. *a,c*: Limestone. *b*: Granite. Arrows in *a,c* show extent of wear-polish; *b* polished on whole surface save ends. Scale ¼.

surfaces normally equally worn; ends squarish. The single granite specimen, a fragment, is thicker than the average flat mano and may have been reduced by long wear from an originally quadrangular form.

Aberrant, 7 (fig. 18). Limestone, 6; granite, 1. All limestone examples, save one cylindrical fragment (the only one

ment of Uaxactun is suggested by household refuse in many chambers and courts.

Because the specimens are almost all late they fail to provide data as to whether or not changes took place during the long occupancy of Uaxactun in the forms of metates and manos or in the kinds of stone of which they were made.

Nor do those from Group E recorded by Mrs. Ricketson (RR, p. 193; fig. 124; pls. 64, 65) yield information on this point, for they too were preponderatingly from superficial deposits; and although a somewhat larger percentage were of granite and conglomerate, they appear not to differ significantly from those of Group A. No large metates with legs, however, were noted. In the Mamom midden beneath the plaza of Group E neither metates nor manos were found. A little material from dwelling sites (Wauchope, 1934, pl. 5) is also inconclusive as regards chronological changes. The metates seem all to be large, legless, and of the same pitted limestone as those from Groups A and E. Manos are both flat and quadrangular in section.

From San Jose, Thompson (1939, p. 172; pl. 27,c) reports large legless metates also of convex-bottomed, turtleback form and with the same open-ended grinding trough as those of Uaxactun. The trough, however, is less curved laterally. The specimens are of limestone, sandstone, and red and gray granites, the latter, Thompson believes, from the Mountain Pine Ridge, some 50 km. south of San Jose. This may also have been the source of the Uaxactun granites. The San Jose manos give evidence of chronological change both in material and shape. Those of San Jose I or II are almost all of limestone, with rounded ends, and either round in section or with a single grinding surface. Those of the later periods, mostly of granite, have tapering ends and a square section, all four surfaces having served for grinding; they are thus much like the quadrangular-section manos of Uaxactun, although Thompson notes the absence of the Uaxactun tendency toward rhomboidal sections.

The metates and manos of Benque Viejo are again similar. Thompson (1940, p. 27) says: "Metate fragments (all surface finds except one) were of polished gray or reddish granite and of the turtle-backed type without feet or decoration. Mullers (all surface finds) were also of polished granite, usually gray, and tapered at the ends. In cross section they were square with rounded corners and sometimes approached circular. Typically they were 6 by 6 cm., with lengths perhaps 20–25 cm."

At Lubaantun great numbers of fragments of three-legged metates were found, the fill of one terrace containing nearly 40 legs. These metates were all of lava and had flat grinding surfaces. The manos were cylindrical (Joyce, Cooper-Clark, and Thompson, 1927, p. 313; Thompson, 1939, p. 173). Being from structural fill, the legged metates, at least, are probably older than the run of material from Uaxactun and San Jose. At Baking Pot, Ricketson (1931, p. 8) found a legless metate, presumably of limestone, which measured 40 by 31.5 cm. A mano 23.5 cm. long lay in the "concave grinding face." As these specimens lay well underground and near, perhaps with, a burial, they are also evidently fairly old. Baking Pot yielded pottery comparable to

that of both Tzakol and Tepeu, but to which phase the metate and mano should be assigned is uncertain.

The small metates from Group A (fig. 51,a,b) and those from Group E (RR, pl. 64) being more carefully shaped and, in the case of one of the Group E specimens having an ornamental opening in the slablike, terraced near leg, were presumably made for some purpose other than household meal grinding. There is no record of similar specimens from the Peten or British Honduras.

Mortar (?), fragment (fig. 19). Purplish white crystalline limestone. If vessel was evenly rounded, as would appear from the 8-cm. length of rim remaining, its diameter must have been about 33 cm. The curve of the lower part suggests that the bottom was nearly flat. Interior highly polished by long use, exterior indifferently smoothed.

FIG. 19—MORTAR (?)

Fragment of rim. Limestone. Scale ½.

COMMENT. Mrs. Ricketson (RR, p. 193, pl. 65,c) records but two mortars, both from late deposits in Group E. One is a rough block of limestone with a hemispherical depression in one side, the other a fragment of a better-made, bowl-like piece not unlike the present specimen. The latter is from Stratum 3, Pit 2, and therefore not later than Tzakol 2. Nothing identifiable as a pestle has been found at Uaxactun.

Rarity and lack of standardization of stone mortars and the absence of specially shaped pestles seem to consitute a negative trait of lowland Maya material culture, and, indeed, of that of Mesoamerica as a whole. The Ganns (1939, p. 49) mention, but do not describe, mortars and pestles from graves of uncertain date in mounds east of Nohmul, British Honduras. Strong (1935, p. 22) mentions a small stone specimen accompanying an apparently late urn burial at Utila, Bay Islands. A little lava mortar with incised decoration and a pair of crude pestles from eastern Salvador are figured by Longyear (1944, pl. XII, 4; no data as to age). Crude pear-shaped pestles are found in the Ulua Valley, Honduras (Mus. Amer. Ind.); ones of this shape and others of truncated conical form occur at the post-Classic (plumbate horizon) site of Tajumulco in southwestern Guatemala, as well as a few small mortars (Dutton and Hobbs, 1943, p. 47, fig. 27). Hartman (1901, pl. 34,6) notes that a bell-shaped specimen from Chircot was the only pestle found by him in the highlands of Costa Rica; apparently there were no true (i.e. deeply cupped) mortars; the small zoomorphic lava plates (Hartman, 1901, pl. 56,3), so abundant in that region, and which are usually called metates, may well have served as mortars. A pestle with expanding base and animal head is reported from Alojuca, Puebla (Linné, 1942, fig. 75); one with a human head from

depression 1 cm. deep. Shallow groove on rim. Bottom flat. Not carefully finished. Possibly for grinding paint.

COMMENT. From above latest floor, North Court. Like mortars, small stone dishes of this sort evidently were not commonly made in Mesoamerica. The only two records I can find, both of rectangular specimens of igneous rock, very similar to this one, are from San Agustin Acasaguastlan (Smith and Kidder, 1943, fig. 57,f) and from Misantla, Veracruz (Strebel, 1885–89, II, pl. VII, 2).

Alabaster bowl. Fragment of wall of bowl. D apparently about 15 cm.; T .4 cm., in flutings .3 cm. Admirably finished. Exterior with close-set vertical (?) flutings about .8 cm. wide. East Court, above latest floor.

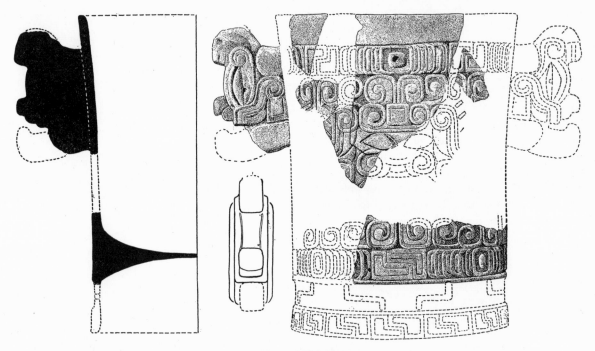

FIG. 20—MARBLE VASE

Ulua type. Base restored from specimen illustrated in Stone, 1937, fig. 6. Original H about 22 cm.

Arroyo Cajete, Veracruz (Strebel, 1885–89, II, pl. VIII, 57). Strebel also figures (pls. V,5; XXVI,45) small three-legged mortars from San Isidro and Quimistlan. These seem to have been a local Veracruz product in relatively late prehistoric times. Farther north on the Gulf coast bell-shaped pestles occur in the Panuco region (Ekholm, 1944, fig. 56); no mortars were found. Only in Chihuahua, which should probably not be considered as part of the Mesoamerican field, and in the Hohokam region of southern Arizona do the mortar and pestle come into their own. In both these areas, and particularly the latter, small mortars occur very commonly and are often tastefully ornamented (Sayles, 1936; Sayles *in* Gladwin et al., 1937).

Lava paint (?) *dish* (fig. 78,b). Fragmentary. W 7.4 cm., T 3 cm., L probably about 10 cm. Rectangular working

Marble vase, fragments (fig. 20). Original H about 22 cm., D orifice 17 cm., T wall .7 cm. Carving averages about .1 cm. deep. Opaque white stone. Well polished inside and out. Annular base cut away, presumably after it had become damaged. That it had been decorated with openwork is indicated by traces of two perforations at base of wall. Although head does not make contact with other fragments, it doubtless belonged to this vessel and was one of two placed on opposite sides, as shown in Sr. Tejeda's restoration. Above latest floor, East Court.

COMMENT. This is obviously an importation from the Ulua Valley of northwestern Honduras, as it corresponds in every particular to the beautiful marble vessels of that region. (See Hamy, 1896; Harry-Hirtzel, 1925; Gordon, 1921; Stone, 1937; Kelemen, 1943, pls. 94, 95.)

Almost all of the score or more known specimens have come from the Ulua drainage, but one, which evidently found its way southward in trade, emanates from the Guanacaste area of Costa Rica (Lines, 1942) and one of the several fragments of marble vessels from San Jose, British Honduras, bears the intricate low-relief carving typical of these vases (Thompson, 1939, fig. 92,*p*). The exact age and the cultural affinities of the marble vases have not yet definitely been established. As far as I know, none of those from the Ulua has been found in the course of stratigraphic excavations. The Uaxactun specimen is from a very late deposit perhaps laid down after the Acropolis had ceased to be a ceremonial center. The piece from San Jose is likewise from late (San Jose V) debris that also contained Yucatecan slate ware and probably copper. Thompson (1941, p. 43) therefore believes the type to date from post-Classic times or, at the earliest, from the very end of the Classic Period. It should be remembered, however, that precious objects such as these might, like jades, have long been treasured as heirlooms. Further evidence, which, when Honduranean ceramic types can more accurately be fitted into the general Mesoamerican archaeological picture, should be of value for dating the marble vases, is provided by pottery vessels resembling them in shape, in decoration, and in possessing two opposed biomorphic lugs. These have been found by Strong (1935, p. 93; pl. 24,*b*) on the Bay Islands in association with Bay Island Polychrome pottery; by Strong, Kidder, and Paul (1938, p. 44; pl. 6,*e,f*) on the Ulua together with Upper Ulua Polychrome; and by Stone (1941, p. 22; fig. 5) on the Agalta River, east of the Ulua. Such pieces have usually been considered imitations of the marble vases, but Stone suggests that they may have been prototypes. This deserves careful consideration, as monochrome pottery with elaborate opposed lugs was firmly rooted in the "Paya" culture of Honduras and on the Bay Islands; and opposed lugs of this sort are also seen in much of the Ulua and Yojoa polychrome ware. Strong (letter of May 24, 1945) has kindly given me the following opinion: "I 'guess date' the Ulua marble vase-like pottery as ca. 800–1300 in the Ulua region, with neither terminal positive. Since no true Ulua marble vase has yet been found in stratigraphic association, we cannot say whether the pottery imitation was contemporary, basic, or derivative and later. Personally, I believe the pottery is an imitation; hence the marble bowls should be as old as, and perhaps a bit older than, the earliest pottery imitations. This would give them a 'guess date' of ca. 800 A.D. on in Honduras."

Presumably also related to the marble specimens in some way are lugged cylindrical vessels of lava discovered by Spinden (1925, fig. 1) in "Chorotegan" territory on the Plantain River still farther to the east, although, as Stone (1937, p. 10) points out, their carved decoration differs from that of the Ulua specimens.

Turning to the west, Maya influence seems to have played no part in the development of the marble vases, for opposed lugs of the Honduras type are foreign to Maya work in either pottery or stone. Thompson goes still farther afield in the search for origins. He recognizes (1941, p. 44), "a south Mexican inspiration for the marble vessels." This opinion is based on the occurrence in Veracruz, particularly in collections from the Isla de Sacrificios, of beautifully fashioned vases of *tecali,* the so-called "Mexican onyx" (see Nuttall, 1910; Mason, 1943, fig. 6). Thompson points to their possession of annular and tripod supports, but admits that the pear-shaped body, so typical of the Sacrificios examples, is not found in the Ulua area. Furthermore, I think the Ulua specimens must be somewhat older than those of tecali from Sacrificios, which Thompson is doubtless right in believing to be of the post-Classic Period characterized by plumbate and fine orange wares. I question his linkage of the curvilinear decoration of the Ulua vases with that of "Totonac" stonework, for not only does such decoration fail to appear on the supposed tecali prototypes but, since Thompson wrote, a find at Kaminaljuyu, Guatemala, indicates that the "Totonac" carvings are probably older by several centuries than either the Sacrificios or the Ulua examples (see KJS, p. 237).

HAMMERSTONES

Spherical, 17 (fig. 78,*d,e*; RR, pl. 62,*b*,1–7; Wauchope, 1934, pl. 4,*a*). D 5–8 cm. Well rounded but seldom truly spherical. Flint and crystalline limestone.

COMMENT. Much Uaxactun stonework, as seen in such architectural elements as veneer slabs and faced vault stones, in sculpture, and in metates, manos, and celts gives evidence, in the form of minute pittings, of having been shaped by the pecking or, as Holmes (1919, p. 330) has termed it, the crumbling process. The rougher work was doubtless done with the nodules of flint next to be mentioned, but the finishing touches were probably given with smaller, spherical stones of the sort under discussion. They may, of course, have had other uses: in games; or, sewed in leather, as clubheads; or for grinding—Dutton and Hobbs (1943, p. 48) found one in the hollow of a mortar—although never at Uaxactun and seldom elsewhere are they polished as if by such service. They should not be confused with the much smaller, more smoothly finished, and more perfectly spherical stones from Group E (RR, p. 191; pl. 62,*b*,9–11). The function of these is unknown.

Amorphous (not counted). Because of their weight and difficulties of transport only a few of these were collected. They are nodules of flint or pieces of extra-hard limestone that show severe battering. Evidently pieces of convenient size, they were put to use without shaping and seem usually to have been discarded when their more salient parts had been so reduced that they were no longer as serviceable as unworn ones, which could be picked up anywhere about the site.

RUBBING STONES

Six. Of these, four are thick limestone discs (fig. 78,*c*; RR, pl. 62,*c*,1). D 7.5–11.5 cm., T 2.5–5 cm. Two, including the one figured, are of hard limestone, well shaped, and highly polished by use on one side; the other two of softer stone, less regular in outline, and without signs of wear. There is also a waterworn quartz pebble (cf. RR, pl. 62,*c*,3), L 9.5 cm., T 3.5 cm., with fine striations on one face, the ends battered. This was seemingly used both for rubbing and as a hammerstone. Finally, there is a similarly shaped piece of pumice, L 7.5 cm., T 4 cm., that has been worn to its present form apparently by use as an abrasive.

COMMENT. The object of pumice is from above the floor of the North Court, the others from Tzakol and later deposits. That the excavations in Group E and the more extensive work at Groups A and B produced so very few implements of this sort is noteworthy in view of the enormous amount of plaster smoothing and work on room and plaza floors that had to be done. It indicates, as stated in the introduction, how extensively wooden tools must have been used. Another striking lack is that of stone pot polishers, none having been found in Group A and in Group E only one specimen which might have served that purpose (RR, p. 190, fig. 121,*a*).

TROUGHED STONE

One (fig. 78,*a*; RR, pl. 62,*c*,3). L 6 cm. Soft, abrasive stone. The longitudinal trough has apparently been made by sharpening implements of wood or bone. The object superficially resembles the arrowshaft smoothers of the Great Plains and Southwest, but it cannot have been so used, as the trough sags at the middle.

PERFORATED DISC

One (fig. 78,*f*). Greatest D 13 cm. Friable limestone, roughly shaped, perforation biconically drilled. Mrs. Ricketson records several better-made discs, some of which were drilled partly through on one or both sides, and a disc with four notches in the edge and a central perforation (RR, p. 192, pl. 63,*a*,5–7; *c*).

BARK BEATERS

Eight (fig. 78,*g-j*; RR, pl. 62,*a*,4–6; Wauchope, 1934, pl. 4,*a*,5). L 6.5–10.3 cm., W 5.4–6.5 cm., T 3.3–5.7 cm. Continuous round-bottomed hafting groove on one short and two long sides, second short side ungrooved. Faces with longitudinal parallel scorings, those on one face wider spaced than those on the other. Figure 78,*j* is exceptional, one end being slightly broader than the other; the parallel scor-

ings on one face are shallow scratchings rather than evenly cut troughs, and the other face bears a design of incised lines and drilled pits. All are of fine-grained limestone save one fragment (not figured) which is a gray, nonvesicular lava.

COMMENT. Most of the bark beaters in the present collection are from superficial deposits, but that they came into use in relatively early times is proved by one specimen (fig. 78,*h*) from a Tzakol stratum in Pit 2, Group A. They were also present on approximately the same chronological horizon in the Guatemala highlands, having been found in Esperanza phase mounds at Kaminaljuyu (KJS, p. 142; it is there erroneously presumed that all Uaxactun bark beaters are from the Tepeu horizon). In the report just quoted references are given to literature concerning the distribution of this implement in Mesoamerica and it is pointed out that no example has come to light in any pre-Classic site.

CELTS

Eleven—seven complete, four fragmentary (figs. 78,*k-q*). L 4.7–17.3 cm. Fine-grained dark green or dark gray igneous rock susceptible to high polish. Greatest width normally at or close above convex cutting edge, which is at right-angles to long axis. Sides rounded. Edge-bevel and forward part of both faces polished; rest of surface peck-finished, in two cases (fig. 78,*l*,*o*) smooth but unpolished. All but one (fig. 78,*p*; Tzakol) are of Tepeu date.

COMMENT. I greatly regret that I have not had opportunity to make a comparative study of Mesoamerican celts, grooved axes, and adzes, which I am sure would yield important information as to the prehistory of that region. As a matter of fact, such a study, extended to cover the entire New World, might well throw light on intercontinental contacts, or lack of them. What little is now known of the typology and distribution of these tools suggests numerous interesting and very far-reaching problems. How early, for example, did the celt, which seems surely to have antedated the grooved axe, come into use in the Americas? Was it an independent New World invention or was it an importation from the Old? This question, like so many others involved in the origin of American artifacts, requires much more knowledge than is now available regarding the cultures of northeastern Asia and their dating relative to those of the Indians. And what about the grooved axe? It occurs in both North and South America and many specimens from the two continents are practically identical. There appears, however, to be a very great gap between the areas in which they are found. Again we must ask whether this is a case of diffusion or of independent invention. At present one cannot do more than guess. The trouble is that Americanists have allowed themselves to become concerned so exclusively with the fields in which they happen to be working that they tend to lose sight of the broader aspects of New World prehistory. We very badly need a recrudescence of interest in such general problems as were attacked by Holmes and Dixon and Nordenskiöld. I can think of no more rewarding career for a young archaeologist than to devote himself to the comparative study of American artifacts.

SPHERES AND HEMISPHERES

Incised sphere, 1 (fig. 21,*d*). D 2.4 cm. Pinkish, fine-grained limestone. Well finished. Quartered by two equatorial, deeply and evenly incised lines.

Cupped subspherical objects, 2 (fig. 21,*a,b*). D 3.5, 3.6 cm.; T 2.4, 2.9 cm. Yellowish flint and white crystalline

of Structure A-V and therefore not later than Chicanel. The third (fig. 21,*c*) is from a Tepeu deposit. All the hemispheres listed by Mrs. Ricketson (RR, p. 191) are of Period I, i.e. Mamom. The only practical use I can suggest for these cupped subspheres and hemispheres is as headpieces for bow-drills, but they seem rather small for such service. No small, smooth stone spheres of the sort found in Group E (RR, pl. 62,*b*,9–11) came to light in subsequent excavations.

SPINDLE WHORLS

Five (fig. 22; RR, fig. 123). D 2.2–2.5 cm. Yellowish brown flint (fig. 22,*b,d,e*), white and pinkish limestone (*a,c*). All symmetrical and well finished save *a*, which is a waterworn pebble slightly evened by rubbing. Incised

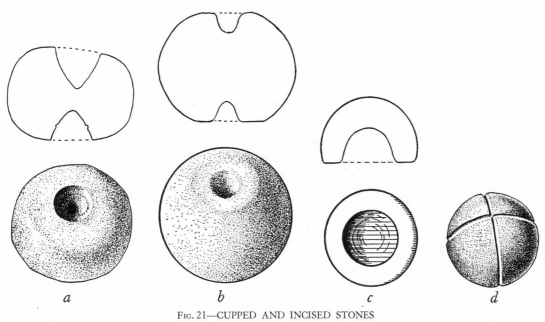

FIG. 21—CUPPED AND INCISED STONES

It is possible that *a-c* were headpieces for bow drills; *a*, however, may represent an abandoned attempt to perforate a large bead. Natural size.

limestone. Each with two opposed conical holes (see sections).

Cupped and uncupped hemispheres, 3 cupped (fig. 21,*c*; RR, fig. 122,*b,c*), D 1.7–3.2 cm.; 1 uncupped (cf. RR, fig. 122,*a*), D 2.9 cm. Yellowish and light brown flints. Highly polished.

COMMENT. The incised sphere appears to be unique. It is not later than Tzakol. I have seen nothing exactly like the subspherical stones with opposed cuppings, those from Tajumulco (Dutton and Hobbs, 1943, p. 51, fig. 28,*f*) being larger, cruder, and made of tuff. The smaller Uaxactun example (fig. 21,*a*) is from a probably Tzakol horizon, the larger (fig. 21,*b*) from a surface deposit in the East Court. The uncupped hemisphere is equally late, but two of those with cups are definitely early, one being from a Mamom midden in Group E, the other from beneath the lowest floor

decoration. All bores seem originally to have been biconical, all perhaps later reamed, those of *c,e* to almost cylindrical form.

COMMENT. All the above except *e*, which was found on the dump, are from above-floor deposits and the specially made, as distinguished from perforated potsherd, spindle whorls of clay (p. 67) are also late. Relative recency of such whorls, both stone and the much more abundant clay examples, seems to obtain throughout Mesoamerica. None, so far as I know, has been found at any Middle Culture site, and in most regions they seem not to have appeared until post-Classic times. The earliest formed whorls of clay of which I can find record are of Teotihuacan II or III date at Xolalpan and Tlamimilolpa (Linné, 1934, 1942) and on the Lower II horizon at Cerro de las Mesas (Drucker, 1943a, p. 66). Those from Tres Zapotes are all from late deposits (Drucker, 1943, p. 86). There is the greatest need for a thoroughgoing study of clay spindle whorls, which vary significantly both geographically and chronologically and which, wherever they occur, are usually abundant. Stone whorls, on the other hand, are very rare. Three, similar in shape and incised decoration to that shown in figure 22,*e,* are from Holmul (Merwin and Vaillant, 1932, p. 85; specimens in Peabody Mus. Harvard); all were with burials, two of Holmul V date (i.e. contemporaneous with Tepeu), one Holmul III (Tzakol). Records from British Honduras: Baking Pot, 1, an apparently late (Tepeu horizon) burial, fine limestone (not illustrated, Ricketson, 1929, p. 14); Tzimin Kax, 1, from burial of Holmul V period, apparently closely similar to figure 22,*a* (Thompson, 1931, p. 317, pl. XLIX, 8); San Jose, 3, "apparently of marble," one with a burial (Thompson, 1939, fig. 91,*m*) like figure 22,*c* in shape and incised decoration, two (Thompson,

EAR (?) ORNAMENT

One (fig. 56,*d*). L 4.2 cm. Fine-grained white limestone. Same shapes as shell examples (fig. 56,*a-c*) but shank longer and the shallowly cupped head rectangular rather than round. Between upper and lower floors, second story, Structure B-XI; probably Tzakol. For comment on objects of this type, see p. 64.

MINOR SCULPTURES

Two (fig. 24). Both are waterworn quartzite pebbles, one pink and yellow the other brown, unaltered save for the sawing of a slot to represent an animal's mouth and the drilling of two holes for the eyes.

COMMENT. These two little objects, both from Tepeu deposits, are interesting examples of the rendering more realistic of a natural form that suggested in the one case a

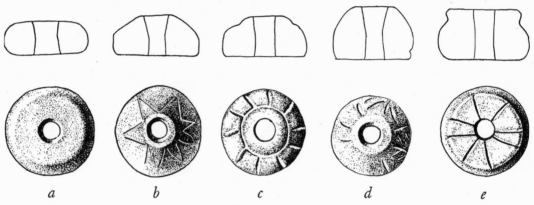

FIG. 22—STONE SPINDLE WHORLS
Natural size.

fig.91,*o,p*) undecorated and in shape much like figure 22,*b* (Thompson's *p* is San Jose III [Tepeu horizon], *m* and *o* are San Jose V [post-Tepeu]); Nohmul, 3, limestone (not illustrated, Gann and Gann, 1939, p. 36). Roatan, Bay Islands, Honduras, 1, gray-green talc, incised design, ceremonial deposit associated with copper. It is to be noted that most of the above are of late date and played mortuary or ceremonial roles.

STONE STAMP (?)

One (fig. 23,*a*). L 9.1 cm. Beautifully fashioned of compact, purplish gray limestone. Four sides and ends ground flat, incised hachure on ends. Apparently unique, possibly a stamp for textile or flesh marking—no pottery at Uaxactun bears the imprint of such a stamp. Surface find, Group A.

CYLINDRICAL STONE

One (fig. 23,*b*). L 8.8 cm. Yellow-brown flint. Excellently shaped and polished. Function unknown. From under latest plaza floor east of Structure A-II.

frog, in the other a monkey's head. A third example is a small pendant (RR, fig. 125) which has been given the semblance of a human face, again by sawing a mouth and drilling eyes. This sort of adaptation, but more fully carried out, was much practiced by the jadeworkers of Kaminaljuyu (KJS, figs. 148, 149). Of more formal small carvings in stones other than jade, only two have been found at Uaxactun (RR, p. 194, pl. 66). As a matter of fact, nonjade small sculptures were seemingly seldom produced by the lowland Maya at any time. In this they differed sharply from the people of the Quiche region, who turned out great quantities of the little stylized human figures locally called *camahuiles* (Lothrop, 1936, fig. 102), as well as more realistic squatting figures with a tiny bowl in the lap or on the head. None of these, I believe, has been figured; there are examples in the Robles and Sandoval collections in Quetzaltenango. In Oaxaca also, small stylized stone figures, in many ways resembling the camahuiles, are abundant; and in Salvador there occurs much minor stone sculpture (Longyear, 1940, pl. XII). The paucity of such products in the

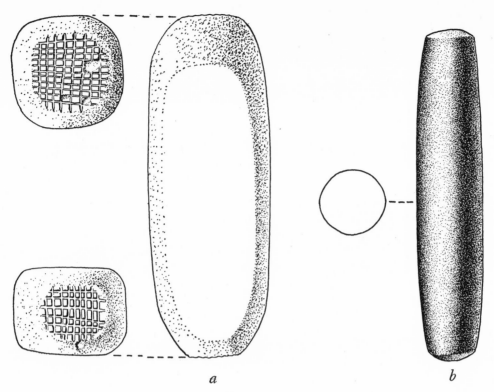

a   *b*

Fig. 23—STONE STAMP (?), CYLINDRICAL STONE
Natural size.

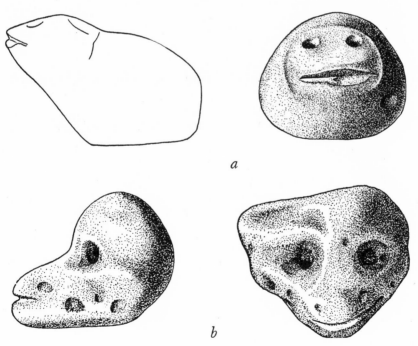

a

b

Fig. 24—MINOR SCULPTURES
Waterworn pebbles whose natural form suggested the addition of sawed mouth and drilled
eyes. Natural size.

Fig. 25—PYRITE BEADS

Sections. Natural size. (See p. 52.)

Maya area cannot be attributed to lack of suitable raw material, for although the limestones of Peten and the northern part of the Yucatan peninsula are not too attractive a

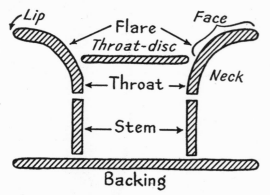

Fig. 26—NOMENCLATURE OF THE COMPOUND EARPLUG

medium for carvings of this sort, there was no dearth of excellent stone at Quirigua and Copan. The phenomenon thus appears to be a further instance of the self-centered conservatism of the Classic Maya.

other hand, came into use early and remained in fashion until the conquest. Because parts of each one were usually of perishable material, very few complete specimens have been recovered, but from those that have and from earplugs shown in stone sculpture, clay figurines, and vase-painting, it is evident that they normally consisted of three elements: backing, stem, and flare (fig. 26). The one nearly whole example with jade flare found at Uaxactun will be described first, then those less complete, and finally, in order to keep all data on earplugs together, two pairs of shell specimens.

Jade and slate earplugs, pair, one very badly crushed (fig. 27). D of backing 4.2 cm., of flare 3.5 cm. Backing a slate disc .15 cm. thick; small, irregular hole punched, not drilled, through center. Upper surface of backing ringed with jade mosaic, mostly gone. Stem of perishable material, probably wood; coated with green stucco, a little of which remains. Flare of Antique Green (Ridgway nomenclature), highly polished jade, shaped with great delicacy, sharp edge, flat face, flat bevel to throat; neck with two tiny, opposite perforations; inner edge of neck irregular, as if broken during earlier use and later remounted. Slate throat-disc set with mosaic of dark jade matching flare so perfectly in color that its elements might well have been cut from the same

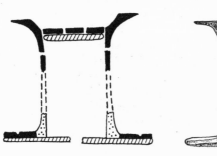
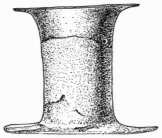
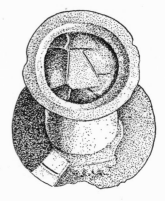

Fig. 27—JADE AND SLATE EARPLUG

In the section, black represents jade; hachure, slate; dots, stucco. Natural size.

JADES

EARPLUGS

Mesoamerican earplugs, other than those of pottery, were of two sorts: one-piece and compound. One-piece earplugs were almost always of obsidian, the beautifully fashioned spool-shaped objects already discussed; but there are examples in jade from Tomb 7 at Monte Alban in the Oaxaca Museum, and one of rock crystal from Ejutla, Oaxaca (Mus. Amer. Ind.). No spool-shaped specimens were found at Uaxactun; indeed, they seem not to have been made anywhere until post-Classic times. Compound earplugs, on the

piece of stone. In the drawing, the stem has been restored; original height uncertain, probably less than shown.

COMMENT. From Burial A-22, Tzakol. Although this specimen corresponds in general make-up to those of the Esperanza phase of Kaminaljuyu (KJS, fig. 143,*a*), the only site from which complete and nearly complete compound earplugs have been recorded, its very thin, sharp-edged flare beveled to the throat has not been duplicated by anything found there or elsewhere. Its round face curving into the neck, the fact that the neck bears small perforations, and the presence of a throat disc, all ally it, however, to the much thicker, unbeveled Type A Kaminaljuyu flares (KJS, p. 106; fig. 143,*a*).

Jade, slate, and shell earplugs, pair (figs. 28; 79,*a,b*). D of backing 6.1 cm. Backing a concavo-convex Spondylus (?) shell disc with small, drilled central perforation. Slate disc with large central perforation cemented to shell disc and covered with mosaic of .1-cm.-thick jade mosaic. Mosaic encircled by round to somewhat oval jades, flat on under sides, upper sides gently convex and highly polished. A number of these are obviously from subspherical beads sawed in two at right-angles to bore, as they retain half the biconical perforation typical of such beads. Others (marked *y* in fig. 28) were cut at a different angle and show merely one edge of the perforation. It is probable that the rest are also parts of beads. In one of the two backings (fig. 28) every third piece is perforated. The hole, in most, probably originally in all, such pieces in both specimens, was concealed by plugging it with a bit of jade of matching color

fig. 147,*j*). Tomb A-IV also contained miniature flares of the same fine color as these, with similarly perforated neck, and one of them with the same four tiny holes in the edge of the face. Because, in the Uaxactun tomb, each of the little flares lay with a backing, and because their necks fitted exactly the central holes in the backing's slate disc, they were glued into place as shown in the photograph (fig. 79,*a,b*). The Kaminaljuyu flares, however, were found mounted on cylindrical rods of copal (KJS, fig. 147,*h*) and they lay near a pair of jade flares at some distance from the sawed bead-set backings. The latter accompanied flares of copal (KJS, fig. 147,*h*). I therefore think it probable that the Uaxactun earplugs had perishable flares and that their miniature jade flares were set on equally perishable rods, perhaps protruding from the mouths of the postulated perishable flares. Whether or not this was the case, the near-

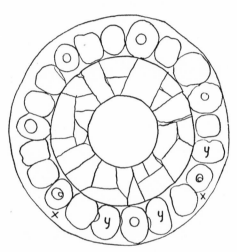

FIG. 28—JADE, SLATE, AND SHELL EARPLUG

In the section, black represents jade; hachure, slate; white, shell. Face view of backing shows arrangement of thin plates of jade mosaic (inner ring) and of thicker jades (outer ring), every third one of which, and perhaps all, were sections sawed from beads. For photos see fig. 79,*a,b*. Natural size.

shaped to perfect fit. In those marked *x* the plugs have been lost.

Lying with each backing was a miniature flare (fig. 28) with four tiny conical holes drilled from lower surface of face, the opening on upper surface being less than .1 cm. in diameter. A very slight cupping was drilled at upper orifice, apparently somewhat to enlarge it. In neck are two opposed conical perforations, drilled from exterior. Each flare has a slate throat-disc covered with fitted pieces of jade of same color as flare.

COMMENT. These two specimens, from either side of the skull in Burial A-29, a rich Tzakol tomb, are of special significance because of their extraordinarily close resemblance to objects found in the Esperanza phase Tomb A-IV at Kaminaljuyu, which produced two shell backings with an inner ring of mosaic and an outer ring of sawed beads (KJS,

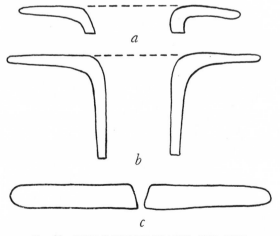

FIG. 29—JADE EARPLUG FLARES AND DISC

Sections. For photos see fig. 79,*c-f*. Natural size.

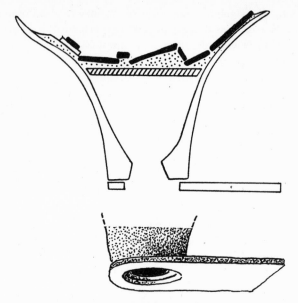

FIG. 30—JADE-INCRUSTED SHELL EARPLUG

a: Section (black represents jade; hachure, slate; dots, stucco; white, shell). For photos see fig. 70,*g-k*. *b*: Perspective of base. Natural size.

identity of the Uaxactun and Kaminaljuyu specimens indicates that both sets were products of the same school, perhaps even of the same workman, and whether they were made in the one place or the other, or were acquired from a third, they add to the steadily growing body of evidence that the Tzakol and Esperanza phases were contemporaneous.

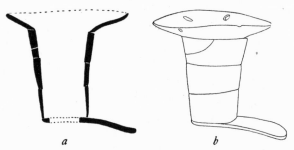

FIG. 31—SHELL EARPLUG

Salmon-colored stucco (largely scaled away and not shown in drawing) originally covered entire object, masking joints between elements and defects in flare. Scale ½.

Jade flares, 2. Larger one (figs. 29,*b;* 79,*f*), D 7.1 cm., H 2.7 cm. Court Gray mottled with Pea Green, Sage Green. Neck without side perforations well polished all over. Smaller (figs. 29,*a;* 79,*e*), D 6.1–6.5 cm., H .8 cm. Clouded (rather than sharply mottled) Mineral Gray and Vivid Green. Somewhat translucent. Face more highly polished than under side. In contour of face less regular than foregoing. Very short neck.

COMMENT. From rich Tzakol cache in Structure A-XVIII (p. 26), which also contained a large jade figurine (fig. 37) and eccentric flints (fig. 66,*d*). The two probably not a

pair, as flares found at the sides of skulls in burials at Kaminaljuyu and elsewhere, and therefore certainly pairs, normally match much more closely in size, shape, and color than do these cache specimens. The larger approximates the Kaminaljuyu Type A flare (KJS, fig. 143,*a*) but has no perforations in neck. The almost neckless one is apparently unique.

Jade discs, 2 (figs. 29,*c;* 79,*c,d*). D 7.2, 7.3 cm.; T .5, .6 cm. Celandine Green with slightly darker clouding. Surfaces even, well polished; edges rounded. Conical perforation at center. Small fragment from edge of a third closely similar disc is from fill of Structure A-II (fig. 80,*e,*6).

COMMENT. Having been found at the head of the skeleton in Burial A-66, Tzakol, these very well made discs doubtless were worn in the ears, but whether they comprised the entire ornaments or were backings for compound earplugs, the other parts of which had decayed, is unknown. Jade discs of about the same size and thickness, but with much larger central perforations, were found in the great cache at Cerro de las Mesas (Stirling, 1941, pl. VIII).

Shell earplugs, jade, shell, and hematite incrustation, pair (figs. 30; 79,*g,k*). D 7 cm., H 4.8 cm. Trumpet-mouth body a single piece of shell, apparently cut from a large conch. Backing (see fig. 30) a flat piece of shell, its inner end rounded to accommodate lower end of body and perforated to match body's lower opening. Slate disc (figs. 30,*a;* 79,*i*) with edge beveled to fit throat. Over disc and remainder of concave face was spread a layer of white plasterlike substance into which incrustation was embedded. Nose, in high relief, made of three triangular pieces of jade accurately fitted; eyes of jade rings with shining black crystalline hematite pupils; mouth (or nose-ornament?) a single jade oval. Horizontal forehead band overlaps eye-rings and upper end of nose. Rest of face of very thin jade plates. Beard (or fangs?) of equally thin plates. Ornament over face is a shell rectangle set with three small jade discs, a jade ring at each corner. Of rest of incrustation, of thin plates of darker jade, most had become detached, but enough loose pieces were found to have covered now nearly bare surface surrounding face. Many of them, like one still in place at right, were curved or otherwise shaped and it is probable that they formed part of a design. Pieces immediately to right of face overlap each other slightly, like scales of a fish. Although entire incrustation of second earplug had fallen away, its elements (triangular nose-pieces, eye-rings, "beard" pieces, etc.) so closely duplicate those of its better-preserved mate that the two were evidently identically decorated. With each were found flakes of green stucco which probably coated outer surfaces and backing.

COMMENT. These remarkable earplugs lay at the two sides of the skull in Burial A-31, Tzakol. The face seems surely to be that of Tlaloc.

Shell earplugs, pair, one very badly rotted (fig. 31). D

6.7 cm., H 6 cm. White shell. Flare a strongly concavo-convex disc, heavily attacked by parasitic marine worms; perforation shown in drawing may therefore not be artificial. Stem composed of three shell rings of decreasing diameter, a defect in the uppermost neatly patched. Backing an oval piece of shell with round perforation somewhat smaller than lowermost ring. All elements originally attached to each other with adhesive and whole specimen coated within and without with hard salmon-colored plaster which concealed joints between elements and ravages of parasitic worms. Much of this remains.

COMMENT. From Burial A-22, Tzakol. A pair of similarly constructed shell earplugs is from an Esperanza phase tomb at Kaminaljuyu (KJS, fig. 143,*d*). From the Pavon site, near Tampico, Ekholm (1944, p. 469) reports an earplug

80,*d*,4,5), D 2.3–2.7 cm., 2.4–2.5 cm. Narrow face sloping steeply into large mouth. Opposed conical perforations near base of neck. Pistachio Green. Traces of cinnabar in mouth.

Neck removed, 3 (fig. 32,*c-e*). Greatest L 2.4–2.5 cm., 2 vaguely rectangular, 1 triangular; all with radiating sawed lines on face. The rectangulars surely, the triangular probably, had had necks, which have been cut off. All are dark green, near Andover Green. Traces of cinnabar in radiating lines.

Without neck, 3 (fig. 80,*e*,1,3). Greatest L 1.7–2.5 cm., T .4–.6 cm. Irregular, flattish ovals. Never possessed necks. Oriental Green stone.

COMMENT. None of the above specimens is of the type represented by the miniature flares found with the jade-incrusted shell backings (figs. 28; 79,*a,b*), a type of which many examples were also found in the Esperanza tombs at Kaminaljuyu (KJS, figs. 146,*a-h*; 147,*a,h*). The latter, in some cases at least, were set on one end of a rodlike cylinder

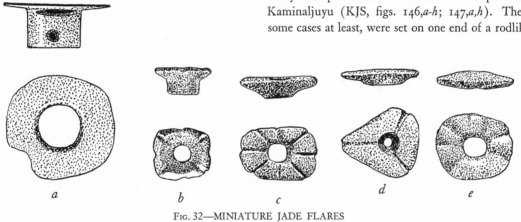

FIG. 32—MINIATURE JADE FLARES
D of *a*, 3.5 cm.

"made of two pieces: a short shell tube fitting at one end against a thin rectangular shell plaque."

MINIATURE FLARES

With neck, 5. *Largest* (fig. 32,*a*), D 3.5 cm.; a beautifully made piece, uniform Bottle Green color. Very thin, flat face breaking sharply into cylindrical neck. Two opposed conical holes near base of neck. On exterior of neck just below where it joins face are marks of sawing on four sides, one slightly cutting through neck. Whether these are remains of sawing done in original shaping of flare (see KJS, p. 124, fig. 153), one cut having unintentionally carried too deep, or whether neck was in process of removal, is uncertain, but three flares found with this one seem to have had necks sawed off (fig. 32,*c-e*). *Broken flare* (fig. 80,*e*,4), D 2.5 cm. Trumpet-shaped face, narrow neck mostly gone but had at least one conical perforation. Vetiver Green stone. *Very small flare* (fig. 32,*b*), rectangular face, 1.6 by 1.9 cm., with four radiating ornamental sawed lines; short, thick-walled neck. Dark Yellowish Green stone. *Pair of flares* (fig.

of copal or other substance (KJS, fig. 147,*h*) and, so mounted and held in position by pins introduced into their neck perforations, were presumably used as the forward-protruding elements of elaborate compound earplugs (cf. Spinden, 1913, figs. 8, 10; see also the noseplugs of serpents, his figs. 30, 42). The relatively large Uaxactun specimen (fig. 32,*a*) may have played the same role, or may originally have served as flare for a small, perhaps a child's, earplug. It was found with the six pieces that were neckless or had had the necks removed. These, it would seem, had studded a headband, as apparently did a group of similar objects from Piedras Negras (Mason, 1933). All seven came from Burial A-34, Tepeu horizon. Like three of these, the piece shown in figure 32,*b* has radiating lines on the face, but it still retains its neck. It is from Burial A-40, also Tepeu. The two large-mouthed miniature flares (fig. 80,*d*,4,5) from Burial A-23, Tepeu, are unlike any of the others. The perforations in their necks suggest, however, that they too may have been set on rods.

4

CARVED PENDANTS

Human face (fig. 33,*a*). H 5 cm. Unmottled Antique Green. Carving in broad, shallow lines. After carving and polishing, fine lines were incised to emphasize mouth, nose, forehead plate; to produce ovals over eyes and glyphlike device on forehead plate. Eyes inlaid with nacreous shell, inset pupils of crystalline hematite. Single transverse, biconical

shading to Elm Green. Well smoothed but unpolished. Eyes, mouth produced by small hollow drill; rest of carving in narrow straight lines. Biconical suspension holes connect back and sides, not visible from front. Burial A-49, Tepeu.

Human face (fig. 34,*b*). W 4.3 cm. Oriental Green with

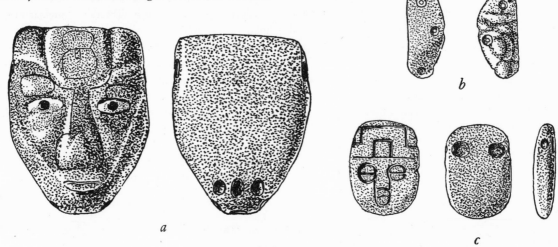

FIG. 33—CARVED JADE PENDANTS

a: Human face with shell and crystalline hematite eyes. *b*: Non-realistic (?) carving. *c*: Human face. Natural size.

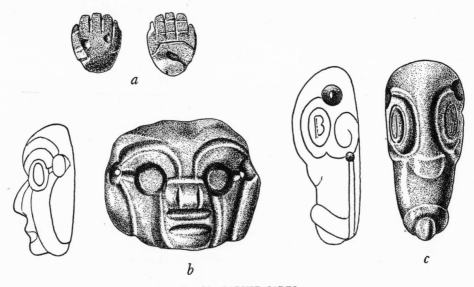

FIG. 34—CARVED JADES

a: Human hand. *b*: Human face. *c*: Alligator (?) head. Natural size.

perforation through forehead; three close-set, biconical borings through chin from back to under side, not visible from front.

COMMENT. Found in a cache, 2 m. below Temple Court floor under south doorway of Room 10, Tzakol. Doubtless designed to form the centerpiece of a necklace, the three chin holes for suspension of smaller ornaments.

Human face (fig. 33,*c*). H 2.6 cm. Light Elm Green

small areas of Vivid Green. Irregular waterworn pebble, back and edges unaltered. Naturally rounded front modified by broad, shallow lines, into which polish extends; eyes deeply cut with hollow drill. Biconical suspension holes at eye level.

COMMENT. The natural broad, flat shape of this piece of jade evidently suggested a face and the likeness was heightened by judicious carving, thereby economizing both work and precious material. Such adaptation was often practiced at Kaminaljuyu, but more commonly for profile than for full-front representations of human and animal forms (KJS, figs. 148, 149). In front view the large eyes and vertical nostrils give the present specimen a monkeylike appearance, but the prominent nose and nonprotruding mouth (see profile, fig. 34,*b*) are unmistakably human. Burial C-2, Tzakol.

Alligator (*?*) *head* (fig. 34,*c*). L 4.8 cm. A little darker than Mineral Green with distinct yellowish cast. Very shallow carving into which polish extends. Eyes in relief, with horizontal groove giving "coffee bean" effect. Lateral biconical perforation. On each side at corner of mouth a small conical drilling.

COMMENT. From Burial C-1, Tzakol. The identification as an alligator is of course uncertain; the curling element at the back of the mouth is seen in many Maya renderings of the serpent. The small drillings at the corners of the mouth are characteristic of La Venta jade carving. A piece similar to this in general shape and in possessing the roll crossing the end of the snout, but with hollow-drilled eyes, is from an Esperanza tomb at Kaminaljuyu (KJS, fig. 148,*b*). I have seen another in brown micaceous stone from the surface of a ruin at Piedra Parada, a few kilometers west of Guatemala City on the road to San Salvador (private collection). Other not dissimilar pendants (RR, pl. 67,*a,b*) were found at Uaxactun in Cist E-2, Tepeu; and under Stela 15, believed to date from late Baktun 8. Additional records of alligatorlike jade heads: Ratinlixul, Dept. of Quiche (Mason, 1927, fig. 7); Kendal, British Honduras (Gann, 1918, p. 92).

Small carved pendant (fig. 33,*b*). L 2.2 cm. Oriental Green. Same type of shallow carving as above. Small biconical perforations at top and middle of one edge; abandoned drilling from back at bottom. Possibly an attempt to represent an animal head. Burial A-40, Tepeu.

MISCELLANEOUS SMALL JADES

Plain pendant. L 2.3 cm., W 1.3 cm., T .4 cm. Antique Green. Thin oval, biconical perforation near one end; one side polished, other dull. Surface Group A.

Human hand (fig. 34,*a*). L 1.7 cm., T .3 cm. Vivid Green with small white cloudings. Very realistically rendered by a few sharply incised lines and sawed notches. Traces of drilling suggest that this piece may have been cut down from some different, earlier form. No means of suspension. From debris of Structure B-XIII. Period uncertain.

Loaf-shaped object (fig. 80,*e*,12). L 3.2 cm., T .8 cm. Andover Green. Flat bottom, strongly rounded top. Indifferently polished. Biconical perforation at each end, drilled from end and bottom to meet at an angle. Above floor, East Court.

Small loaf-shaped object (fig. 80,*e*,11). L 1.5 cm., T .8 cm. Glaucous. Shaped much like foregoing, but unperforated. Burial C-1, Tzakol.

Adorno (fig. 35,*b*). L 2.7 cm., T .6 cm. Andover Green, yellowish clouds. Back flat, face undulant. Well polished. Biconical perforation in center of deeply cut hollow-drill circle. Found in back-dirt from Structure A-V. Period unknown.

Fragment (fig. 35,*a*). L 2.5 cm., T 1.2 cm. Storm Gray. Lower side flat, unpolished; upper side strongly and evenly carved, well polished. Broken off at either end. Trench, west side of Structure B-XIII. Period unknown.

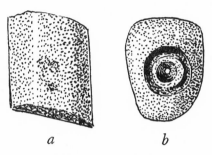

FIG. 35—SMALL JADES
a: Fragment of elongated object. *b*: Adorno. Natural size.

Jointed object, serpent (*?*), bird head (*?*), insect larva (*?*) (fig. 36). Total L 7.5 cm. Mottled Light Bice Green and Bice Green. Four pieces found, as assembled in drawing, at pelvis of Burial A-29, Tzakol. Presumably once attached to each other with adhesive. Upper surface of two larger segments polished, lower surface rough. "Tail" or "beak" pieces polished on all surfaces. A unique specimen.

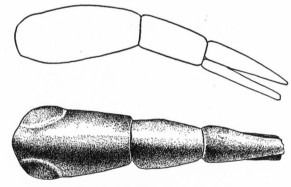

FIG. 36—JOINTED JADE OBJECT
Serpent (*?*), bird head (*?*). Natural size.

HUMAN EFFIGY

One (figs. 37, 74). H 26 cm. Most of body near Niagara Green, some parts brighter, upper part of head slightly tinged with brown. Left side of body, of shoulder, and of head with micaceous inclusions. Smooth, even finish but not highly polished. Thirteen pairs of conical holes, each pair meeting at an angle, junction only large enough to accommodate a thread. Pairs situated as follows: forehead, top of head, sides of top of head (2), sides of head above ears (2), upper side of forearms (2), lower side of wrists (2), calf of right leg, ankles (2). Nostrils indicated by similar pair of meeting holes. More ample biconical holes through ears. Fingers and fingernails and ornaments on forehead in accurately incised lines. Cheek ornaments (representing earplugs?) incised with slightly cutaway background. Alae

A-XVIII (see p. 26). The high, hairless head, elongated ears, nude body without navel, cursory treatment of limbs, and incised decorations are all characteristic of La Venta figurines in jade and other stones. The features, however, are not in the La Venta manner. Sr. Miguel Covarrubias,

FIG. 37—JADE EFFIGY
Cf. fig. 74.   H 26 cm.

of nose emphasized by curved incisions. Rectangular eye-depressions perhaps once held inlays, but when object was found were colored, as was mouth, with red oxide of iron.

COMMENT. This remarkable sculpture formed part of the Tzakol period cache of ceremonial objects in Structure

the leading student of La Venta art, has seen the drawings and photographs of the specimen. He agrees that it is in the La Venta tradition. The characteristics of La Venta sculpture are admirably defined in a recent paper by Covarrubias (1946).

MOSAIC

Although objects bearing jade mosaic had been present in a number of graves, they had for the most part been of materials that had decayed and the mosaic had fallen away, its elements becoming disarranged beyond hope of reassembly. The two pairs of shell earplugs already described (p. 42; fig. 79,*a,b,g*) were the only examples recovered in reasonably good preservation. They illustrate clearly the way in which such work was done. It should, perhaps, be called incrustation, for in the majority of cases only jade seems to have been employed, and there was little use of elements of contrasting colors to produce designs, as in true mosaic. Shell, however, entered into some of the arrangements, and even when nothing but jade was utilized the pieces were sometimes shaped and set in such a way as to form patterns.

Two sorts of elements occur at Uaxactun. The most common are little plates of jade, usually of fine color, from less than .1 cm. to a rare maximum of .2 cm. thick, highly polished on one side, dull on the other. They might be irregular in outline, cut to formal, straight-edged or curved shapes, or fashioned into more elaborate forms. The second, rarer, type of element, apparently never combined with the foregoing, are pieces of poorer color, .3–.5 cm. thick, often with rough edges, but with one side well polished. It will suffice to describe one example of each sort and to state merely the general nature and provenience of the others.

Mosaic of thin plates (fig. 82,*d*). About 175 mosaic elements of jade and a number of shaped pieces of shell, many rotted beyond recovery, were found in the lap of a seated male skeleton (Burial C-1, Tzakol). As the skull was also in the lap, it was at first thought that the jade and shell might have formed the decoration of a mosaic mask. But laboratory study showed them to have been parts of a large circular object, probably a breast ornament, for there were just enough pieces with the correct curvature to have been set in a circle with outer diameter of 10 cm. There were also enough narrower pieces to have made a less certain inner circle (see fig. 82,*d*), and sufficient other bits to have filled the center. Some of the latter were of odd shapes, doubtless elements of a design in which the shell probably also played a part. The jade elements were of clear gray-green stone. There were, in addition, a few small, round, flat-based convex-topped pieces of brilliant green jade, like much of that from Kaminaljuyu. In the same lot were thin, flat bits of a greenish substance, perhaps adhesive or possibly stucco from the back of the ornament, the body of which was presumably wood.

Mosaic of large, thick plates (fig. 86,*b*). Nearly 100 pieces lay at the pelvic region of the extended male skeleton of Burial A-29, Tzakol. The largest of these measures 3.5 by 2.7 cm. and range in thickness from .3 to .5 cm. One side of each is faintly convex and well polished, the other

flat and dull. The edges of some are rounded, of others rough. In color the stone is a gray-green, with darker veins and mottlings. There was no way of determining how these elements were set, but there were enough of them to have covered a sizable ornament. It is conceivable that the strange jointed jade object (fig. 36), also found at the pelvis of Burial A-29, may have had some connection with these plates.

Other finds of mosaic elements: Burial A-29, not directly associated with the foregoing: 27 pieces of the thin, fine type, bright green, some rectangular, one circular. Tzakol.

Burial A-20: 30 or more (some broken) pieces of thin type, mostly gray-green, one bright green; 25 pieces flat and dull on one side, convex and polished on other, one conically perforated. These perhaps sawed from beads as were those of the incrusted earplugs (fig. 79,*a,b*). Tzakol.

Burial B-1: miscellaneous lot containing: 2 pieces of jade and fragment of another, whole pieces about 2 by 3 cm., one .1 cm. thick, the other .2 cm., both with raw edges, well polished on one side; small oval piece of jade polished on both sides; several pieces of badly corroded pyrite. This assemblage possibly from a disintegrated pyrite-incrusted plaque, a type of ornament sometimes bearing jade incrustation (see KJS, p. 127). Tzakol.

In cache pot, Structure A-I: 17 typical thin plates, 2 jade discs D .8 cm. Period uncertain.

General digging, not associated with burials or caches: fragment of disc (fig. 80,*e*,6); rough-edged piece, indifferently polished (fig. 80,*e*,5); thin triangular piece (fig. 80,*e*,8); small square piece, highly polished one side; piece of thick type, 2 by 3 cm., both surfaces polished, one much more highly than other (fig. 80,*e*,9).

Grooved elements, 10 (fig. 80,*e*,10). Whether or not these should be considered mosaic elements is uncertain, but as they are not perforated it is probable that they were set on some sort of backing, possibly a bracelet (cf. KJS, p. 116, fig. 147,*i*). Four are vaguely rectangular, L 1.2–1.5 cm., W 1–1.1 cm., T .3–.5 cm., blue-green; five oval, L 1.4–1.7 cm., W 1–1.3, T .3–.5 cm., yellowish green. Each has two longitudinal grooves. One of the oval pieces has a longitudinal biconical groove on the back, perhaps half the perforation of a bead that had been cut in two; it also differs from the others in that there is a protuberant ridge between the two grooves, and on this are two short crossgrooves (upper right, fig. 80,*e*,10). Burial A-48, Tepeu.

BEADS

Subspherical, 118 (figs. 38,*a,b*; 39,*a,d*; 80,*a*; 80,*b*,3,5–7, 10,11,13–28; 80,*d*, except 4,5; RR, pl. 67,*a,b*). Smallest (figs. 38,*a*; 80,*b*,7), D .6 cm.; T .4 cm. Largest (figs. 38,*b*; 80,*b*,24), D 3.6 cm., T 2.5 cm. Almost perfect gradation between these extremes, commonest size about midway. An unstandardized lot: a very few nearly perfect spheres (figs.

80,*b*,27; 80,*c*), some flattish (figs. 80,*a*; 80,*d*,1–3,17), some irregular in outline (fig. 80,*b*,17,23). Biconical perforation standard (exceptions shown in fig. 39,*a-d*). In most cases well polished. Only one subspherical bead bears decoration (figs. 80,*b*,5; 80,*d*,9): on either side a small incised circle, apparently not hollow drill work, in which is a tiny scroll; between circles a pair of very small conical drillings .1 cm. deep. Almost all subspherical beads of gray-green stone; handsomely colored light or dark greens rare. Descriptions of individual beads of this and following categories are contained in the Uaxactun catalog on file at the Peabody Museum of Harvard University.

and one of 78 disc-beads from Burial E-9, Mamom (RR, pl. 63,*b*). There were seldom more than one or two beads in a grave, or more than one in a cache (see table of occurrences, p. 51). They occurred in Mamom, Tzakol, and Tepeu graves; no jade could surely be assigned to Chicanel, but this is probably due to the fact that so few and such poorly equipped graves of that phase were found. There seem to have been no significant changes in form or nature of stone from early to late. Only one example with a single conical boring occurred (fig. 39,*b*); that method of perforation was very common at Kaminaljuyu (KJS, p. 111; fig. 46,*b*).

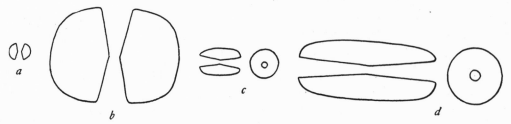

FIG. 38—JADE BEADS

Sections. *a,b*: Smallest and largest subspherical. *c,d*: Smallest and largest barrel-shaped (longitudinal and transverse). Natural size.

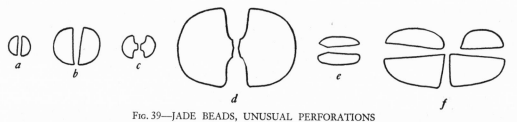

FIG. 39—JADE BEADS, UNUSUAL PERFORATIONS

Sections. *a*: Cylindrical. *b*: Single conical. *c*: Biconical with secondary cylindrical. *d*: Biconical with secondary biconical. *e*: Biconical, unequal lengths. *f*: Triple conical with natural cavity. Natural size.

COMMENT. The subspherical form was standard for jade beads throughout Mesoamerica. Such beads were normally not of the best grades of stone, but those of Uaxactun are unusually poor, both in color and regularity of contour. They were also relatively rare, considering the number of

FIG. 40—FLARED TUBULAR JADE BEAD

Natural size.

burials opened. There were no long necklaces of beads of this type such as those of the Esperanza tombs at Kaminaljuyu (KJS, p. 111; fig. 152), the only jade necklaces being one of 29 subspherical beads from Burial A-20, Tzakol,

Barrel-shape, 10 (figs. 38,*c,d*; 39,*e,f*; 80,*b*,1–4; 80,*c*; RR, pl. 63,*d*). Smallest (figs. 38,*c*; 80,*b*,4), L 1.4 cm., D .8 cm. Largest (figs. 38,*d*; 80,*c*), L 3.3 cm., D 1.6 cm. Considerable variation in proportions, but greatest diameter usually at middle. Round to oval in transverse section. Biconical perforation. Stone and finish average finer than in subsphericals.

COMMENT. These specimens are referred to by Mrs. Ricketson (RR, p. 195) and in the Uaxactun catalog as "tubular" or "subtubular," but it seems best to distinguish them from the truly tubular, i.e. cylindrical or nearly cylindrical, beads with square ends which occur elsewhere but of which none came to light at Uaxactun. The barrel-shaped beads were found in Mamom, Tzakol, and Tepeu graves.

Flared-end tubular, 1 (fig. 40; RR, fig. 127,*a*). L 2.8 cm. Storm Gray to white. Biconical perforation. Lower end square (somewhat damaged). Round in section, tapers very slightly. Well polished.

COMMENT. Differs from Kaminaljuyu examples (KJS, fig. 150,*a*) in that the flare is wider and more abrupt and that there is no encircling groove just below it. The

Kaminaljuyu beads are also less perfectly round in section. Tzakol.

Disc beads. None found save single string with the Mamom Burial E-9 (RR, p. 196; pl. 63,*b*).

OCCURRENCES OF JADE

As mortuary offerings:

BURIAL	AGE AND SEX	NATURE OF SPECIMENS	CERAMIC PHASE
E-3	Ad.m.	2 beads (RR, fig. 127,*d,e*)	Mamom
E-9	Ad.	78 beads (RR, pl. 63,*b*)	
E-10	Inf.	1 bead (RR, pl. 63,*d*)	Chicanel
A-20	Ad.	29 subsph. beads (3003); 30 mosaic plates (3013,14)	Tzakol
A-22	Ad.m.	15 beads (figs. 80,*a*; 80,*d*,8), 2 earplugs (fig. 27)	"
A-29	Ad.m.?	13 beads (fig. 80,*b*,1,3–6), serpent (?) (fig. 36), earplugs (fig. 79,*a,b*); 93 mosaic plates (fig. 86,*b*)	"
A-31	Ad.m.	4 beads (fig. 80,*b*,10,15,17,20), 14 flat rough beads (3532-43), earplugs (fig. 79,*g*)	"
A-66	Inf.	1 bead (fig. 80,*b*,13), 1 oval bead (4610), 2 discs (fig. 79,*c,d*)	"
B-2	Ad.f.	7 beads (fig. 80,*c*)	"
C-1	Ad.m.	5 barrel-shaped beads (1408,10); mosaic plates (fig. 82,*d*), pendant (fig. 34,*c*)	"
E-4	Inf.	71 pieces scrap jade (RR, pp. 170, 197)	"
E-21	Ad.	9 beads, 2 miniature flares (RR, p. 150; pl. 67,*a,c*)	"
C-2	Ad.f.?	1 pendant (fig. 34,*b*)	"
A-2	Ad.m.	2 subsph. beads (994)	Tepeu
A-6	Ad.m.	1 subsph. bead (1125)	"
A-16	Child	2 barrel-shaped beads (1892,3), 1 small flare (fig. 80,*e*,4)	"
A-23	Ad.	1 bead (fig. 80,*d*,9), 2 miniature flares (fig. 80,*d*,4,5)	"
A-34	Ad.m.?	7 miniature flares (figs. 32,*a,c-e*; 80,*e*, 1,3)	"
A-40	Ad.m.	2 subsph. beads (3668,9), miniature flare (fig. 32,*b*), pendant (fig. 33,*b*)	"
A-41	Ad.f.	1 subsph. bead (3790)	"
A-43	Ad.m.	3 beads (fig. 80,*b*,2,12,22)	"
A-45	Ad.m.	2 subsph. beads (4001,2)	"
A-48	Inf.	10 grooved objects (fig. 80,*e*,10)	"
A-49	Child	1 pendant (fig. 33,*c*)	"

In caches:

No.	LOCATION	NATURE OF SPECIMENS	CERAMIC PHASE
A-16	Str. A-I,B	1 subsph. bead (1403)	Chicanel
A-15	" ",C	1 " " (1304)	Tzakol
A-6	" ",D	1 " " (1012,b)	"
A-24	Str. A-V,Ic	1 " " (4154), 1 pendant (fig. 33,*a*)	"
A-31	Str. A-XVIII	1 bead (fig. 80,*b*,26), 2 earplug flares (fig. 79,*e,f*), 1 figurine (fig. 37)	
B-8	Stela 4	1 undrilled bead, 1 pendant, 5 unworked frags. (RR, p. 159; pl. 67,*e*)	"
D-1	Stela 15	1 bead, 1 pendant (RR, p. 162; pl. 67,*b*)	"
D-2	Stela 16	1 subsph. bead (1014)	Tepeu
E-5	Str. E-VII,Cist 11	3 beads (RR, p. 152; fig. 126,*a,d,e*)	Tzakol
E-6	Str. E-VII,Cist 12	1 cylindrical bead (RR, p. 72, fig. 127)	"
B-2	Str. B-XI,Pit 1	3 pieces crude jade, 1 bead (uncat.)	"
C-1	Str. C-I	1 piece crude jade (uncat.)	"
A-3	A-I,E	1 subsph. bead (1014)	Tepeu
A-4	" "	2 small beads, 17 unworked bits (1010)	"
A-37	Stela A-15	4 beads (fig. 80,*b*,18,19,20, 24)	"

GENERAL COMMENT ON JADES. As we have seen, jade was in use throughout the occupancy of Uaxactun. It served solely for ornaments and all that was recovered, save a few odd beads and scraps, came from graves or ceremonial caches (see above table of occurrences). The specimens are, on the whole, an unimpressive lot, rather few in number, limited in range of forms. Workmanship is not outstanding, little of the stone is of gem quality. Especially noteworthy is the entire lack of beautiful carvings such as plaques bearing low-relief human figures seated cross-legged and half-round, full-front representations of typical Maya faces (see Kelemen, 1943, pls. 238,*b*; 240,*c,d,f*; 241,*b,d*; 245,*h*). Pieces of this sort seem certainly to have been products of the Classic Maya; their absence from Uaxactun, an important city in the very heart of the Classic Maya area, is puzzling. It may, of course, have been due to niggardliness in the matter of mortuary offerings and caches. The great distance that separated Uaxactun from any source of raw material may have caused a lack of interest in jade carving. But even if there had been no local school of craftsmen it is strange that no fine pieces were imported, for we know that jade was widely disseminated in trade. Perhaps the most probable explanation is that the best work was done in some other part of the Maya area at a relatively late period and that failure to find examples was due to the fact that all the Tepeu graves discovered at Uaxactun were modest interments, presumably of persons not sufficiently important to have been accorded offerings of precious imported jewels. At the nearby site of Holmul, however, graves of Holmul V, a period equating chronologically with Tepeu, and containing the bodies of individuals evidently of distinction, held no outstanding jades (Merwin and Vaillant, 1932). As a matter of fact, little jade was found in any Holmul grave, nor did much appear at San Jose, British Honduras (Thompson, 1939). Gann's many excavations in various parts of British Honduras did not produce any great amounts of jade. Thus, although little digging has been done in central Peten, it seems that wealth of this stone was not characteristic of that apparently nuclear region of the Classic Maya area.

That the plaques, beads, and other fine pieces were late and that they were not turned out in central Peten are, of course, assumptions, for the provenience and date of jades are at present almost impossible to ascertain because of their above-mentioned wide distribution in trade and also because they were often long treasured as heirlooms before finally coming to rest in tombs, caches, or such sacrificial deposits as the Sacred Cenote at Chichen Itza. Furthermore, no single specimen of this type, so far as I know, has been found in a controlled excavation. Nevertheless, their great sophistication and their stylistic resemblance to stone sculptures of the second half of the Classic Period convince me that they were made during the era characterized at Uaxactun by Tepeu pottery. And, again on stylistic grounds, I would guess that the center of their manufacture was the Usumacinta valley. The assignment by Miss Proskouriakoff (1944) to Piedras Negras of a head from the Sacred Cenote, which is executed in this style, and its tentative dating at around 9.14.0.0.0 bear out that supposition. Also several specimens of the fine type are from Ococingo, not overly distant from the Usumacinta cities.

To return to the jades found at Uaxactun, only a few can be related to specimens from other regions. The figurine (fig. 37), as already mentioned, has strong La Venta traits. The micaceous stone of which it is made is apparently not found, however, in any other example of La Venta style. Its presence in a cache laid down in Tzakol times seems to bear out a feeling (KJS, p. 257) that the remarkable La Venta development should be equated chronologically with the first half of the Maya Classic Period, but there is always the likelihood that such an object may have been centuries old when it was cached. Final solution of the problems of the age of the La Venta culture and of its relationship to that of the Maya will presumably have to be made on the basis of ceramic studies rather than on occurrences of La Venta jades.

Very close resemblances exist between the earplug backings set with sawed jade beads (fig. 79,a,b) and those from Kaminaljuyu. The same is true of the miniature flares found with them. The mosaics of Uaxactun are also much like those of Kaminaljuyu. Only one Uaxactun subspherical bead, on the other hand, was perforated by a single conical bore, a very common practice at Kaminaljuyu. Other differences are the lack, at Uaxactun, of large carved beads made of waterworn pebbles whose original shape was little altered (KJS, figs. 148, 149), of large uncarved "blobs" (KJS, fig. 151,d), of cylindrical beads (KJS, fig. 150), and of Type B flares (KJS, fig. 145,a,b). Extremely few Uaxactun jades are of the beautiful clear light green and emerald green stone so characteristic of Kaminaljuyu.

PYRITE

Beads, 32 (fig. 25). Thick discoidal, biconical perforation, aperture at junction of bores about .1 cm. D .45–.9 cm., T .3–.5 cm. One egg-shaped, L .7 cm. biconical perforation at small end (fig. 25,c). Brownish black matrix with specks of "fool's gold." Burial B-2, Tzakol.

Worked piece, 1. Shape of miniature celt. L 1.7 cm., greatest D 1.6 cm., T .8 cm. Burial A-41, Tepeu.

COMMENT. In view of the rich mortuary offerings in a number of the Uaxactun burials, it is strange that no certain pyrite-incrusted plaques came to light, for these objects have been found in the more pretentious tombs in many parts of Mesoamerica and were particularly common at Kaminaljuyu and in Alta Verapaz sites inhabited during the centuries during which Uaxactun was occupied. Only a single doubtful specimen was found in the several rich graves at Holmul. These plaques, therefore, seem not to have been much in use, or at least not favored as funerary offerings, in central Peten. A few examples, however, have been noted from British Honduras and one from Piedras Negras. The distribution of pyrite-incrusted plaques is discussed in KJS, p. 132.

CRYSTALLINE HEMATITE

The largest find of this black mineral was made in the rich Burial A-20, Tzakol. It consisted of 75 pieces from .2 by .3 cm. up to 1.5 by 2.5 cm. in area and varying little from .1 cm. thick. Their surfaces are true planes. One side of each has a glassy luster, reflecting as perfectly as the finest mirror; the other is dull and bears series of fine parallel scratches, often in crisscross order. The edges of many have been worked smooth, but they are irregular, rather than straight and beveled as are the pyrite plates of incrusted plaques (see KJS, p. 127). There are enough to have covered an area about 6 cm. square if, as seems probable, they had been used as elements in a mosaic. Several small pieces of the same substance worked in the same way were in Cache B-2, Tzakol; and two in Cache B-8 under Stela 4 (8.15.0.0.0?). Similar plates were set on the face of an earplug from Kaminaljuyu (KJS, fig. 143,g).

LIGNITE (?)

Three small bits of a soft, light black mineral formed part of Cache A-4, Tepeu.

ROCK CRYSTAL

Single small, irregular piece. Burial C-1, Tzakol.

COMMENT. In Mesoamerica, this beautifully limpid stone failed to come into its own as raw material for ornaments and small sculptures until after Classic times. There seem to be no records at all of such objects from Middle Culture sites and but one from a Classic Maya site, a single spherical bead found in a pair of Spondylus shells at Copan (information from G. Strömsvik). Only by the supremely skillful lapidaries of Central Mexico who, as we have seen, also achieved such remarkable results with obsidian, was rock crystal extensively utilized. Most famous of their products is the full-size skull in the British Museum (Kelemen, 1943, pl. 255,b). There are small skulls from Texmilincan, Guerrero (Garcia Payon, 1941, figs. 6–8) and others, presumably from in or near the Valley of Mexico (Univ. Pa. Mus., Mason, 1943, fig. 9; Musée de l'Homme, Nuñez y Dominguez, 1942, fig. 11; Mus. Amer. Ind.; and several in Mex.

Nat. Mus.). Other carvings represent frogs (Kelemen, 1943, pl. 256,*a*; several more are in Mex. Nat. Mus.) and rabbits (Toscano, 1944, p. 297). I seriously doubt the authenticity of the "man in the moon" possessed by the Musée de l'Homme (Kelemen, 1943, pl. 256,*b*). There is a superb rock crystal goblet, some 11 cm. high, from Tomb 7 at Monte Alban (Kelemen, 1943, pl. 255,*a*). Earplugs of the spool type are from the same tomb (Oaxaca Mus.), from the Valley of Mexico and Ojitlan, Oaxaca (Mex. Nat. Mus.), and from Ejutla, Oaxaca (Mus. Amer. Ind.). Other personal ornaments are "top hat" labrets, probably from the Valley of Mexico (Mex. Nat. Mus., Amer. Mus. Nat. Hist., Chicago Nat. Hist. Mus.), biconically perforated spherical and subspherical beads averaging 2 cm. in diameter (Valley of Mexico, Mex. Nat. Mus.; Chichen Itza, High Priest's grave, a very fine string, Thompson and Thompson, 1938, fig. 17,*b*; Labna, from a chultun, E. H. Thompson, 1897a, pl. X; Dept. of Santa Rosa, Guatemala, Mus. Amer. Ind.), a fragmentary tubular bead about 1.5 cm. in diameter (Chichen Itza, Sacred Cenote, Peabody Mus. Harvard), uncarved pear-shaped and triangular pendants (Valley of Mex.,

Mex. Nat. Mus.; Gualupita, Morelos, from a late deposit, S. B. and G. C. Vaillant, 1934, fig. 7; Jiquilpan, Michoacan, Noguera, 1944, figs. 20, 22). Rock crystal seems seldom to have been worked in highland Guatemala in spite of the fact that the material is common in Baja Verapaz (Sierra de Chuacus and vicinity of Salama, Termer quoted by Dutton and Hobbs, 1943, p. 55 and information from Robert Sayre). Lothrop (1936, fig. 63,*b*) figures a small egg-shaped object said to be from Zacualpa and there is a thick, crudely chipped point about 9 cm. long from Alta Verapaz (Univ. Pa. Mus.); a single small pendant was found by A. L. Smith in a tomb contemporaneous with late Tzakol, at Nebaj, Quiche. Unworked crystals, however, have been found at Tajumulco, and in that vicinity they still form part of the equipment of Mam shamans (Dutton and Hobbs, 1943, p. 55); one was taken from a cave at Campur, Alta Verapaz, by Seler (1904, p. 90); another from a late Classic grave at Tzimin Kax, British Honduras (Thompson, 1931, p. 314); and Strong (1935, pp. 49, 111) reports them from ceremonial caches in the Bay Islands off the north coast of Honduras.

2

Objects of Bone

The collection of bone implements and of unworked bones is not extensive. That this is to some extent due to the perishability of bone under tropical conditions is suggested by the fact that most of the bone specimens came from rooms and from architectural fill, situations in which they were more or less protected from moisture. Conversely, little bone was found in the surface refuse that produced so large a percentage of the stone objects. Even so, however, there is less bone material than one might expect. Its relative rarity might have been caused by paucity of game in a thickly inhabited region. But, on the other hand, if the milpa system of agriculture was being practiced—and there is good reason to suppose that it was—large tracts of land must constantly have been in process of reforestation and have provided cover for all sorts of animals and birds, as is the case today even in well-populated parts of Yucatan. A third factor that should also be taken into account is the abundance in the Peten of extremely hard woods which could have served quite as effectively as bone for awls, scrapers, flakers, etc.

Because it is so subject to decay, there is little likelihood that we shall ever obtain collections of bone that are adequately representative of all Mesoamerican periods and cultures. It is therefore improbable that it will become as important an archaeological criterion as ceramics or artifacts of stone. Nevertheless, all specimens should be recorded,

for they can throw light on some aspects of technology, of art, and of cult practices which are not illustrated by objects of other materials. And in a region such as Mesoamerica, in which time has dealt so severely with all products of human hands, every scrap of evidence as to ancient customs and ceremonies is precious.

AWLS

Mammal Bone

Metapodials, 4 (fig. 82,*c*,1–4). L 6.8–14.3 cm. Made from metapodials, apparently of deer, split on median anterior-posterior line, remaining half of articular end left unaltered, but edges of shaft smoothed and shaft tapered to sharp point, round in section. One with carved butt (fig. 82,*c*,4).

Unidentifiable bones, 20 (fig. 82,*c*,6–12; RR, fig. 134,*c*). All either too fragmentary or with articular ends too much worked down to permit identification. L (few complete) from 7.5 to over 13 cm. Made from heavy-walled bones, apparently mostly split metapodials. Worked all over, but some trace of central canal usually remains; and although actual points of most specimens lost, nature of shaft's taper indicates two sorts of points: sharp, round in section (10 cases, fig. 82,*c*,6–9; 6,7 are pointed at both ends); less acute, flat in section (10 cases, fig. 82,*c*,10–12). Points of the few of latter class that retain whole of flattened tip show considerable wear, as if used for some purpose other than perforating.

Fragments of shafts, 7. Presumably of awls of above types.

Unidentifiable bones, carved, 8 (fig. 41,*c-j*). L of *c,* only complete specimen, 17.9 cm. Whether these objects actually served as awls, or whether they were ornamental pins for hair or costume, is unknown. The complete piece is from Burial A-45, Tzakol; the others from refuse or structural fill.

Human Bone

Two. (1) L 34.5 cm. Adult femur (fig. 84,*b*), apparently male, split on median anterior-posterior line. Half distal articular end serves as butt; about two-thirds of shaft worked away at butt; from there shaft tapers gradually to round-section point. (2) L (point missing) 29 cm. Adult fibula (fig. 41,*a*), apparently male. Whole distal articular end remains. Upper part of shaft much thinned and rounded but central canal not exposed; at 11 cm. from butt canal cut into and from that point downward shaft is progressively

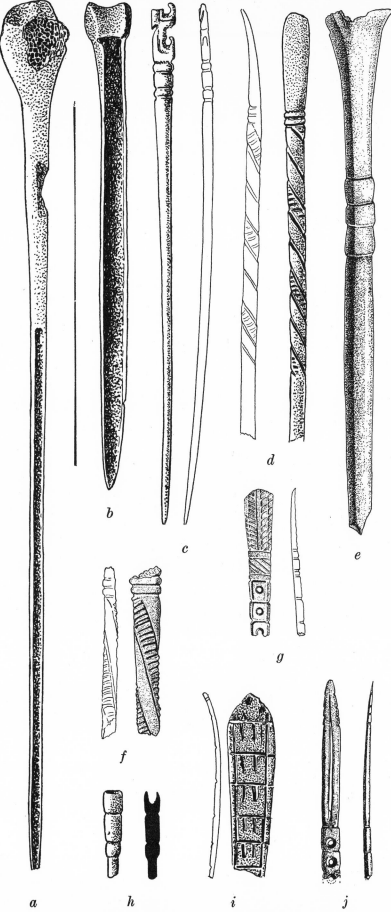

a   *h*   *i*   *j*

Fig. 41—BONE AWLS AND CARVED BONES

a: Awl cut from human fibula. *b*: Awl of bird bone (photo fig. 86,*m*). *c*: Awl-like object with carved butt. *d-j*: Fragmentary carved bones, apparently of awl form. L of *a*, 29.7 cm.

tapered until only about one-eighth remains at break. Point probably of flat type. Articular end and first 12 cm. of shaft painted red.

BIRD BONE

Three (figs. 41,*b*; 82,*c*,13). L of only complete specimen 16.6 cm. Ulna of large bird, articular end unworked, shaft

FIG. 42—BONE SMOOTHING OR RUBBING TOOL

Scale ½.

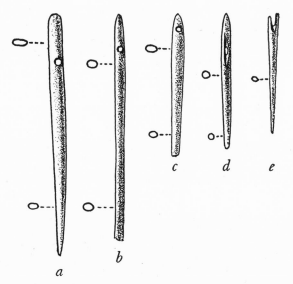

a   *b*   *c*   *d*   *e*

FIG. 43—BONE NEEDLES

Note drilled eye of *a-c*, scraped eye of *d,e*. Natural size.

split and a little more than half removed. Point flat. Other two fragments apparently from similar implements.

FLAKERS (?)

Three. One, L 11 cm. Rough splinter of thick-walled bone, one end bluntly conical and scratched as if by use in flaking. Other two, L 13.2, 13.5 cm., resemble deer-metapodial awls, but points are blunt and somewhat scored.

SMOOTHER

One (fig. 42). L 10.8 cm. Broad fragment of heavy bone, perhaps human femur; fractured edges left raw, but softened by use; ends V-shaped in section and highly polished, apparently by service in smoothing or rubbing.

NEEDLES

EYE DRILLED

Four (fig. 43,*a-c*). L of only whole specimen 6.5 cm., others apparently about same length. Thick oval in section, point keen. Eyes cylindrically drilled, D .1–.2 cm. Well finished, delicate implements.

EYE SCRAPED

Four (fig. 43,*d,e*). L of only whole specimen 3.7 cm., but broken examples indicate lengths up to 7 cm. Perforated end flatter, shaft more nearly round in section, than needles with drilled eyes. Eye made by scraping longitudinally from both sides until narrow oval aperture was produced.

COMMENT. Whether or not the above types differed in function is unknown. There seems to have been no chronological distinction, as specimens of each sort were found in both Tzakol and Tepeu deposits. Furthermore, Tomb I at Copan held one example of each type (Peabody Mus. Harvard) and both occurred in Period V deposits at the Las Flores site in the Panuco region on the Gulf coast of Mexico (Ekholm, 1944, p. 485, fig. 53,*o-t*). Needles with scraped holes were found by E. H. Thompson (1897, fig. 15) in the Loltun Cave in Yucatan. These and the Las Flores examples appear to be the only ones of this type that have been recorded from Mexico. Those from the Middle Culture site at Ticoman are drilled (Vaillant, 1931, pl. XC), as are those from Teotihuacan (Gamio, 1922, pl. 119,*c*; Linné, 1934, figs. 333–35; 1942, figs. 261, 291) and Tenayuca (Noguera, 1935a, pl. LV, 14). It may be significant that no true needles were found in Group E, where most of the artifacts recovered came from early (Mamom) deposits. All Group E eyed implements were broader and flatter and so are better termed bodkins (RR, p. 206).

BODKIN

One (cf. RR, fig. 134,*d,e*). L (broken at eye) probably 5 cm., W .7 cm. Broader and flatter than the needles. Eye scraped from both sides. This specimen is from a Tepeu horizon in Pit 14, whereas the bodkins from Group E were all from the subplaza Mamom midden. One of the Group E bodkins (RR, fig. 134,*d*) is unique in possessing a scraped perforation at each end.

SPINDLE WHORL (?)

One (fig. 84,*a*,3). D 3.2 cm., T .5 cm. Cut from skull, apparently human. That the .5-cm. perforation is cylindrical rather than biconical and therefore well adapted to accommodate a spindle shaft adds to the probability that this is a whorl.

TUBULAR BONE OBJECTS

Thirty-two (figs. 44;81,*b-d;* RR, fig. 135). Although certain of these specimens probably served as beads, others as whistles, and some perhaps as hafts or batons, identification in any given case is so doubtful and the pieces differ so widely that I have not attempted a classification. All, however, are alike in being sections of hollow bones (for remarks on methods of cutting, see Dr. Ricketson's discussion of worked human bones on p. 58).

PENDANTS

Two. One (fig. 45) a very neatly and realistically carved representation of a deer hoof; the other (fig. 84,*a,*2) a two-pronged object apparently cut from the articular end of a long-bone or from a vertebra, D of drilled perforations in prongs .4 cm.

SMALL ORNAMENTS

In two piles behind the head of the extended skeleton in Burial A-2, Tepeu (R. E. Smith, 1937, fig. 8) were 230 little bone objects, apparently of bird bone (fig. 46). Most of them were rotted and broken, but from the fragments and a few nearly whole specimens it could be determined that all were closely alike, exactly 2.3 cm. long, with four notches at the thinner end, an incised V in which were tiny drilled punctations, the thicker end plain or with a smaller V. As they have no suspension holes, they could not have been strung as a necklace; and their curving backs and thin ends render them unsuitable for inlays. Nothing similar has been recorded.

PERFORATED ANIMAL TEETH

Twenty-three (fig. 81,*a*). Molars of large dog, whole or cut vertically in two, 4 (1–4); tusks of peccary, 3 (11,12); canines of carnivors, 16 (5–10, 13–19), among which are identifiable those of puma, ocelot, and dog. In each case a single biconical suspension hole was drilled through root.

COMMENT. In spite of the fact that the perforated teeth undoubtedly served as ornaments, only 10 of the 23 were in graves, 8 in Burial A-45, Tepeu (fig. 81,*a*,10–15, 2 too badly rotted to photograph), 2 in Burial A-46, Tepeu (6,16). Three of the dog molars were in a Tepeu cache with *Marginella apicina* shells and snake vertebrae (fig. 82,*b*). The rest were single finds in Tzakol and later deposits. For discussion of the use of perforated teeth in Mesoamerica, see KJS, p. 155.

FIG. 44—CARVED BONE
Possibly a three-stop whistle. Scale ½.

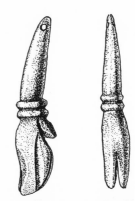

FIG. 45—BONE PENDANT
Represents deer hoof. Natural size.

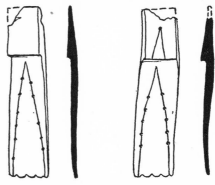

FIG. 46—BONE ORNAMENTS
Twice natural size.

PORTIONS OF HUMAN SKULL, WORKED

Two. One (Stratum 2, Pit 14, a Tzakol deposit) frontal portion of adult skull, strong frontal deformation. Supraorbital ridges and root of nose form front, but edges there are raw and facial portions may originally have been attached. Coronal suture forms rear edge; this and sides worked smooth. At center of rear edge a .3-cm. broken-through (not drilled) hole and what seem to be beginnings of two drilled holes on inner surface 1.5 cm. forward of center of coronal suture. Second specimen (East Terrace, Group B, period uncertain) same portion of adult skull, also with strong frontal deformation. All edges worked.

COMMENT. If the facial bones once formed part of the first piece, it may have served as backing for a human face modeled in stucco. Skulls or parts thereof (the rear portions of both are lost) were so used in two specimens from the Quiche region (Rossbach coll., Guatemala Nat. Mus.; see Muños, 1941; KJS, p. 154). These were probably architectural embellishments, and the skulls may be presumed to be those of sacrificed persons. In Yucatan, at the time of the conquest, however, the skulls of the distinguished dead were sometimes supplied with an artificial face. Landa (1941, p. 131) describes the process as follows: "They used to cut off the heads of the old lords of Cocom, when they died, and after cooking them they cleaned off the flesh, and then sawed off half the crown on the back, leaving the front part with the jaws and teeth. Then they replaced the flesh which was gone from these half-skulls by a kind of bitumen, which gave them a perfect appearance characteristic of those whose skulls they were."

I suspect that a similar custom may have obtained at Uaxactun, because of the above-described fragments and because of the fact that the frontal portions of the skulls of three adult skeletons (Burials A-20, A-22, B-12) had been removed. The individuals in Burials A-20 and A-22, both Tzakol interments, were evidently persons of much importance. Burial B-12 was a simple inhumation of Chicanel times. Not only had the skull been cut, but both femora were missing (RR, p. 145, fig. 99). This is of interest in connection with the transected human long-bones, on which Dr. Ricketson has prepared the following notes.

CUT HUMAN LONG-BONES

Oliver G. Ricketson

During the excavations of 1933 in Structure A-V there were recovered 107 cut human bones. These were found above the floors within the structure, most frequently in the corners of rooms, but also in corners outside the building. The specimens were chiefly the heads of long-bones severed from the shafts, although in some instances the shafts themselves were recovered. The cylinders formed by the latter were apparently the desired pieces, possibly for use as beads; the heads were apparently discards. Since the pieces of shafts were usually neatly cut at both ends, and sometimes grooved longitudinally (fig. 83,c,10,11), it is

obvious that the work was not done in order to extract the marrow, which could have been obtained much more easily by splitting. The longitudinal cuts, deep grooves following the long axis of the shaft, were evidently made to obtain a strip of bone. In some instances such cuts were made before the head was removed; often the strip was freed by a short transverse cut between grooves (fig. 83,a,8). Such pieces could have been used to make awls or punches, or could have been carved for ceremonial or decorative use.

The cutting on the bones is of two kinds: first, a ringing of the shaft to remove the articular portions; second, a cut following the long axis. Longitudinal cuts were not infrequently made prior to the circumferential cuts, no doubt because the shaft could be gripped more firmly with the head attached (fig. 83,b,12). Again, cylindrical sections of the shafts were sometimes cut in two lengthwise and the edges smoothed (fig. 83,c,6–9). The use of these sections is not clear; they could, of course, have been further split into strips for the manufacture of small tools, such as needles.

The work was done with a sharp instrument, possibly an obsidian chip, for under a magnifying glass individual cuts are visible. Gashes on either side of the actual cut may also be seen as though when beginning the cut, the instrument, worked with a sawing motion, had slipped. No cuts were made by scraping or by attrition with an abrasive; all are roughly V-shaped in section. Sometimes they are carried neatly through the bone from the external surface to the marrow cavity, producing a relatively smoothly finished surface (fig. 83,a,1); in other specimens the cut was made only sufficiently deep to allow the bone to be broken, thus leaving a rough surface at the area of the break (fig. 83,a,3). All cuts were made by rotating the bone, never by sawing straight through.

Most of the bones are of adults, and many exhibit the prominent muscular attachments characteristic of males. Identification of the bones as those of adult males is corroborated by specimens of the femur showing the head, neck, and that portion of the shaft as far down as the lesser trochanter. Although no actual measurement of the neck-shaft angle is feasible (since the shaft is mostly gone), it is possible to hold the specimen vertically in a position approximating that of life. Of the 18 specimens of the upper end of the femur, I have sexed 14 as male on the criterion of the obtuse neck-shaft angle; the remaining 4 could not be sexed. Furthermore, of the distal articulations of 18 humeri, only two had perforate olecranon fossae. This latter statement is made for what it is worth; the writer knows of no studies which bear upon the reliability of the olecranon perforation as a sex criterion among the ancient Maya.

The following bones were represented: femur, 31 (18 heads, 8 condyles, 5 shafts); tibia, 13 (4 proximal ends, 7 distal ends, 2 shafts); fibula, 3 (all proximal ends); humerus, 31 (9 proximal ends, 18 distal ends, 6 shafts); ulna, 20 (19 proximal ends, 1 distal end); radius, 5 (3 proximal ends, 2 distal ends); unidentifiable pieces cut from shafts, 9. For notes on two pathological specimens see caption of figure 83,*d*.

COMMENT. Although the above were all from surface deposits and therefore of late date, the cutting up of human long-bones was practiced in earlier times, very much earlier if the femora of the Chicanel skeleton in Burial B-12 were removed for that purpose. It was certainly being done during the Tepeu phase, as a femur head and the distal end of a tibia were taken from Room 43 and from the fill beneath the floor of Room 70, both Tepeu constructions. These articulations had been removed by sawing in exactly the same way as those just described. Dr. Ricketson is doubtless correct in believing that such treatment of human bones was to obtain sections of shaft for working up in one way or another, and that the articular ends are discards. But attention may be called to the fact that femur heads were set like bosses in the plastered walls of the inner chamber of the buried temple in the Castillo at Chichen Itza. The latter, it is to be supposed, were the bones of sacrificial victims, for human sacrifice is known to have been extensively carried on at Chichen Itza during the Mexican Period. The Uaxactun cut bones, together with the several cases of severed skulls in Group E caches (RR, p. 150 ff.) and the decapitated skeleton in Temple E-VII (RR, p. 69), suggest that the more ancient Maya can by no means be acquitted of common indulgence in this practice.

ANTLER

Three. (1) Horn of spike buck with small portion of skull attached, tip sharpened and shows wear (in masonry of wall of Room 39, Tepeu). (2) Calcined fragment of base, part of burr remaining, no work showing (Cache A-30 in Structure A-XV). (3) Rotted fragments in Tepeu Burial A-2 (R. E. Smith, 1937, fig. 8). Only one specimen was found in the extensive midden excavations in Group E, a three-pronged antler with burr removed (RR, p. 207; pl. 69,*d,1*).

TURTLE CARAPACE DISC

One (fig. 47). D 7 cm. Badly broken, decayed. About edge of convex surface a band of incised face-glyphs, painted red, spaces between glyphs white. Undecorated central portion fresh, unworked, unworn, suggesting that it may originally have been covered with stucco. Concave surface worked smooth. Unique specimen; function problematical, possibly pendant whose suspension hole was in part now lost; possibly earplug backing, but lacks central perforation normally found in backings. Fragments of the carapace of a small turtle and a piece of a large, thick carapace seemingly worked to rectangular form were in the Tepeu Burial A-2 (R. E. Smith, 1937, fig. 8).

STING-RAY SPINES

Nineteen. Seven large, apparently unworked, none complete but one at least 24 cm. long; 9 small, 6–8 cm. long (fig. 75), proximal ends apparently smoothed, in one case acutely pointed; 3 gently S-shaped, pathological?

COMMENT. The large spines were all single finds: one each at the pelvis of the skeleton in Burials A-2 (Tepeu, R. E. Smith, 1937, fig. 8), A-22, A-23, A-29 (Tzakol), one at about the position of the navel in Burial A-6 (Tepeu,

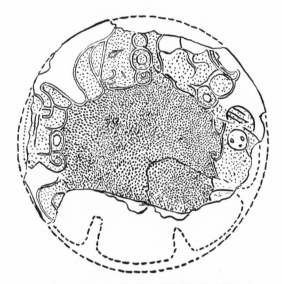

FIG. 47—ORNAMENT OF TURTLE CARAPACE
Natural size.

R. E. Smith, 1937, fig. 14), one in a pottery vessel cached in Structure B-XI, one under the floor of the west gallery above the capstones of Rooms 43 (Tepeu). The nine small spines were in a bowl in Burial A-22, Tzakol. The number of these is interesting in view of the frequent occurrence of eccentric flints and incised obsidians in groups of nine. The three curved specimens were in a cache with eccentric flints below Stela 26 (Tzakol). Two spines were found in a Mamom deposit in Group E (RR, p. 205). The evident ceremonial significance of sting-ray spines is discussed and other occurrences are listed in the report on Kaminaljuyu, at which site they were also found at the pelvis of skeletons (KJS, p. 156).

SNAKE VERTEBRAE

Sixty-five (fig. 82,*b*). Unworked vertebrae of a colubrine snake cached with many small perforated shells (*Marginella apicina*, see p. 62) in fill of the Tepeu phase.

MAMMAL, BIRD, REPTILE BONES

From general digging (including specimens from Group E, see RR, pp. 204, 205)

MAMMALS

Opossum, large (*Didelphis yucatanensis* ssp.)
Opossum (*Marmosa murina*)
Opossum, small (*Metachirops opossum* ssp.)
Short-tailed shrew (*Cryptotis* sp.)
Short-tailed bat (*Carollia subrufa*)
Fruit bat, large (*Artibeus jamaicensis* ssp.)
Vampire bat (*Desmodus rotundus* ssp.)
Coati (*Nasua narica* ssp.)
Tayra (*Tayra barbara* ssp.)
Dog (*Canis familiaris*)
Gray fox (*Urocyon parvidens*)
Jaguar (*Felis onca* ssp.)
Ocelot (*Felis pardalis* ssp.)
Long-tailed cat (*Felis glaucula* ssp.)
Cougar (*Felis concolor* ssp.)
Spiny pocket rat (*Heteromys* sp.)
White-footed mouse (*Peromyscus* sp.)
Rice rat (*Oryzomys* sp.)
Native mouse (*Ototylomys* sp.)

Cotton rat (*Sigmodon hispidus* ssp.)
Agouti (*Dasyprocta punctata* ssp.)
Paca (*Cuniculus paca* ssp.)
Rabbit (*Sylvilagus* sp.)
Collared peccary (*Pecari angulatus* ssp.)
White-lipped peccary (*Tagassu pecari* ssp.)
White-tailed deer (*Odocoileus* sp.)
Brocket (*Mazama* sp.)
Tapir (*Tapirella dowii*)

BIRDS

Ocellated turkey (*Agriocharis ocellata*)
Quan (*Penelope* sp.)
Chachalaka (*Ortalis vetula*)
Curassow (*Crax globicera*)
Quail (*Colinus leucopogon hypoleucus*)

REPTILES

Lizard (*Ctenosaura similis*)
Turtle (*Dermatemys maivii*)
Turtle (*Kinosternon cruentatum*)

AMPHIBIAN

Rhynophrynus dorsalis

3

Objects of Shell

Almost all specimens of shell were ornamental or ceremonial objects from graves and caches. No surely utilitarian implement was found. Of the thirteen identifiable species, ten are from the Atlantic, as are all those from Group E (RR, p. 199). Shell objects from Group E of types not represented in the present collection are: little figurines (RR, fig. 128), a conch shell trumpet (RR, pl. 69,c) a small death's-head mask (RR, pl. 69,a), and a great number of irregular fragments of shell, many with a single drilled perforation (RR, pl. 68,a). All but the figurines were from subplaza deposits of the Mamom phase, and are therefore earlier than the materials from the other groups.

SPECIES REPRESENTED

(Asterisks indicate presence in Group E)

Atlantic Ocean:
Busycon perversum
Cyphoma gibbosa
Fasciolaria gigantea
Marginella apicina *
Melongena melongena
Murex pomum
Nassa vibex
Oliva reticularis
Strombus pugilis *

Venus campechiensis
Xancus angulatus
Pacific Ocean:
Arca pacifica
Pecten subnodosus
Spondylus crassisquama
Provenience uncertain:
Chama sp.
Crepidula sp.
Nerita sp.
Olivella sp.
Ostrea sp.
Fresh-water:
Unionid shells
In Group E the following additional species, all from the Atlantic, were found (RR, p. 199):
Arca noae
Cardium magnum
Cardium muricatum
Cerithium floridanum (?)
Fasciolaria distans
Nerita praecognita
Strombus gigas

UNWORKED SHELLS

Arca pacifica (under Platform I, Chicanel, 2; Room 2, Tzakol, 2).

Busycon perversum (under Platform I, Chicanel, 1).

Crepidula sp. (Burial A-22, Tzakol, 1).

Murex pomum (Burial A-22, Tzakol, 1).

Nerita sp. (Burial A-22, Tzakol, 1).

Ostrea sp. (Buried Pyramid I, Tepeu, 1; Burial B-2, Tzakol, 1).

Spondylus crassisquama (Burials A-2, Tepeu, 4; A-6, Tzakol, 1; A-22, Tzakol, 1; cache in Structure A-I, Tepeu, 9).

Strombus pugilis (S. Court, under floor, Chicanel, 1; Pit 14, Tzakol, 1).

Venus campechiensis (under Platform I, Chicanel, 1).

Xancus angulatus (Room 6, Tzakol, 1).

ORIGINAL FORM LARGELY PRESERVED

BIVALVES PERFORATED FOR SUSPENSION

Pecten subnodosus, 2. Three .3-cm. holes, drilled from exterior, one in each wing of hinge, third in tip between

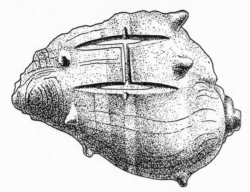

FIG. 48—WORKED SHELL
Natural size.

wings; one of these specimens illustrated in KJS, fig. 162,*c*, upper left. Burial A-31, Tzakol.

Spondylus crassisquama, 27. Two .3–.4-cm. holes about 1 cm. apart, drilled from exterior near highest part of back

Nassa vibex, 1 (fig. 82,*b*). Single small drilled perforation. With first of above-mentioned *Marginella apicina* lots.

Oliva reticularis, 1 (fig. 82,*b*). Single small drilled perforation. Same lot as foregoing. For tinklers of Oliva, see p. 63.

Strombus pugilis, 1. Tip of spire ground off. Under early terrace of Period III, Tzakol.

CUT SHELL

EARPLUGS (described with the jades, p. 42, *supra*)

BEADS (ornamental objects designed for stringing in series, perforated through the center)

Disc, 457 (fig. 49,*a-c*; RR, pl. 63,*b*). D .4–.9 cm., T .1–.5 cm. Biconical bore. All but one (Burial A-55, Tzakol, same size as fig. 49,*a*) formed part of a shell and jade necklace recovered in almost exactly original order from Burial B-2, Tzakol (fig. 80,*c*). Smaller beads, forming upper ends

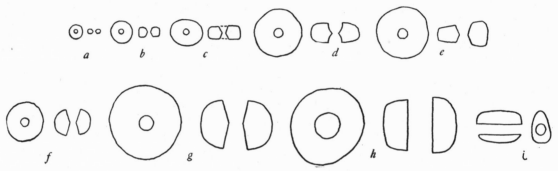

FIG. 49—SHELL BEADS

a-c: Disc-shaped. From necklace (fig. 78). Note range in size. *d,e*: Subspherical. Unusually flat, but more rounded than disc beads. Note bore of *d* produced with round-pointed drill; and wedgelike section of *e*, presumably produced to allow beads to fit snugly in the curve of a necklace. *f,g*: Subspherical. From necklace (fig. 86,*c*). *h*: Subspherical. Possibly not a bead because of very large cylindrical bore. *i*: Tubular, only example of this form. Natural size.

(fig. 82,*a*). Burials A-22, Tzakol, 2; A-29, Tzakol, 15; A-31, Tzakol, 8; A-66, Tzakol, 1; debris of Structure B-XIII, period uncertain, 1.

UNIVALVES PERFORATED OR OTHERWISE SLIGHTLY WORKED

Cyphoma gibbosa, 1. Two holes broken through wall (Burial C-1, Tzakol). Shells of this species similarly perforated were found at Holmul (Merwin and Vaillant, 1932, pl. 35,*z*).

Marginella apicina, 185 (fig. 82,*b*; RR, pl. 63,*d*). Each has a .1–.2-cm. hole broken, not drilled, through back. One lot of 106 in Tepeu cache in Structure A-V with snake vertebrae; second lot of 79, same type of perforation, in Tepeu cache in Structure A-I.

Melongena melongena, 1 (fig. 48). Three sawed cuts, in form of H, perforate wall near orifice. Under early terrace of Period III, Tzakol.

of necklace, are true discs; larger ones farther down seldom have exactly parallel faces (fig. 49,*c*) so that they fit snugly together to allow necklace to curve and constitute as smooth a strand as the seldom perfectly circular shape of individual beads permits. Unlike disc-bead necklace from Burial B-9 (RR, p. 200; pl. 63,*b*), this one was not worked down as a unit to produce a smooth strand. There are other thin, centrally perforated shell discs, but because of large size and cylindrical form of perforations and because not found in strings, they are classed as adornos (fig. 85, *a*,1-3,21).

Tubular, 1 (figs. 49,*i*; 85,*c*,7). L 1.2 cm. Pear-shaped in section, cylindrical bore. Tubular beads referred to by Mrs. Ricketson (RR, p. 200) as having been found in Group A caches are short sections of cases of marine worms (p. 66).

Subspherical, 172 (figs. 49,*d-h*; 85,*c*,8–12; 86,*a*,*c*). D 3 cm., T .6–2.3 cm. All but one (figs. 49,*h*; 85,*c*,11) biconically perforated, two (figs. 49, *d*; 85,*c*,8,10) with round-pointed drill. None truly spherical, some (e.g. fig. 49,*d*; see also several in fig. 86,*c*) might be classed as disc-shaped were it not for their fully rounded edges. One double-strand necklace of 154 beads (fig. 86,*c*, Burial A-22, Tzakol) recovered in original order with its carved shell pendant (fig. 50). Several of its beads have shallow, round, cup-like depressions up to .6 cm. in diameter. One of these is inlaid flush with a bit of jade cut to fit perfectly. It is improbable that the others were plugged with jade, as no loose pieces of proper shape were found in the tomb. They may have been filled with some perishable substance, or with pieces of thin shell that have rotted. Presumably the cups were drilled, as a dentist shapes a cavity, to prepare for plugging holes made in the shell by parasitic marine organisms. The carved pendant is similarly treated (see below) and similar work in shell has been noted elsewhere in Mesoamerica (KJS, p. 149).

PENDANTS (ornamental objects designed for suspension, which are perforated near one edge or one end)

Carved, 2. (1) Anthropomorphic (fig. 50). L 8 cm. Central element of necklace (fig. 86,*c*). Back of head deeply cupped as if to receive inlay; a conical suspension hole opens into cup from each side in such a way that inlay would have concealed string. A biconical perforation pierces headdress laterally; one aperture (on side not shown in fig. 50) tightly plugged with shell disc; other aperture probably once similarly treated. Mouth somewhat suggests La Venta style. (2) Monkey (?) head (fig. 86,*d*,2). L 2 cm. Central element of string of pyrite beads (fig. 25) in Burial B-2, Tzakol. Two cup-like drillings represent eyes, possibly once inlaid with some other substance. No other feature shown but domed forehead and dished face suggest monkey. Transverse cylindrical suspension hole.

Incised, 2 (fig. 51,*a*,*b*). L of complete specimen 11.2 cm., T .8 cm. Apparently cut from lip of conch. Seated human figures in lightly incised lines on concave surface.

COMMENT. Found in late deposit on floor of East Court. A specimen in the American Museum of Natural History, acquired by Lumholtz (1902, 2: 454) in the Valley of Mexico, is so nearly identical to the above in size, shape, number, and position of figures, and in details of incising (fig. 51,*c*) that one can hardly doubt that all three were the handiwork of a single craftsman. They are certainly products of the same school, but whether this was in Peten or in the Valley of Mexico, or in some third region, is unknown. Unfortunately there is no information as to the circumstances under which the Lumholtz piece was found.

"Horse collars," 2 (fig. 52). L of complete specimen 9.8 cm., the second probably about 17 cm. Cut from large,

heavy shells. Marginal nicks on concave side. The same catchword name has been applied to similar shell ornaments

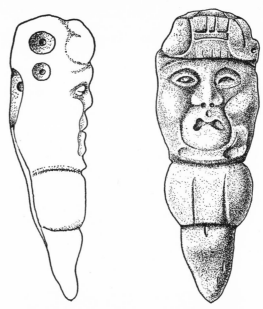

FIG. 50—ANTHROPOMORPHIC SHELL PENDANT
Center ornament of necklace (fig. 86,*c*). Natural size.

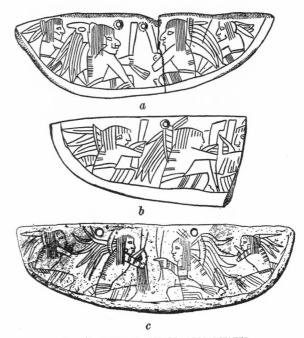

FIG. 51—INCISED SHELL ORNAMENTS
a,*b*: Uaxactun. *c*: Valley of Mexico (after Lumholtz). L of *c*, 12 cm.

from Esperanza phase tombs at Kaminaljuyu (KJS, p. 149; fig. 162,*e*,*h*).

Tinklers, 9 (fig. 85,*d*; RR, fig. 131,*d*; pl. 68,*b*). L 1.8–5 cm. Some surely, others presumably, *Oliva reticularis.* Spire removed in all but three cases (fig. 85,*d*,4,8,9). Per-

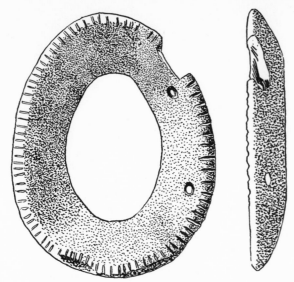

FIG. 52—SHELL "HORSE COLLAR" ORNAMENT
L 9.8 cm.

foration by drilled hole (1,2,5,6) or transverse sawed cut (3,7,9). Method of perforation apparently has no chronological significance, for although all those from Mamom deposits in Group E (RR, p. 201) are sawed, some of those of Tzakol and Tepeu date from Group A are sawed, others drilled. Specimen 4, with four perforations, perhaps designed to be sewn to a backing, rather than suspended as a tinkler. For discussion of distribution of tinklers in Mesoamerica see KJS, p. 148.

Miscellaneous forms, 9 (fig. 86,*d*). Two small discs with off-center perforations (fig. 86,*d*,3,4); Unionid shell with notched edge and two suspension holes (5); oval of heavy shell with two perforations (6); elongated triangular pendant (1); three triangular pendants apparently cut from Strombus (7–9; a similar piece from Group E, RR, fig. 131,*a*); end cut from large pendant (fig. 85,*b*,7).

Ear (?) Ornaments
Four (figs. 56; 85,*c*,3–6; RR, fig. 132,*c*). L 2.4–2.9 cm. Three (fig. 56,*a*,*b*), with head cupped, one (fig. 56,*c*) with perforated head. Latter has tiny biconically drilled hole in rim (diameter of aperture, where drillings meet, less than .08 cm.). Specimen shown in figure 53,*b* possibly an unfinished example.

Comment. The pair (fig. 56,*b*) accompanied a female skeleton in Burial B-2, Tzakol; the limestone specimen (fig. 56,*d*) is also Tzakol, as is that from Group E (RR, fig. 132,*c*); the remaining two are from Tepeu deposits. Objects of this sort have often been called labrets, but because of the length and straightness of their shanks, which would have had to fit between lip and teeth, I think it probable that they were ear ornaments, an identification supported by the occurrence of undoubted earplugs which,

though much larger, had shanks like those of the present specimens (see figs. 30, 31). I have three records of their occurrence in pairs: the one with Burial B-2 and two from graves at Piedras Negras. Mr. L. Satterthwaite, Jr., who has kindly supplied information regarding the latter, tells me that in one case (Burial 2) one of the ornaments was with beads below the skull, the second between the tibiae. In the other (Burial 5) they lay at either side of the jaw just below a pair of earplugs (i.e. toward the feet), the earplugs being in place at either side of the skull. This might indicate that in this instance they had been set in the cheeks. All objects of this sort could not have been worn in cheeks or lips, for of some of them the shanks, which in such positions would have been concealed, are elaborately decorated with openwork (wooden examples from the Sacred Cenote at Chichen Itza—Peabody Mus. Harvard; one of shell from Seamay, Alta Verapaz—Kidder, 1942, p. 39,*a*; a pair of copper from Texmilincan, Guerrero—Mex. Nat. Mus.). The head, however, was evidently always exposed, as it is often decoratively carved (cf. fig. 56,*c*; RR, fig. 132,*c*) and is normally cupped, as if to receive an inlay. Without much question labrets are the "top hat" obsidian objects described above (p. 31, fig. 14). These, as far as I know, are only found in Mexico. The type now under discussion seems to have had a more southerly distribution. From Copan there are examples in shell (Copan Mus.); from the Ulua Valley, of pottery with very short shank, much like one, also of pottery, from Group E at Uaxactun (cf. Gordon, 1898, fig. 22 and

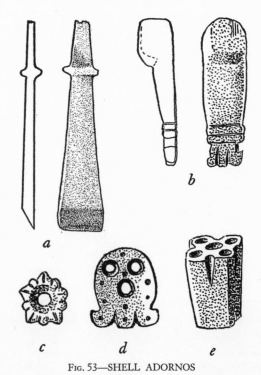

FIG. 53—SHELL ADORNOS
b: Perhaps unfinished ear (?) ornament (cf. fig. 56). Natural size.

RR, fig. 145,*a*); of both pottery and shell are specimens from offertory deposits on Bonaca, Bay Islands, the heads of which have vertical biconical perforations (Strong, 1935, pp. 71, 139; pl. 15,*h-m*); those of shell from Seamay and Piedras Negras and of wood from Chichen Itza have already been mentioned. The only records I have from continental Mexico are of much larger head-and-shank ornaments: of copper from Texmilincan, of clay from Period V deposits in the Panuco region ("flanged earplugs," Ekholm, 1944, fig. 47,*a-g*).

ADORNOS

This is a catchall class comprising ornamental objects to which no specific use, as for beads, pendants, ear ornaments, etc., can be assigned. It would appear that some of them served as inlays, others were perhaps sewed to clothing, still others may have entered into the decoration of ceremonial paraphernalia. The majority have been cut from thick-walled marine shells, a few of the smaller and more delicate specimens from the pearly shells of fresh-water clams.

Round adornos, unperforated, 5 (fig. 85,*a*,17,22; RR, pl. 69,*e*,6,8). D 1–2.5 cm. Plain, well-finished discs, pre-

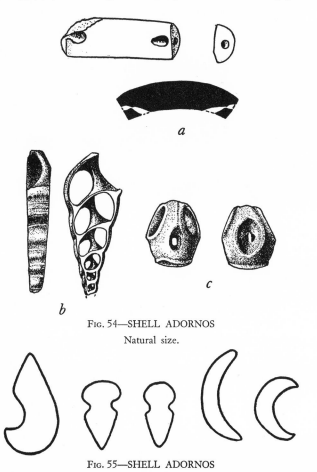

FIG. 54—SHELL ADORNOS
Natural size.

FIG. 55—SHELL ADORNOS
Natural size.

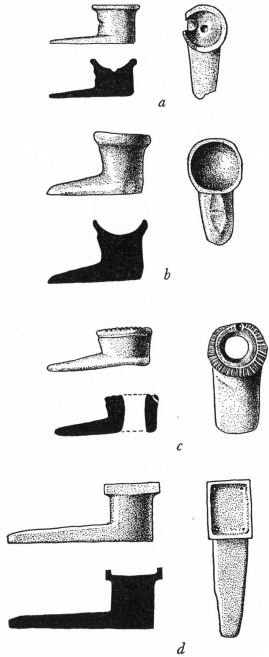

FIG. 56—EAR (?) ORNAMENTS
a-c: Shell. *d*: White limestone. Natural size.

sumably inlays. Three, not illustrated, from cache of shell and jade in Structure A-I, Tepeu.

Round adornos, perforated, plain, 9 (fig. 85,*a*,1–7,21,23). D .8–3.8 cm. Size of perforation varies widely. Smaller specimens (fig. 85,*a*,5–7) might be considered disc beads were it not for relatively large size of central perforations.

Round adornos, perforated, elaborated, 7 (fig. 85,*a*,10–16; RR, figs. 130, 132,*a*). D 1.1–2.2 cm. (fragment with scalloped edges [fig. 85,*a*,16] measured, if circular, about 11 cm. Characterized by scalloped, dentate, or "cogwheel" periphery).

"Rosette" adornos, 3. Greatest measurement 1.2–2.2 cm. Square and hexagonal (fig. 85,*a*,8,9), five-pointed star (fig. 53,*c*). Characterized by incised lines radiating to points.

Inlay (?) adornos, 19 (fig. 85,*b*,1). Av. size 1.2 by 1.7 cm. Oval to nearly circular. Pearly fresh-water clam shell. On faintly concave surface of each are two parallel incised lines. Convex surfaces unworked, bear traces of gummy substance, presumably adhesive. Found with Burial A-48, Tepeu.

Miscellaneous adornos, 19. (1) Slightly curved ornament of heavy shell, two deeply incised parallel lines on convex surface. Single small biconical perforation at each of two opposite corners (fig. 85,*c*,1). (2) Strongly curved, thick, single incised line on convex surface. Biconical perforation at either end. (3) Nose (?) ornament (fig. 85,*c*,2). Slightly curved bar, convex surface rounded. Two conical drillings at each end meet at obtuse angle to form means of attachment not visible from convex surface (fig. 54,*a*). (4,5) Pointed oval and square objects with large round perforations (fig. 85,*a*,19,20). (6) Small ornament in form of glyph Ahau (figs. 53,*d*; 85,*a*,18). (7) Fragment of large adorno with round central perforation; possibly four pointed "petals" like that which remains (fig. 85,*b*,6). (8) Elongated inlay (?) cut from wall of *Oliva reticularis* (fig. 85,*b*,5). (9) Solid, four-sided object, sides of larger end notched, surface of larger end has five shallow cups (fig. 53,*e*). (10) Small univalve with both sides sawed away to expose spiraled interior structure (fig. 54,*b*). (11) Object with five apertures, apparently made from small univalve (fig. 54,*c*). (12–16). One hooklike, two arrowhead-shaped, two crescentic adornos (fig. 55) of thin shell, cached with human figurines of shell (RR, fig. 128,*c,e*) in Structure A-I, Tepeu horizon. (17–19) Spatulate objects, none complete. Two (fig. 85,*b*,3,4) of fresh-water clam, one (figs. 53,*a*; 85,*b*,2) of marine shell. Spatulate end of each is worked to sharp edge, but shows no wear. Because of this and because of fragility of those of fresh-water clam shell, it seems improbable that they served as tools.

PEARLS

Pendants, 2. Egg-shaped, L 2, 2.3 cm. Perforated through small end, one by two conical holes slanting inward and down to meet at an angle (cf. KJS, fig. 63,*f*), the other by two conical holes drilled directly through to a straight junction. With Burial A-29, Tzakol.

Beads, 2. Round, D about .5 cm., biconically perforated. Cache A-4, Structure A-I, Tepeu.

Unperforated, 1. Spherical, D .3 cm. With Burial A-31, Tzakol.

"Blister," 1. Irregular piece from which small discs have been cut, apparently for inlays. Fill of Structure A-I, Tzakol horizon.

COMMENT. Archaeological finds of pearls in Mesoamerica are listed in KJS, p. 152.

CORAL

In fill of Structure A-I, Tepeu horizon, 4 lumps; probably in Cache B-3, Structure B-XI, Tzakol, 1 piece branch coral; in Cache A-4, Structure A-I, Tepeu, 9 pieces branch coral.

COMMENT. The Ricketsons (RR, p. 159, pl. 68,*d*) report two pieces of coral from beneath Stela 4 (9.18.0.0.0?). The only other record, as far as I know, of coral from the Maya area is of a piece from a cache at Hatzcap Ceel, British Honduras, probably Late Classic (Thompson, 1931, p. 273, pl. XXXI, 16).

MARINE WORM CASES

In Cache A-4, Structure A-I, Tepeu, 42, L 1.1–2 cm., D .2 cm., painted red. With Burial A-22, Tzakol, a curved case, L 5 cm., D .5 cm. With Burial C-1, Tzakol, two tapering cases, L .5, 1 cm., D .2 cm.

4

Objects of Clay

The pottery vessels, effigies, and whistles of Uaxactun will be described by R. E. Smith. In the present section are considered the few other clay specimens that were found there.

SPINDLE WHORLS

Perforated potsherds, 39 (fig. 87,*b*, three upper rows; RR, pl. 78,*f*). Discs 2.5–8.5 cm. in diameter, cut from flat or faintly curved potsherds from unslipped or plain red bowls and jars. Central perforation made by drilling from both sides, the "waist" of the biconical bore thus produced subsequently reamed to a diameter not less than .6 or more than .7 cm. This uniformity seems surely to indicate that the identification of the perforated discs as spindle whorls is correct. A single specimen (fig. 58,*g*) bears some crude

incising; its edge is scalloped, as is that of one from Group E (RR, fig. 144,*a*). Made from an unusually thick sherd is a spindle whorl (fig. 57,*c*) that was evidently shaped in imitation of the specially formed examples to be described below. Several unperforated discs (fig. 87,*b*, lowest row) and a few with unfinished drilling from one or both sides (cf. RR, fig. 144,*b,c*) were found. The latter are practically all rough-edged, suggesting that it was customary to work the sherd spindle whorls into their final round shape after they had been drilled. The well-finished, unperforated round sherds may have served other purposes.

Specially formed spindle whorls, 12 (fig. 57; RR, fig. 143). Seven (fig. 57, *d-h*; two others similar to *e*) have flat "platforms" and more or less rounded bodies; two are subhemi-

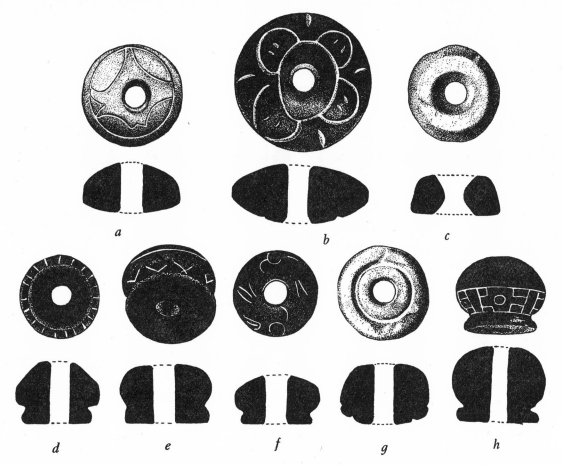

FIG. 57—SPINDLE WHORLS, CLAY

All from very late deposits. *a,d-g*: Dull-finish gray. *b*: Well-smoothed black. *c*: Cut from a thick potsherd. *h*: Highly polished black. Natural size.

spherical (cf. RR, fig. 143,*b*); one (fig. 57,*a*) is thinner than the foregoing, the lower surface slightly convex rather than flat; two (fig. 57,*b*) are elliptical in section. The two sub-hemisphericals are undecorated, the others bear simple designs, incised after the surface had been finished. All are dull unslipped gray ware save two. One of these (fig. 57,*h*)

that of the modeled ones (fig. 57,*c*) was found above the last floor in the East Court.

WORKED POTSHERDS

Under this heading are included all objects made from potsherds except the spindle whorls just listed.

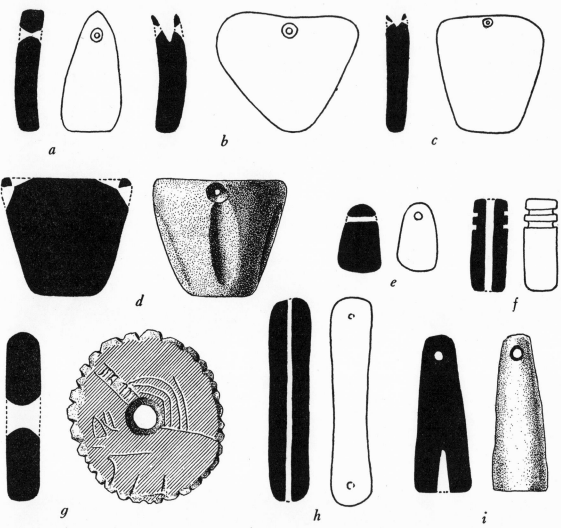

FIG. 58—OBJECTS OF CLAY

a-c,g: Pendants cut from potsherds; *b,c*, found together, have one grooved edge, the biconically drilled suspension hole entering the groove from either side. *d*: Problematical object. *e,h,i*: Specially modeled, i.e. not potsherd, pendants. Three punctations at each end of *h*; perforations of *e,h* made by molding the clay about a slender rod; that of *i* was punched through, conical hole in base was made with a sharp-pointed drill. Natural size.

is highly polished black, the other (fig. 57,*b*) well-smoothed black.

COMMENT. Potsherd spindle whorls emanated from deposits of all periods, those specially formed are all from the latest above-floor debris. The tardy appearance of the latter, as stated in discussing the few stone specimens, is in line with what data we have on the introduction of formed spindle whorls throughout Mesoamerica. It should be noted that the one potsherd example worked to a shape resembling

Discs and rectangles, 2 rectangles, number of discs not recorded. Many discs were found, most commonly of suitable size, had they been perforated, to have served as spindle whorls (fig. 87,*b*, bottom row). Others (fig. 59,*b*) are evidently too small for such use. Found together in a Tepeu deposit was a set of five little discs 1.5 cm. in diameter, their edges neatly rounded. They were made from piece of a red-on-black ware bowl. The decoration being on only one side, they might have served as dice or counters for gaming.

Pendants, 3 (fig. 58,*a-c*). All are from plain red potsherds, the edges carefully ground. One (*a*) is simply drilled for suspension through the small end, the other two (*b,c*) are, as far as I know, unique in that a groove was sawed longitudinally the length of one edge and the suspension hole was drilled from either side to enter the groove.

Backing for plaque (?), 1. Sherd from almost perfectly flat base of red-slipped bowl accurately cut to a 9-cm. disc with beveled edge; two .4-cm. holes drilled from the beveled side near opposite edges. This almost perfect duplicate of the typical stone backing of pyrite-incrusted plaques (KJS, figs. 52, 53) provides another hint that such objects may have been in use at Uaxactun. It bears no trace either of adhesive or of pyrite staining. Potsherd backings are not unknown, Thompson (1939, p. 176) having found one at San Jose, British Honduras, with the pyrite mosaic in place; Saville (1922, fig. 7) one at Cuilapa, Oaxaca, with mosaic of crystalline hematite. The present specimen is from an early Tepeu deposit.

Pair of problematical objects, 2 (fig. 87a). L 15.5 cm. Made from pieces of very large, gray, unslipped jars with raked exterior. Edges show no wear beyond original rounding. At middle of convex surface of each an approximately 3.5 cm. circular area has been slightly flattened as if by wear. From the richly stocked Tzakol Burial A-22.

MODELED OBJECTS

Problematical object, 1. In size and shape much like the foregoing, but is somewhat thicker and the rounded smaller end is brought to a sharp edge. It is covered with polished red slip. Surfaces and edges show no wear. From fill of Buried Pyramid I, a Tzakol structure.

Pendants, 4 (fig. 58,*e,h,i*). Three (one shown at *e*). L .8 cm., T .1 cm. Found together with a tubular clay bead (*f*) in a Tepeu structure. Of the rather crudely modeled *e,* the suspension hole was punched through while the clay was soft; traces of blue paint. The fourth (*h*) is from a Tzakol deposit. L 4.2 cm., T at base 1.9 cm. In the flat base a deep hole has been bored with a sharp-pointed drill.

Beads, 3 (fig. 58,*f,h*). One is a nicely made cylinder ringed at one end by two squarely cut grooves. L 2.5 cm., T .9 cm. Coated with white stucco. Tepeu. A somewhat larger and more ornate bead of the same sort was found in a deposit of doubtful period in Group E (RR, fig. 145,*d*). The second (fig. 58,*h*) is also cylindrical, but less well

modeled. L 5.5 cm., T 1 cm. Its long bore was made by packing the clay about a slender rod or twig. Chicanel. The third, found with the foregoing, is a tiny pat of clay folded on itself to form a bead .8 cm. long.

Cylindrical stamp (?), 1 (fig. 59,*c*; RR, fig. 145,*e,f*). L 5 cm., T 2.5 cm. Crudely modeled, gray, roughly carved. This would appear to be a roller stamp, but its narrow, irregular longitudinal bore may indicate that it was a large bead. Mrs. Ricketson (RR, p. 221) is also in doubt as to the function of two fragmentary carved clay cylinders from Group E. The present specimen was also found in Group E, during R. E. Smith's supplementary excavation in Mamom refuse.

Small covers (?), 2 (fig. 59,*a*). The one illustrated: D 4.2 cm., H 2.5 cm.; unslipped, brown; nicely modeled; bird head with low bosses for eyes, wings, and body in

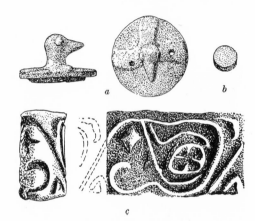

FIG. 59—OBJECTS OF CLAY

a: Possibly cover for small vessel. *b*: Disc cut from potsherd. *c*: Cylindrical stamp. Scale ½.

conventionalized low relief; two small perforations. The second: D 2.2 cm., H 1.3 cm.; red slip; only head shown, boss eyes; two perforations as in foregoing. Both these little objects are of Tzakol age, the former from Structure B-XIII, the latter from Pit 14, Group A. The disc on the lower surface of the larger would fit nicely in the mouth of a small vessel.

Problematical objects, 2 (fig. 58,*d*). H 3.2 cm., greatest W 3.5 cm. The one illustrated has fine longitudinal grooves and in the edge of its broader end are two opposite perforations. The second is of about the same size and shape, also has fine longitudinal grooves, but the broad end is slightly cupped. No perforations. Both Tepeu.

5

Perishable Materials

It is most deeply to be regretted that our knowledge of the arts and crafts of the Classic Maya should be limited to the few classes of objects which have survived the ravages of time and an intensely humid tropical climate. It cannot be doubted that these people were at least as skilled as their sixteenth-century descendants or as the Mexicans whose handiwork so astonished the conquerors. Sculpture in stone and clay, wall and vase paintings, the three surviving codices, all testify to the extreme richness of the prehistoric culture in textiles, featherwork, and various ceremonial paraphernalia; while the Chichen Itza lintels, and even more so those at Tikal, indicate that woodcarving had reached a

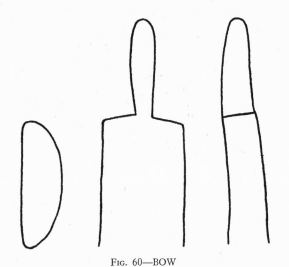

FIG. 60—BOW

Section at middle, front and side views of end. Natural size.

high degree of perfection. At Uaxactun, however, there were recovered only the few remnants listed below.

WOOD

Aside from structural timbers, which will be described in A. L. Smith's report on the excavations, the only wooden object recovered was a bow found in Structure A-XVIII (A. L. Smith, 1937, p. 19; pl. 13,c). It is so perfectly preserved that although it lay on the floor of a room under 2.5 m. of fallen masonry, Mr. Smith believes that it must have been left in the building by some wandering hunter long after the abandonment of Uaxactun. It is of heavy, dark brown, wavy-grained wood, well finished but with short, transverse, parallel scratches on its convex front surface. One end is broken away, the present length being

1.2 m. It would seem that a piece not more than 10–15 cm. long is missing. At the middle it is 2.3 cm. wide, 1.2 cm. thick. The drawing (fig. 60) shows median section and the nature of the square-shouldered string nock. The latter is cut across very cleanly, as if by a steel tool, although it is possible that when the wood was green the work might have been done with an obsidian flake-blade. It should be noted that modern Lacandon bows have no nock, the bowstring being held in place on the evenly tapered shaft by a wrapping of cord.

CLOTH

In Burials A-22, A-40, Tzakol; A-28, A-43, A-52, A-74, Tepeu; and from Tepeu construction in a late terrace, were imprints of plain basket-weave cloth. That from the terrace was sufficiently clear to permit a thread count of about 20 warps and 20 wefts per centimeter (50 by 50 per inch). For record of other finds of textiles in Mesoamerica, see KJS, p. 99.

MATTING

Imprints of twilled matting in plus 2–minus 2 weave of strands about .5 cm. wide were in clay under the skeleton in Burial A-40, Tzakol. The field notes mention less distinct prints in several other graves. It was evidently customary to wrap the bodies of the dead in mats of this sort.

CORDAGE

In Burial A-75, Tzakol, in fill below the top floor of Structure A-XV were found bits of a charred two-strand cord about .5 cm. in diameter of coarse fibres tightly twisted counterclockwise. There was an impression of a thin cord in Burial A-74, Tepeu.

CODICES (?)

Multiple layers of very thin stucco bearing traces of red and green paint, but so badly crushed that their nature could not be ascertained, were in Burials A-6, A-29, Tzakol. It is possible that these were remains of codices.

COMMENT. According to Landa (1941, p. 130), codices were sometimes buried with Yucatecan Maya priests of the sixteenth century. Thin laminations of pink and green stucco, much like those from Uaxactun, occurred in a Magdalena phase tomb at San Agustin Acasaguastlan (Kidder, 1935, p. 112).

OTHER ORGANIC SUBSTANCES

Copal (?). Lumps apparently of this material were in Burials A-20, A-38, Tzakol, and on the floor of a room in Structure A-XVIII.

Rubber (?). Bits of a shiny black substance, which when burned gave off a rubbery smell, were among the mortuary offerings in Burial A-66, Tzakol.

Cacao beans. Two well-preserved specimens, identified by Dr. Paul Vestal, were found with Burial A-40, Tzakol.

Pumpkin. A carbonized stem of *Cucurbita moschata* came from Burial A-37, late Tepeu. Identification by Dr. Vestal (1938; in this paper is discussed the problem of the area in which *C. moschata,* an important element of pre-Columbian agricultural economy, was first brought under cultivation; see also Carter, 1945, and reviews of Carter by Jones, Willey, and Roberts in *American Antiquity,* vol. 11, no. 4).

Maize. A single cob, preserved in the rubble of structure E-II, Tepeu, "does not differ noticeably from the corn characteristic of the region at the present time. The ear was apparently immature as the grains were in some places *in situ* and undeveloped" (RR, p. 208, pl. 68,*e*).

Discussion

Richly accoutered figures carved on the monuments of the Maya, persons and objects depicted in paintings on the walls of their ruined temples and in the decoration of their pottery, testify to the excellence of their work in wood and leather, the beauty of their basketry and textiles, the magnificence of their ceremonial regalia; but of all these products of countless artists and craftsmen, laboring through the centuries, hardly a vestige has survived. Nothing remains but stone implements and jade ornaments, a few bone tools, and, where conditions have been unusually favorable, certain objects of shell. The poverty of each new collection from the Maya country brings home with keen poignancy how cruelly time and tropical climate have dealt with the handiwork of one of the most brilliant peoples of the pre-Columbian New World.

That from Uaxactun is no exception. What was recovered there represents but a fraction of a fraction of the material culture of that ancient community. It, also, fails to provide adequate evidence as to the history of any single industry throughout the occupancy of the site. This is due not so much to the relatively small number of specimens as to their uneven distribution in time, most of the utilitarian objects illustrating only the earliest and latest periods, whereas nearly all ceremonial and mortuary equipment dates from the intermediate Tzakol phase; and the full archaeological value of what did come to light cannot be realized until much fuller information is available as to artifacts made at various periods in the rest of the lowland Maya region and in other parts of Mesoamerica.

In the matter of utilitarian implements, there seem to have been no very great changes at Uaxactun, from beginning to end. Stemmed points of flint or obsidian were not found in the earlier deposits, short-bladed points with tapering stem (fig. 2,c) occurred only above the latest floors. Specially shaped, as distinguished from perforated, potsherd spindle whorls, also came into use very late, and even then sparingly. The bark beater apparently was not introduced until Tzakol times. It is probable that there were shifts in the forms of metates and manos, for although we have no examples surely attributable to the Mamom or Chicanel horizons and the only adequate series of these objects is from the closing years, Thompson observed chronological variations in those of San Jose, a site which ceramically rather closely parallels Uaxactun; but by and large, one gets the impression that, as far as common everyday tools and weapons are concerned, a rather simple pattern was established early, and was held to with little modification throughout the life of the city.

Work in stone, both chipped and ground, was in general not outstanding. Projectile points and knives are rare and no strongly standardized forms appear. Arrowheads are absent, as are well-made drills; scrapers are uncommon and also unstandardized. The eccentric flints, with which one might expect extra care to have been taken, are larger, more crudely flaked, and of simpler forms than those from Tikal and in all these respects far inferior to Piedras Negras eccentrics.

The low average quality of Uaxactun chipped implements may well have been due, as suggested in a preceding section, to the fact that the almost iron-hard woods of Peten probably served for various sorts of implements that in other regions were made of stone. The further fact that obsidian chips and flakes and flake-blades could be put to many uses without reshaping, would seem to account for failure to develop the several types of knives and scrapers found elsewhere. Native flints, too, were not of the best grades.

Substitution of wood for stone, dependence on unretouched obsidian, lack of suitable raw materials are responsible perhaps for the rarity of fine chipped implements throughout the whole Yucatan Peninsula. Yet from some cities there come a few superlatively excellent pieces. The "sacrificial knives," often of honey-colored flint (RR, pl. 54a,10; Strömsvik, 1941, fig. 30,b), the white atlatl dart points from Chichen Itza (fig. 3), and the elaborate dark flint eccentrics (Thompson, 1936) are cases in point. Obviously, these were made by experienced hands, but had such craftsmen been residents of the districts where the specimens were found one would expect to encounter many more examples of first-class workmanship than actually occur. It, therefore, is to be suspected that there were centers, in regions yielding unusually good stone, where chipping was a highly specialized art and whose product was widely disseminated in trade.

Objects of ground stone, aside from manos and metates in the field of utilitarian implements and jades in that of ornaments, are also scantily represented in the Uaxactun collection. There are very few celts or bark beaters, mortars and pestles are practically absent; stone vessels, except for fragments of certainly imported marble vases, are entirely lacking. Small stone sculptures are represented by a single crude little figure (RR, fig. 66). Great scarcity of such sculptures is characteristic of the whole area occupied by the Classic Maya, whereas they are abundant in Salvador, highland Guatemala and the Gulf Coast of Vera Cruz and Tabasco. In the case of the Yucatan Peninsula, this might be attributed to want of suitable raw material, were it not that small sculptures appear to be equally rare, possibly absent, at Copan and Quirigua, where fine stones were readily obtainable, and where stela and architectual carving attained great perfection. This might be explained if one believes, as do most students, that the highly specialized Maya religion had its origin in the Tikal-Uaxactun district, where neither the soft limestones nor the intractable white flints are conducive to the development of minor carvings. If so, the making of little stone figures, which wherever found in Mesoamerica seem surely to have been cult objects, might not have become a part of the Maya ceremonial complex that spread outward from north-central Peten.

Another object represented at Uaxactun by but a single specimen, and that not certainly identified (see p. 52), is the so-called "mirror," a thin disc, normally of stone, incrusted with pyrite mosaic; and Miss Proskouriakoff, who has made a detailed study of Peten sculpture, tells me that these showy ornaments seem never to form part of the elaborate trappings of personages represented on the stelae. Yet, as mortuary furniture, "mirrors" occur commonly in adjacent regions—the Motagua, Alta Verapaz, northern Quiche, Kaminaljuyu—where they appear in greatest numbers in graves contemporaneous with the richly stocked Tzakol tombs of Uaxactun and those of the nearby site of Holmul, which also contained no certainly identifiable "mirrors." The Peten Maya seem, indeed, to have been a conservative lot. No metal, for example, has come to light in tombs or caches attributable to the Classic Period, although Boggs (1945) has shown that copper ornaments were in use at Tazumal, in western Salvador, during late Classic times, i.e. contemporaneous with Uaxactun Tepeu. Strömsvik (1941) found parts of a gold figurine in a sub-stela deposit at Copan that dates from 9.17.12.0.0, and A. L. Smith (Smith and Kidder, 1943) recovered from a tomb at San Agustin Acasaguastlan a bit of gilded sheet copper of approximately the same age. Thus it is clear that metal was known to neighboring peoples well before the abandonment of Uaxactun. Specimens, of course, may yet turn up there or elsewhere in the Peten, for the burials of the Tepeu phase contained relatively modest offerings and may have been those of individuals not sufficiently important to be accorded rare and costly gifts.

If metal eludes further excavation in late Classic sites of Peten, its absence will have to be attributed to reluctance to adopt new customs rather than to lack of knowledge, because it is evident that a lively commerce was carried on with neighboring peoples. The list of imports includes obsidian in great quantities, dark-colored flint, granites and lavas for metates and manos, fine-grained igneous rocks, jade, marble vases, shells from both Atlantic and Pacific, and presumably quetzal feathers. What was passed outward in exchange for these commodities is unknown, probably manufactured goods and tropical products of one sort or another; a pure limestone country such as Peten certainly yielded no exportable minerals.

Because of our almost complete ignorance regarding the artifacts of other Peten sites, paucity of information as to those of northern Yucatan, and the spottiness and very uneven quality of data for the regions to the east, west, and south, it is impossible to draw valid conclusions as to the exterior affiliation of Uaxactun. Ceramically, it appears to form part of an area including most of the Department of Peten and British Honduras, with extensions into Alta Verapaz and northern Quiche. Whether or not there was also similarity of artifacts throughout this region remains to be determined. All nonceramic materials, as a matter of fact, cannot properly be lumped together, for the distribution of common, everyday utensils and weapons may well have differed from those of ceremonial objects and articles of personal adornment, the former group reflecting fundamental cultural cleavages, the latter more superficial spreads of cults and fashions.

The Uaxactun collection contains representations of both categories and, in spite of many serious lacunae and although it does not have the immediate usefulness of pottery as a criterion of culture change and culture contacts, it can be counted upon, when more is known of other regions, to reveal relationships and divergences that are not made apparent by pottery, particularly by the finer decorated wares that, to date, have received the lion's share of attention. Furthermore, these specimens supply the only information we can ever hope to obtain as to many important aspects of life at Uaxactun.

To serve the purposes of archaeology, artifacts no less than pottery must be intelligently classified, accurately described, and above all adequately illustrated. At first this may result in the recording of much detail which will ultimately prove to be of no significance. Some classes of specimens may tell us much less than others, and we shall doubtless go up more than one blind alley. But that is inevitable at the beginning of any serious research. We must, at this stage of the game, make note of everything. Unless we do so, other students cannot be sure that this or that was not found, and absence of certain sorts of objects may be quite as important as the presence of others. Nor can aberrants, although an annoyance in classification, be neglected. They may, it is true, be the result of passing individual whims and therefore do no more than show what amount of variation from cultural norms could take place. On the other hand, they may indicate the breaking down of an established trait, the copying of a nonlocal form, or they may be actual importations evidencing the extent and direction of trade. In short, one cannot pick and choose. The great value of the thorough study of artifacts, on a sound conceptual basis, is made clear by the work of Osgood and Rouse on the cultures of the West Indies.

References

BATRES, L.
n.d. Antigüedades mexicanas falsificadas: falsificación y falsificadores. Mexico.
1902 Exploraciones en Monte Alban. Mexico.
1902a Exploraciones arqueológicas en la Calle de las Escalerillas. Mexico.
1906 Teotihuacán. *Memoria que presenta Leopoldo Batres al XV Cong. Int. de Amer.*, Quebec, 1906. Mexico.

BLOM, F.
1932 Commerce, trade and monetary units of the Maya. *Middle Amer. Research Ser., Tulane Univ.*, 4:531–56. New Orleans.

BOGGS, S. H.
1945 Informe sobre la tercera temporada de excavaciones en las ruinas de "Tazumal." *Tzunpame*, 4:33–45. San Salvador.

BOWDITCH, C. P.
1910 The numeration, calendar systems and astronomical knowledge of the Maya. Cambridge.

BRANSFORD, J. F.
1881 Archaeological researches in Nicaragua. *Smithsonian Contrib. to Knowledge*, vol. XXV. Washington.

BRETON, A. C.
1902 Some obsidian workings in Mexico. *Proc. 13th Int. Cong. Amer.*, pp. 265–68. Easton, Pa.

BROWNE, J.
1938 Antiquity of the bow. *Amer. Antiquity*, 3:358, 359. Menasha.

BURKITT, R.
1924 A journey in northern Guatemala. *Univ. Pa. Mus. Jour.*, 15:115–44. Philadelphia.

BUTLER, M.
1940 A pottery sequence from the Alta Verapaz, Guatemala. *The Maya and their Neighbors*, pp. 250–67. New York.

CARTER, G. F.
1945 Plant geography and culture history in the American Southwest. *Viking Fund Pubs. in Anthropol.*, no. 5. New York.

CASO, A.
1928 Las estelas Zapotecas. *Monogr. del Mus. Nac. de Arq., Hist. y Etnog.* Mexico.
1932 Las exploraciones en Monte Alban, temporada 1931–32. *Inst. Panamer. de Geog. e Hist.*, Pub. 7. Mexico.
1932a Monte Alban, richest archaeological find in America. *Nat. Geog. Mag.*, 62:487–512. Washington.

DANZEL, T. W., AND E. FUHRMANN
1922–23 Mexico. *Kulturen der Erde*, vols. 11–13. Hagen and Darmstadt.

DIAZ DEL CASTILLO, B.
1908–16 The true conquest of New Spain. Translated into English by Alfred P. Maudslay. *Hakluyt Soc.*, 5 vols. London.

DIESELDORFF, E. P.
1926 Kunst und Religion der Mayavölker im alten und heutigen Mittelamerika. Berlin.

DRUCKER, P.
1943 Ceramic sequences at Tres Zapotes, Veracruz, Mexico. *Bur. Amer. Ethnol.*, Bull. 140. Washington.
1943a Ceramic stratigraphy at Cerro de las Mesas, Veracruz, Mexico. *Bur. Amer. Ethnol.*, Bull. 141. Washington.

DUTTON, B. P., AND H. R. HOBBS
1943 Excavations at Tajumulco, Guatemala. *Monogr. School Amer. Research*, no. 9. Santa Fe.

EKHOLM, G. F.
1942 Excavations at Guasave, Sinaloa, Mexico. *Amer. Mus. Nat. Hist., Anthrop. Pap.*, vol. 38, pt. 2. New York.
1944 Excavations at Tampico and Panuco in the Huasteca, Mexico. *Amer. Mus. Nat. Hist., Anthrop. Pap.*, 38:320–512. New York.

ESPEJO, A.
1945 Las ofrendas halladas en Tlaltelolco. *Tlaltelolco a traves de los Tiempos*, 5:15–29. Mexico.

FOLLETT, P. H. F.
1932 War and weapons of the Maya. *Middle Amer. Research Ser., Tulane Univ.*, 4:373–410. New Orleans.

GAMIO, M.
1909 Restos de la cultura Tepaneca. *Anales del Mus. Nac. de Arq., Hist. y Etnol.*, 1:233–53. Mexico.
1922 La población del Valle de Teotihuacán. Mexico.

GANN, T. W. F.
1893–95 An exploration of two mounds in British Honduras. *Proc. Soc. Antiq. London*, 2d ser., 15:430–34. London.
1918 The Maya Indians of southern Yucatan and northern British Honduras. *Bur. Amer. Ethnol.*, Bull. 64. Washington.
——, AND M. GANN
1939 Archaeological investigations in the Corozal district of British Honduras. *Bur. Amer. Ethnol., Anthrop. Pap.*, no. 7. Washington.

GARCIA PAYON, J.
1941 Estudio preliminar de la zona arqueológica de Texmilincan, Estado de Guerrero. *El Mexico Antiguo*, 5:341–64. Mexico.

GLADWIN, H. S., E. W. HAURY, E. B. SAYLES, AND N. GLADWIN
1937 Excavations at Snaketown: material culture. *Medallion Pap.*, no. 25. Globe.

GORDON, G. B.
1921 The Ulua marble vases. *Univ. Pa. Mus. Jour.*, 12:53–74. Philadelphia.

HAMY, E. T.
1896 Etudes sur les collections américaines reunies à Gênes à l'occasion du IV centenaire de la découverte de l'Amérique. *Jour. de la Soc. des Amer. de Paris*, 1:1–31. Paris.

HARRY-HIRTZEL, J.-S.
1925 Collections d'antiquités guatémaltèques du Musée d'archéologie de Gand. *Proc. 21st Int. Cong. Amer.*, pp. 668–72. Göteborg.

HARTMAN, C. V.
1901 Archaeological researches in Costa Rica. *Royal Ethnog. Mus.* Stockholm.

HOLMES, W. H.
1919 Handbook of aboriginal American antiquities: the lithic industries. *Bur. Amer. Ethnol.*, Bull. 60. Washington.

HRDLIČKA, A.
1903 The region of the ancient Chichimecs, with notes on the Tepecanos and the ruin of La Quemada, Mexico. *Amer. Anthrop.*, n.s., 5:385–440. Lancaster.

JOYCE, T. A.
1920 Mexican archaeology. London.
1927 Maya and Mexican art. London.
1929 Report on the British Museum expedition to British Honduras, 1929. *Jour. Royal Anthrop. Inst.*, 59:439–59. London.
1932 The "eccentric flints" of Central America. *Jour. Royal Anthrop. Inst.*, 62:xvii–xxvi. London.
——, J. COOPER CLARK, J. E. THOMPSON
1927 Report on the British Museum expedition to British Honduras, 1927. *Jour. Royal Anthrop. Inst.*, 57:295–323. London.
——, T. GANN, E. L. GRUNING, R. C. E. LONG
1928 Report on the British Museum expedition to British Honduras, 1928. *Jour. Royal Anthrop. Inst.*, 58:323–50. London.

KELEMAN, P.
1943 Medieval American art. New York.

KELLY, I. T.
1938 Excavations at Chametla, Sinaloa. *Ibero-Americana*, no. 14. Berkeley.

KIDDER, A. V.
1932 The artifacts of Pecos. *Pap. Southwestern Expedition, Phillips Acad., Andover*, no. 6, New Haven.
1938 Arrow-heads or dart-points? *Amer. Antiquity*, 4:156,157. Menasha.
1942 Archaeological specimens from Yucatan and Guatemala. *Carnegie Inst. Wash., Div. Historical Research, Notes on Middle Amer. Archaeol. and Ethnol.*, no. 9. Cambridge.
——, J. D. JENNINGS, AND E. M. SHOOK
1946 Excavations at Kaminaljuyu, Guatemala. *Carnegie Inst. Wash.*, Pub. 561. Washington.

LANDA, DIEGO DE
1941   Relación de las cosas de Yucatán. Translated and edited by A. M. Tozzer. *Pap. Peabody Mus. Harvard Univ.*, vol. 18. Cambridge.

LE PLONGEON, A.
1896   Queen Móo and the Egyptian sphinx. New York.

LINES, J. A.
1942   Dos nuevas gemas en la arqueología de Costa Rica. *Proc. 8th Amer. Sci. Cong.*, 2:117–22. Washington.

LINNÉ, S.
1934   Archaeological researches at Teotihuacan, Mexico. *Ethnog. Mus. Sweden*, n.s., Pub. 1. Stockholm.

1942   Mexican highland cultures. *Ethnog. Mus. Sweden*, n.s., Pub. 7. Stockholm.

LONGYEAR, J. M., III
1944   Archaeological investigations in El Salvador. *Mem. Peabody Mus. Harvard Univ.*, vol. 9, no. 2. Cambridge.

LOTHROP, S. K.
1933   Atitlan: an archaeological study of ancient remains on the borders of Lake Atitlan, Guatemala. *Carnegie Inst. Wash.*, Pub. 444. Washington.

1936   Zacualpa: a study of ancient Quiche artifacts. *Carnegie Inst. Wash.*, Pub. 472. Washington.

LUMHOLTZ, C.
1902   Unknown Mexico. New York.

MALER, T.
1901   Researches in the central portion of the Usumacintla Valley. Report of explorations for the museum, 1898–1900. *Mem. Peabody Mus. Harvard Univ.*, vol. 2, no. 1. Cambridge.

1912   Lista de las ilustraciones para una proyectada publicación, de Teoberto Maler, en el libro de recuerdos del Congreso de Americanistas. *Proc. 17th Int. Cong. Amer.*, added plates. Mexico.

MASON, J. A.
1933   Jade ornaments from Piedras Negras. *Univ. Pa. Mus. Bull.*, 4:53–56. Philadelphia.

1935   Preserving ancient America's finest sculptures. *Nat. Geog. Mag.*, 68:535–70. Washington.

1937   Late archaeological sites in Durango, Mexico, from Chalchuites to Zape. *Pub. Phila. Anthrop. Soc.*, 1:127–46. Philadelphia.

1943   The ancient civilizations of Middle America. *Univ. Pa. Mus. Bull.*, 10:1–64. Philadelphia.

MERWIN, R. E., AND G. C. VAILLANT
1932   The ruins of Holmul, Guatemala. *Mem. Peabody Mus. Harvard Univ.*, vol. 3, no. 2. Cambridge.

MORRIS, E. H., J. CHARLOT, AND A. A. MORRIS
1931   The Temple of the Warriors at Chichen Itza, Yucatan: description of the Temple of the Warriors and the edifices related thereto. *Carnegie Inst. Wash.*, Pub. 406. Washington.

MOTOLINIA, T. DE
1858   Historia de los indios de la Nueva España. *Col. de Doc. para la Hist. de Mex.*, vol. 1. Mexico.

MÜLLERRIED, F. K. G., AND H. VON WINNING
1943   El "Cerrito" al este de Tepotzotlán, Mex., en el Valle de Mexico. *El Mexico Antiguo*, 6:131–39. Mexico.

MUÑOZ, J. F. T.
1941   Piezas arqueologicas Mayas. *Los Mayas Antiguos*, pp. 137–42. Mexico.

NOGUERA, E.
1935   Antecedentes y relaciones de la cultura de Teotihuacán. *El Mexico Antiguo*, 3:3–95. Mexico.

1935a   La cerámica de Tenayuca y las excavaciones estratigráficas. In *Tenayuca*, 1935, pp. 141–201.

1944   Exploraciones en Jiquilpan. *An. del Mus. Michoacano*, ep. 2, no. 3, pp. 37–52. Morelia.

NORDENSKIÖLD, E.
1926   Miroirs convexes et concaves en Amérique. *Jour. Soc. des Amer. de Paris*, n.s., 18:103–10. Paris.

NUÑEZ Y DOMINGUEZ, J. de J.
1942   La colección de objetos mexicanos del "Museo del Hombre" de París. *Rev. Mex. de Estudios Antrop.*, 6:5–18. Mexico.

NUTTALL, Z.
1910   The Island of Sacrificios. *Amer. Anthrop.*, n.s., 12:257–95. Lancaster.

ORCHARD, W. C.
1927   Obsidian ear-ornaments. *Indian Notes, Mus. Amer. Indian*, 4:216–21. New York.

PALACIOS, E. J.
1937   Arqueología de México: culturas Arcaica y Tolteca. *Enciclopedia Ilustrada Mex.*, no. 4. Mexico.

PEÑAFIEL, A.
1899   Teotihuacan (album of plates). Mexico.

1903   Indumentaria antigua. Vestidos guerreros y civiles de los Mexicanos. Mexico.

POPENOE, D. H.
1928   Las ruinas de Tenampua. Tegucigalpa.

1936   The ruins of Tenampua, Honduras. *Ann. Rept. Smithsonian Inst. for 1935*, pp. 559–72. Washington.

POPENOE, W., AND D. H. POPENOE
1931   The human background of Lancetilla. Reprinted from *Unifruitco Mag.*, Aug. 1931, n.p.

PROSKOURIAKOFF, T.
1944   An inscription on a jade probably carved at Piedras Negras. *Carnegie Inst. Wash., Div. Historical Research, Notes on Middle Amer. Archaeol. and Ethnol.*, no. 47. Cambridge.

1946   Album of Maya architecture. *Carnegie Inst. Wash.*, Pub. 558. Washington.

RICKETSON, O. G., JR.
1929   Excavations at Baking Pot, British Honduras. *Carnegie Inst. Wash.*, Pub. 403, Contrib. 1. Washington.

——, AND E. B. RICKETSON
1937   Uaxactun, Guatemala: Group E—1926–1931. *Carnegie Inst. Wash.*, Pub. 477. Washington.

RIDGWAY, R.
1912   Color standards and color nomenclature. Washington.

RUBIN DE LA BORBOLLA, D. F.
1940   Types of tooth mutilation found in Mexico. *Amer. Jour. Phys. Anthrop.*, 26:349–65. Philadelphia.

1944   La orfebreria tarasca. *Cuadernos Americanos*, 15:125–38. Mexico.

SAUER, C., AND D. BRAND
1932   Aztatlán, prehistoric Mexican frontier on the Pacific Coast. *Ibero-Americana*, no. 1. Berkeley.

SAVILLE, M. H.
1925   The wood-carver's art in ancient Mexico. *Contrib. Mus. Amer. Indian, Heye Found.*, vol. 9. New York.

SAYLES, E. B.
1936   An archaeological survey of Chihuahua, Mexico. *Medallion Pap.*, no. 22. Globe.

SELER, E.
1901   Die alten Ansiedelungen von Chaculá im Distrikte Nenton des Departements Huehuetenango der Republik Guatemala. Berlin.

1904   Antiquities of Guatemala. *Bur. Amer. Ethnol.*, Bull. 28, pp. 77–121. Washington.

SMITH, A. L.
1932   Two recent ceramic finds at Uaxactun. *Carnegie Inst. Wash.*, Pub. 436, Contrib. 5. Washington.

1937   Structure A-XVIII at Uaxactun. *Carnegie Inst. Wash.*, Pub. 483, Contrib. 20. Washington.

——, AND A. V. KIDDER
1943   Explorations in the Motagua Valley, Guatemala. *Carnegie Inst. Wash.*, Pub. 546, Contrib. 41. Washington.

SMITH, R. E.
1937   A study of Structure A-I complex at Uaxactun, Peten, Guatemala. *Carnegie Inst. Wash.*, Pub. 456, Contrib. 19. Washington.

SOCIEDAD DE ARTE MODERNA
1945   Mascaras Mexicanas. *Secretaría de Educación Pública.* Mexico.

SOUSTELLE, J.
1933   Notes sur les Lacandon du Lac Peljá et du Río Jetjá (Chiapas). *Jour. de la Soc. des Amer. de Paris*, n.s., 25:153–80. Paris.

1937   La culture matérielle des Indiens Lacandons. *Jour. de la Soc. des Amer. de Paris*, n.s., 29:1–95. Paris.

SPINDEN, H. J.
1913   A study of Maya art, its subject matter and historical development. *Mem. Peabody Mus. Harvard Univ.*, vol. 6. Cambridge.

STIRLING, M. W.
1941   Expedition unearths buried masterpieces of carved jade. *Nat. Geog. Mag.*, 80:277–302. Washington.

——, AND M. STIRLING
1942   Finding jewels of jade in a Mexican swamp. *Nat. Geog. Mag.*, 82:635–61. Washington.

STONE, D. Z.
1937   Masters in marble. *Middle Amer. Research Ser., Tulane Univ.*, vol. 8, no. 1. New Orleans.
1941   Archaeology of the north coast of Honduras. *Mem. Peabody Mus. Harvard Univ.*, vol. 9, no. 1. Cambridge.

STREBEL, H.
1885–89 Alt-Mexico. Archäologische Beiträge zur Kulturgeschichte seiner Beiwohner, vols. 1, 2. Hamburg and Leipzig.

STRÖMSVIK, G.
1941   Substela caches and stela foundations at Copan and Quirigua. *Carnegie Inst. Wash.*, Pub. 528, Contrib. 37. Washington.

STRONG, W. D.
1935   Archaeological investigations in the Bay Islands, Spanish Honduras. *Smithsonian Misc. Coll.*, vol. 92, no. 14. Washington.

THOMPSON, E. H.
1897   Cave of Loltun, Yucatan. Report of explorations by the museum, 1888–89 and 1890–91. *Mem. Peabody Mus. Harvard Univ.*, vol. 1, no. 2. Cambridge.
1897a The chultunes of Labna, Yucatan. Report of explorations by the museum, 1888–89 and 1890–91. *Mem. Peabody Mus. Harvard Univ.*, vol. 1, no. 3. Cambridge.

——, AND J. E. S. THOMPSON
1938   The High Priest's Grave, Chichen Itza, Yucatan, Mexico. *Field Mus. Nat. Hist., Anthrop. Ser.*, 27:1–64. Chicago.

THOMPSON, J. E. S.
1930   Ethnology of the Mayas of southern and central British Honduras. *Field Mus. Nat. Hist., Anthrop. Ser.*, vol. 17, no. 2. Chicago.
1931   Archaeological investigations in the southern Cayo District, British Honduras. *Field Mus. Nat. Hist., Anthrop. Ser.*, vol. 17, no. 3. Chicago.
1932   The solar year of the Mayas at Quirigua, Guatemala. *Field Mus. Nat. Hist., Anthrop., Ser.*, vol. 17, no. 4. Chicago.
1936   An eccentric flint from Quintana Roo, Mexico. *Maya Research*, 3:316–18. New Orleans.
1939   Excavations at San Jose, British Honduras. *Carnegie Inst. Wash.*, Pub. 506. Washington.
1939a The Moon Goddess in Middle America, with notes on related deities. *Carnegie Inst. Wash.*, Pub. 509, Contrib. 29. Washington.
1940   Late ceramic horizons at Benque Viejo, British Honduras. *Carnegie Inst. Wash.*, Pub. 528, Contrib. 35. Washington.
1941   Dating of certain inscriptions of non-Maya origin. *Carnegie Inst. Wash., Div. Historical Research, Theoretical Approaches to Problems*, no. 1. Cambridge.

TOSCANO, S.
1944   Arte precolombiano de Mexico y de la America Central. *Instituto de Investigaciones Esteticas, Universidad Nacional Autonoma de Mexico*. Mexico.

TOZZER, A. M.
1907   A comparative study of the Mayas and the Lacandones. *Archaeol. Inst. Amer.* New York.
1941   Landa's Relacion de las cosas de Yucatan. A translation. *Pap. Peabody Mus. Harvard Univ.*, vol. 18. Cambridge.

VAILLANT, G. C.
1930   Excavations at Zacatenco. *Amer. Mus. Nat. Hist., Anthrop. Pap.*, vol. 32, pt. 1. New York.
1931   Excavations at Ticoman. *Amer. Mus. Nat. Hist., Anthrop. Pap.*, vol. 32, pt. 2. New York.
1934   The archaeological setting of the Playa de los Muertos culture. *Maya Research*, 1:87–100. New York.
1935   Excavations at El Arbolillo. *Amer. Mus. Nat. Hist., Anthrop. Pap.*, vol. 35, pt. 2. New York.
1935a Artists and craftsmen in ancient Central America. *Amer. Mus. Nat. Hist., Guide Leaflet Ser.*, no. 88. New York.

VAILLANT, S. B., AND G. C. VAILLANT
1934   Excavations at Gualupita. *Amer. Mus. Nat. Hist., Anthrop. Pap.*, vol. 35, pt. 1. New York.

VESTAL, P.
1938   *Cucurbita moschata* found in pre-Columbian mounds in Guatemala. *Botanical Mus. Leaflets, Harvard Univ.*, 6:65–69. Cambridge.

WAUCHOPE, R.
1934   House mounds of Uaxactun, Guatemala, with notes on the pottery by Edith B. Ricketson. *Carnegie Inst. Wash.*, Pub. 436, Contrib. 7. Washington.

WEIANT, C. W.
1943   An introduction to the ceramics of Tres Zapotes, Veracruz, Mexico. *Bur. Amer. Ethnol.*, Bull. 139. Washington.

WILLARD, T. A.
1926   The City of the Sacred Well. New York.

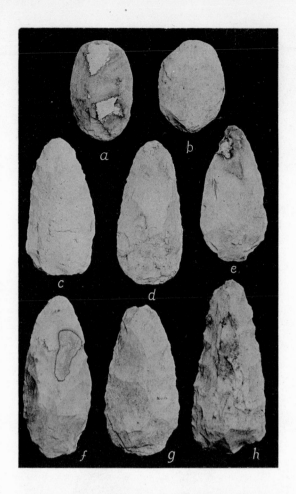

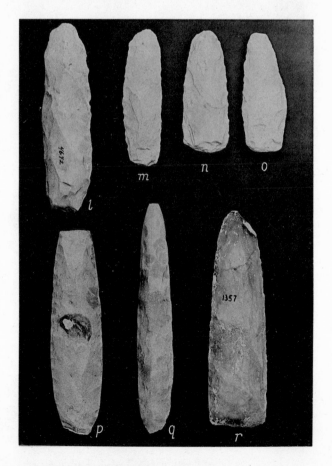

FIG. 61—LARGE CHIPPED IMPLEMENTS, WHITE FLINT

a, a′, b, b′: Chopping (?) tools, standard form, face and side views, ends blunted by use in hammering. *c-h, c′-h′*: Chopping (?) tools, standard form, face and side views. *i*: Chopping (?) tool, standard form. *j*: Chopping (?) tool, extra fine, thin specimen. *k*: Chopping (?) tool, standard form, lower end polished by use in ground (?). *l-o*: Pecking or pounding tools. *p, r*: Chisel-like rubbing tools. *q*: Large drill (??). L of *q*, 18.5 cm.

FIG. 62—FLINT SCRAPERS
L of *d*, 11.5 cm.

FIG. 63—FLINT POINTS, CHICHEN ITZA
a-e: Expanding stem.   *f*: Tapering triangular
stem. All from deposits of Mexican period or
later. L of *f*, 9.3 cm.

a: Points, mostly Tzakol. L of 9, 6.5 cm.

b: Flake blades, lancet type. L of longest, 8.5 cm.

FIG. 64—OBSIDIAN IMPLEMENTS

FIG. 65—KNIVES OR PROJECTILE POINTS, FLINT

a, 1-9: Pointed at both ends.   *a*, 10-13: Tapering stem, short blade. *b*, 1,2: Expanding stem.   *b*, 3-11: Pointed at one end, other rounded.
c, d: Tapering stem, long blade. L of *c*,9, 13 cm.

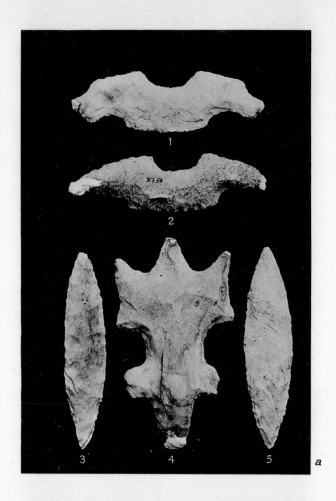

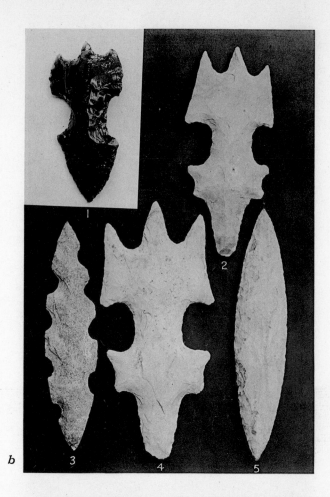

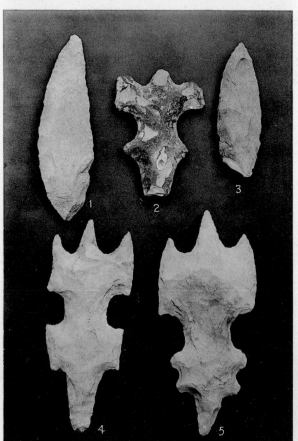

FIG. 66—ECCENTRIC FLINTS AND OBSIDIAN

a: Under Stela 26.   *b*: Under Stela A-15.   *c*: Under latest floor, Structure A-XV (for other flints and obsidians from this cache, see fig. 68, *a*, *d*).   *d*: Cache in upper stairway, Structure A-XVIII.   L of *c*,4, 20.5 cm.

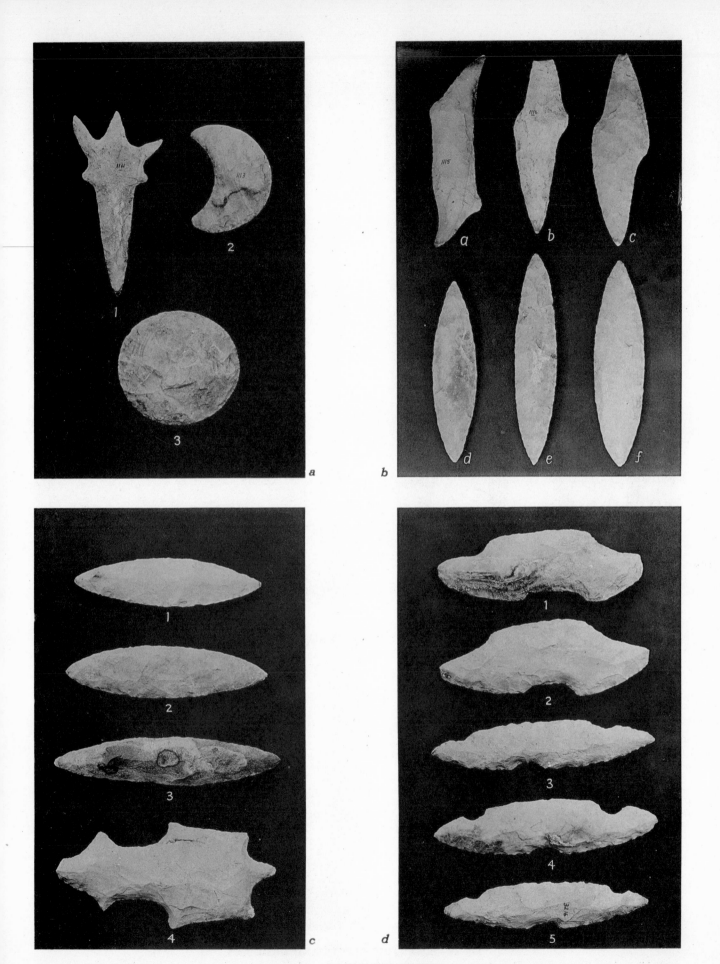

FIG. 67—ECCENTRIC FLINTS
a, b: Under Stela 22.   *c, d*: Shrine 2, Structure A-V.   L of *d*,4, 18.7 cm.

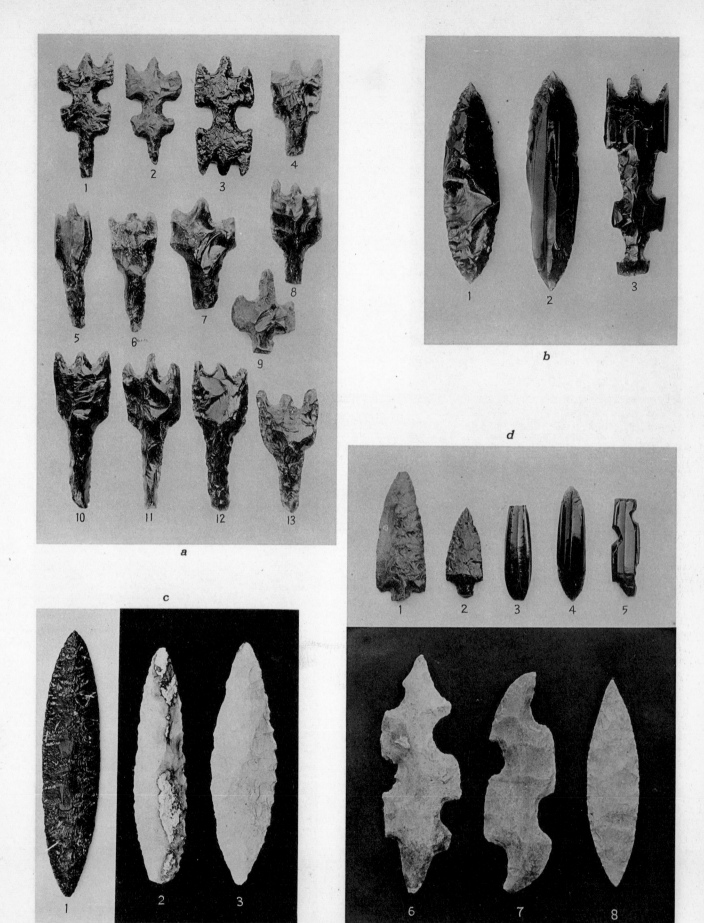

FIG. 68—ECCENTRIC FLINTS AND OBSIDIANS

a: Obsidians from beneath latest floor, Structure A-XV (for other obsidians and flints from this cache, see *d*; and for other flints, fig. 66,*c*). L of 10, 11.7 cm. *b*: Obsidians from cache in upper stairway, Structure A-XVIII (for drawing see fig. 9; and for flints from this cache, see fig. 66,*d*). L of 2, 9 cm. *c*: Obsidian (for drawing see fig. 10) and flints from Pit 1, Structure B-XI. L of 1, 18.8 cm. *d*: Obsidians and flints from beneath latest floor, Structure A-XV (for other obsidians from this cache see *a*; and for other flints, fig. 66,*c*). L of 6, 17.2 cm.

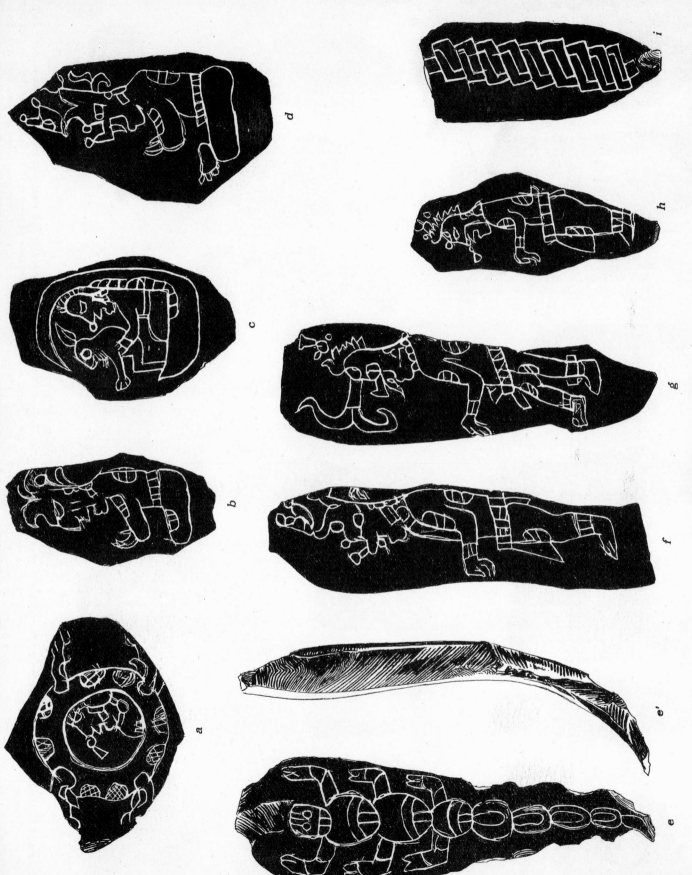

FIG. 69—INCISED OBSIDIANS

Cached together. To date, incised obsidians have been found only at Uaxactun and Tikal (see figs. 70-72). Natural size.

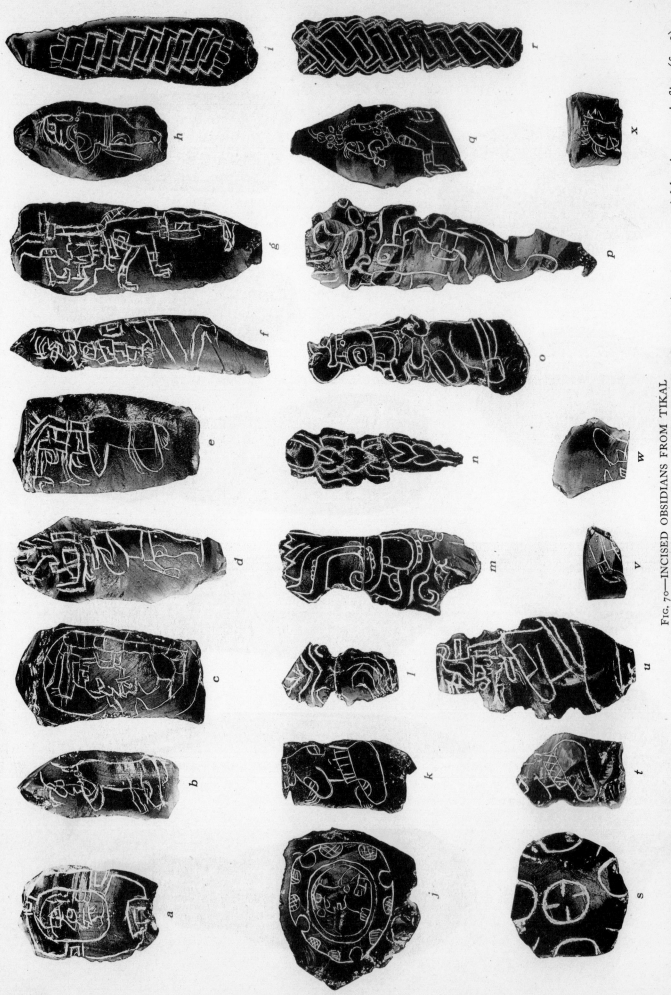

FIG. 70—INCISED OBSIDIANS FROM TIKAL

Specimens found by the Mexico-Guatemala Boundary Commission in 1931. Now in Guatemala National Museum. Of those figured at *j-x*, nine, accompanied by nine eccentric flints (fig. 8), were taken from beneath Stela 16 (9.14.0.0.0). Just which nine are concerned is uncertain, but A. L. Smith, who was present when some of them were being excavated, believes that most of those came from below the plain Stela A21. Scale about 2/3. A second lot of nine (*a-i*), also accompanied by nine eccentric flints (fig. 8, *a-i*), came from beneath the plain Stela A21. Scale about 2/3, with edges chipped to conform to the incising were from Stela 16.

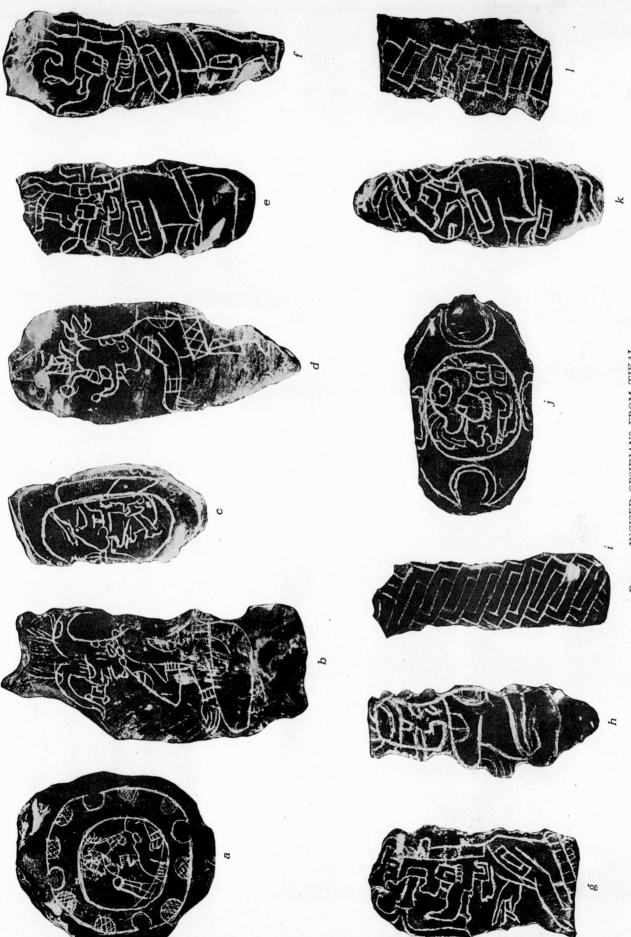

FIG. 71—INCISED OBSIDIANS FROM TIKAL

From beneath stelae. Now in British Museum. Scale about ¾ (after Joyce).

FIG. 72—INCISED OBSIDIANS FROM TIKAL

From beneath stelae. *a,b*: Guatemala National Museum (scale about ⅔). *c*: Peabody Museum, Harvard (natural size).

FIG. 73—CEREMONIAL OBJECTS, COPAN

Shells, jade plaque, eccentric flints, "sacrificial" knife of black flint. Found scattered in debris of Hieroglyphic Stairway; believed to have formed part of a single cache. Scale about ⅓.

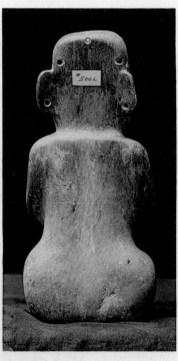

FIG. 74—JADE EFFIGY
For drawing see fig. 37. H 26 cm.

FIG. 75—STING-RAY SPINES
Found at pelvis of skeleton in Burial A-22, Tzakol. L of longest, 8 cm.

FIG. 76—METATES

a,b: Small type; *a* schist, *b* sandstone. *c-f*: Legs of large metates, all of vesicular lava; *c,d,f*, corner legs; *e*, leg at center of one end. *g*: Large legless metate, limestone. L of *b*, 24 cm.; of *f*, 13 cm.; of *g*, 43 cm.

a: Flat type, limestone. 3,4: End views of specimens broken near middle. For sections of 1,2 see fig. 17,*b,a*. L of 1, 15.5 cm.

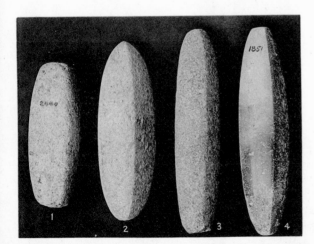

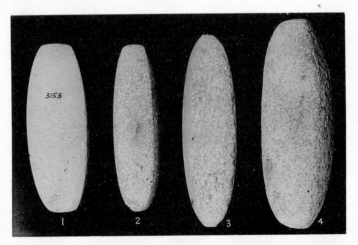

b: Quadrangular in section. 1: Granite. 2-4: Limestone. For sections of 1, 3, 4 see fig. 17,*a,g,c*. L of 4, 22 cm.

c: Quadrangular in section. Limestone. For sections of 1, 2, 4 see fig. 17,*i,f,l*. L of 4, 22 cm.

FIG. 77—MANOS

FIG. 78—MISCELLANEOUS STONE OBJECTS

a: Grooved stone. L 6.4 cm. *b*: Paint (?) dish. L 7.4 cm. *c*: Rubbing stone. D 8.7–9.4 cm. *d,e*: Hammerstones. D 5 and 7 cm. *f*: Perforated disc. D 11.5–13 cm. T 4 cm. *g-j*: Bark beaters. L of *g*, 10.3 cm.; others same scale. *k-q*: Celts. L of *n*, 17.3 cm.; others same scale.

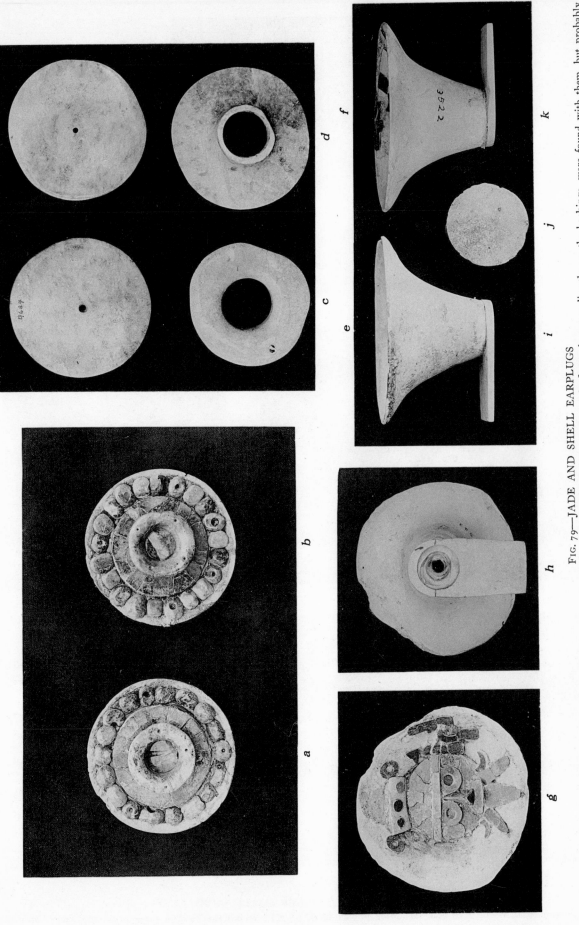

FIG. 79—JADE AND SHELL EARPLUGS

a,b: Shell earplug backings bearing jade mosaic and outer ring of cut-down jade beads. The miniature jade flares, here set directly on the backings, were found with them, but probably were originally raised on mountings of perishable material (see fig. 28,*a*). D 6.1 cm. *c,d*: Jade discs, possibly backings for earplugs whose other parts were of perishable material. *c*, obverse; *d*, reverse. For section see fig. 29,*c*. D of *c*, 7.3 cm. *e,f*: Jade earplug flares. For sections see fig. 29,*a,b*. D of *f*, 7.7 cm. *g,h*: Face and bottom views of shell earplug incrusted with jade, shell, and crystalline hematite. For section see fig. 30. D 7 cm. *i,k*: Side views of foregoing and its mate. *j*: Slate throat disk of *k*, from which incrustation (recovered largely intact in the case of the other earplug) had become detached.

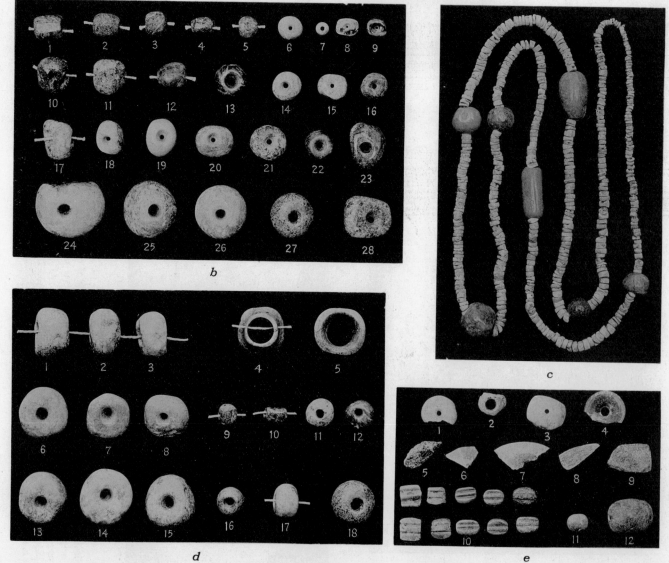

FIG. 80—JADE BEADS AND OTHER SMALL JADES

a: Unusually large subspherical beads. L of bead supporting pendant head, 3.3 cm.   *b*: Selection to show range in size and shape. Strings indicate direction of bore. D of 24, 2.2 cm.   *c*: Jade and shell necklace recovered in approximately original order. L of long bead at center, 4 cm.   *d*: Beads and (4,5) miniature flares. Average D of large subspherical beads (1), 2.4 cm.   *e*: Miscellaneous small jades. L of 12, 2.8 cm.

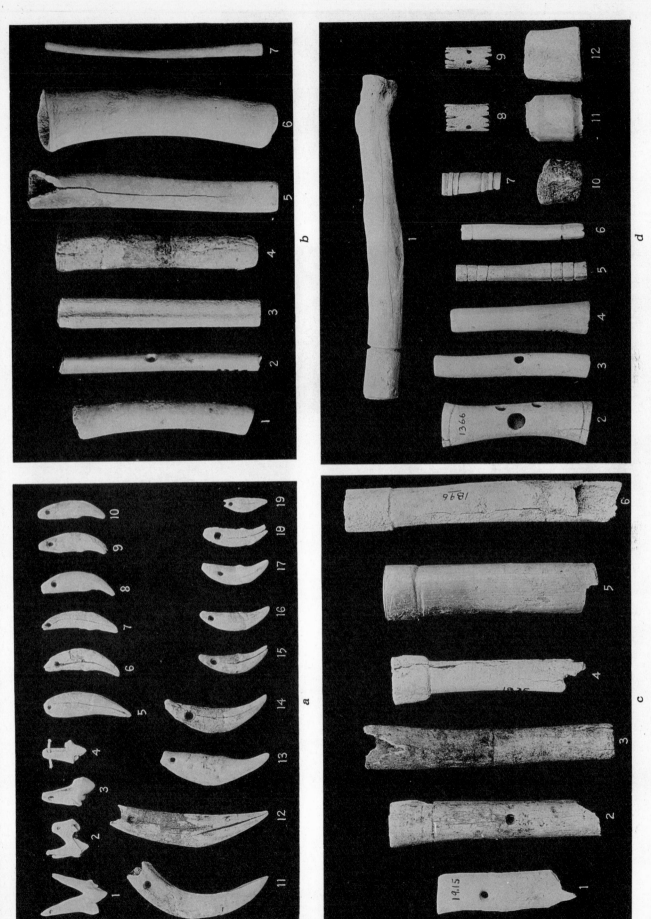

FIG. 81—PERFORATED ANIMAL TEETH AND TUBULAR BONE OBJECTS

a: 1–4, dog molars; 5–10, 15–19, dog and ocelot canines; 11, 12, peccary tusks; 13, 14, puma canines. L of 12, 7 cm. *b*: Bone tubes: 1–6, mammal bone (2 perhaps a whistle; 4, from a burial, bears mark of wrapping); 7, bird bone. Ends of all tubes well worn. L of 5, 10.7 cm. *c*: All may be of human bone. Use unknown. At broken end of 2 are traces of a second perforation at 90° to right of the one shown; 2 and 3, both from graves, bear marks of wrappings. Of 4, 5, 6, the shafts are more or less reduced by scraping to emphasize terminal ring. L of 3 (only complete specimen), 10.8 cm. *d*: Tubular bone objects. 1: Mammal bone, one articular end severed by groove-sawing, second groove started. Had the section been removed it would presumably have been used as a bead, as probably were the pieces at 4–7, 10, 12. 2: Section of bird bone, perhaps a whistle. 3: Whistle (?), mammal bone. 4–7: Tubular beads (?), mammal bone. 8,9: Beads (?) of thin-walled bird bone, each with two perforations. 10–12: Beads (?), apparently of human bone; cut edges of 11 unsmoothed. L of 1, 13.5 cm.

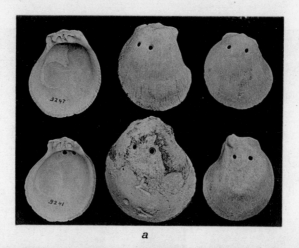

a

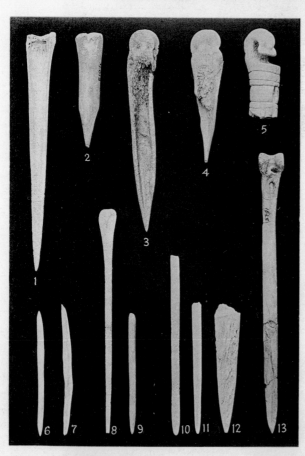

b

c

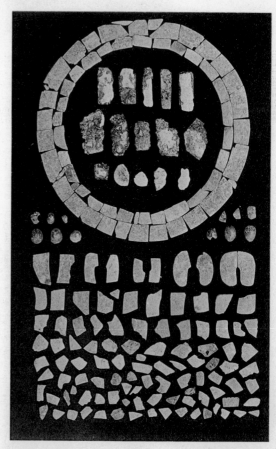

d

FIG. 82—SHELL, BONE, JADE

a: Shells, perforated for suspension. L of longest, 9 cm. *b*: Perforated shells and vertebrae of a colubrine serpent from a Tepeu cache. Average L of vertebrae, 1 cm. *c*: Bone awls. 1–4: Split metapodials, probably deer. 5: Butt of metapodial awl, carved. 6, 7: Double-pointed awls. 8, 9: Awls, round in section. 10–12: Awls with flattened points. 13: Awl of bird bone (for drawing of other side see fig. 41,*b*). L of 13, 16.6 cm. *d*: Elements of a mosaic that disintegrated upon the decay of its presumably wooden backing. The thin jade plates of the two circles replaced in what is thought to have been approximately their original order. The positions of the other jades and the shell elements (in circle) not ascertainable. D of circle about 10 cm.

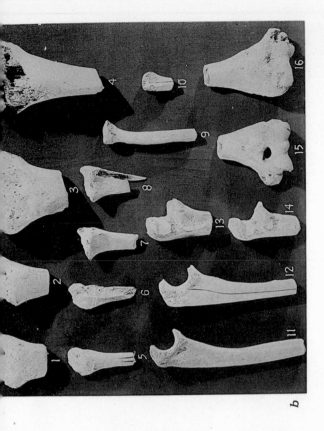

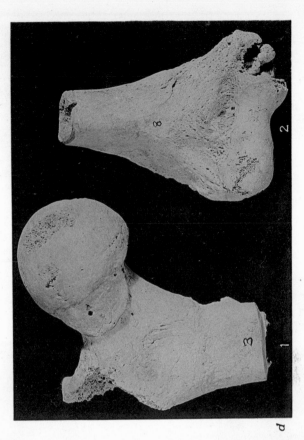

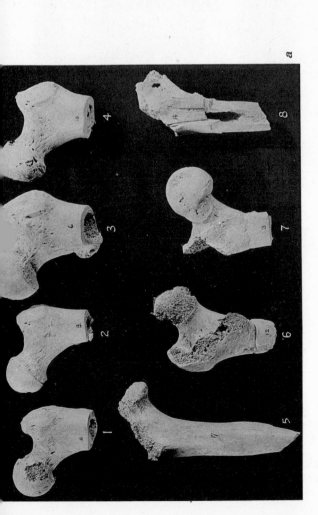

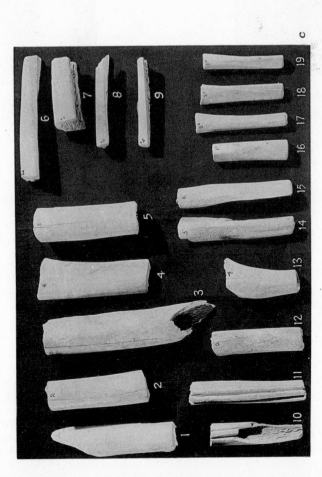

FIG. 83.—WORKED HUMAN BONES

Articular ends cut from shafts, presumably to procure the tubular pieces and strips of bone shown in c. For other specimens of this sort, see fig. 84,c. a: Femur heads. b: Ends of tibia, fibula, radius, ulna, humerus. c: Tubular sections and cut strips. d: Bones showing pathological conditions. At left, head of femur with extensions of articular surface onto anterior and posterior surfaces of neck. Anterior extension 3·7 cm. long, extends 1·6 cm. over surface of neck; posterior 2·2 cm. long, extends 1·4 cm. over surface of neck. Extensions indicate abnormality of joint, probably in acetabulum. At right, distal end of humerus. Median epicondyle shows extensive deep necrosis, apparently healed; this also affected surfaces of bone across adjoining anterior face below joint (but did not affect joint); and across the posterior face, involving olecranon fossa and external condyle, as evidenced by pitting of surface of bone (notes and photos by O. G. Ricketson).

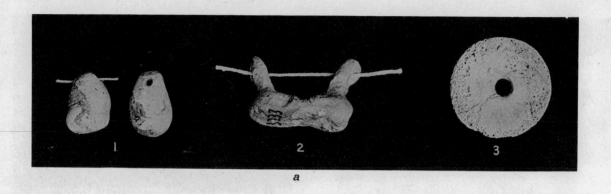

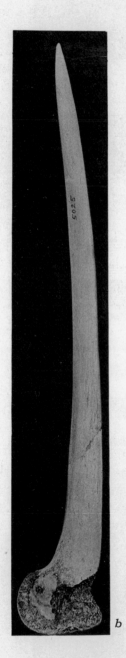

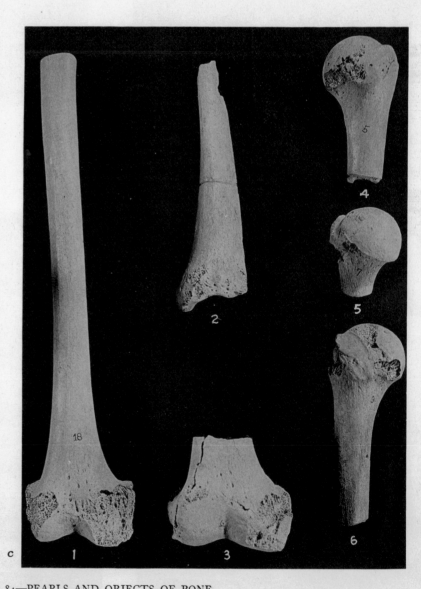

FIG. 84—PEARLS AND OBJECTS OF BONE

a: Pearls, bone pendant, spindle whorl (?). Strings indicate direction of bores. D of whorl, 3.2 cm. *b*: Awl, human femur. L 34.5 cm. *c*: Cut human bones, femur, tibia, humerus (photo by O. G. Ricketson).

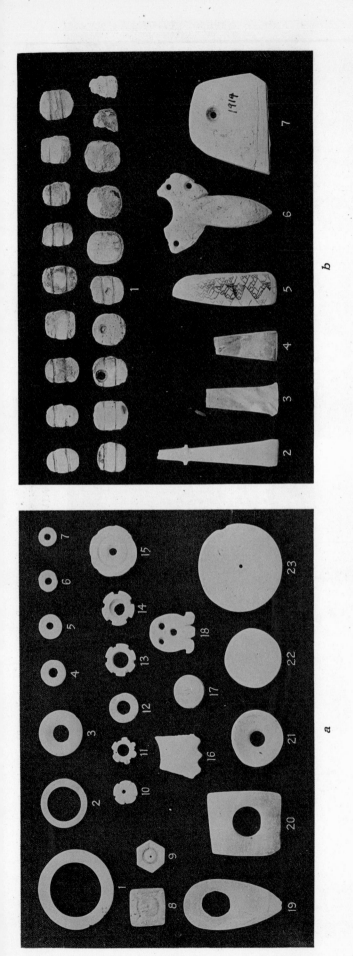

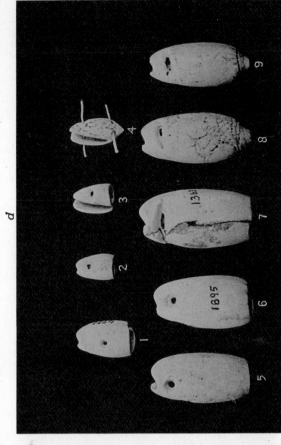

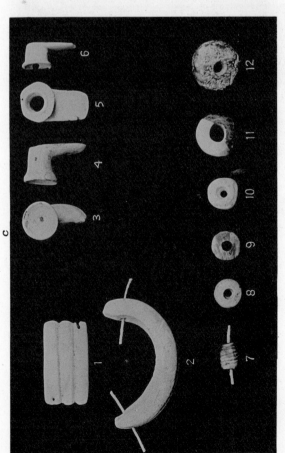

FIG. 85—SHELL ORNAMENTS

a: Adornos of cut shell. L of 19, 4.75 cm. *b*: Inlays and adornos. L of 2, 5.5 cm. *c*: Ornaments, ear (?) ornaments, beads. L of 1, 3.6 cm. *d*: Tinklers. Strings indicate four perforations in 4. L of 7, 5 cm.

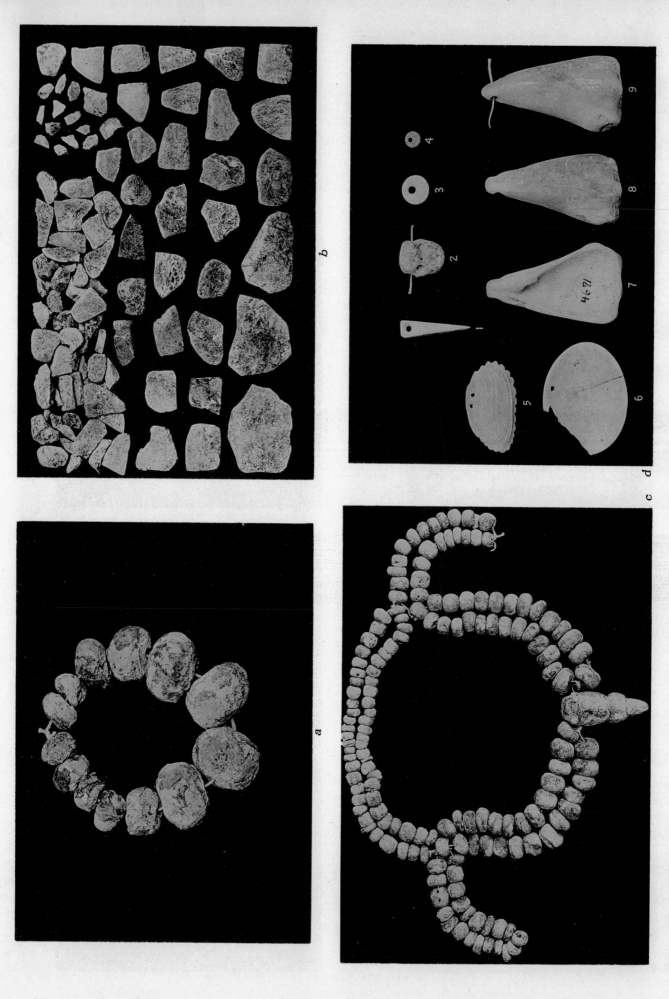

Fig. 86—SHELL BEADS AND ADORNOS, JADE MOSAIC ELEMENTS

a: Unusually large shell beads. D of largest, 3 cm.   *b*: Plates of jade, probably from coarse mosaic. L of piece at lower left, 3.7 cm.   *c*: Shell necklace (for drawing of pendant see fig. 50). L of pendant, 7.25 cm.   *d*: Shell adornos. Strings indicate direction of bores. L of 9, 6.5 cm.

a

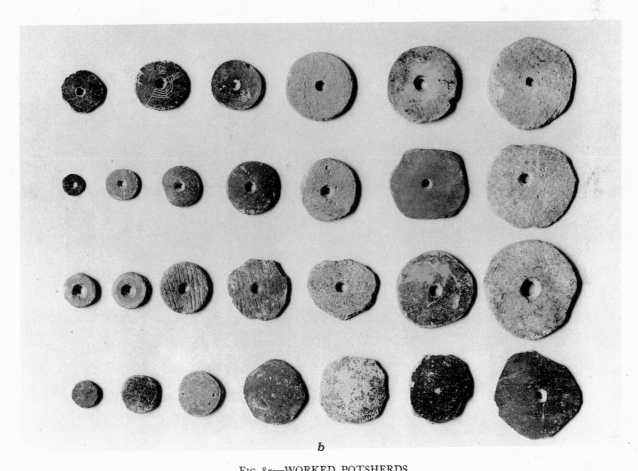

b

FIG. 87—WORKED POTSHERDS

a: Two objects made from fragments of large unslipped gray jar. From Burial A-22, Tzakol. L 15.5 cm.   *b*: Potsherd discs, the well-finished and centrally bored specimens probably spindle whorls; those with rough edges perhaps unfinished whorls; use of unperforated specimens unknown. D of largest about 8.5 cm.

9